AMONG THE
HEADHUNTERS

ALSO BY ROBERT LYMAN

Slim, Master of War

First Victory

Iraq, 1941

The Generals

The Longest Siege

Japan's Last Bid for Victory

Kohima, 1944

Operation Suicide

Into the Jaws of Death

Bill Slim

The Jail Busters

The Real X-Men

The twenty American and Chinese survivors of Flight 12420, shown here (*facing page*) with three USAAF servicemen who parachuted into Pangsha to provide medical care to the injured, pose for a photograph on their way out of the jungle. *Left to right, back row:* Philip Adams, Technical Sergeant Evan Wilder, Colonel Wang Pae Chae, Eric Sevareid, William T. Stanton, Staff Sergeant Joseph E. Clay, Corporal Basil M. Lemmon, Sergeant Glen A. Kittleson, Sergeant Francis W. Signer, and Corporal Lloyd J. Sherrill. *Middle row:* Second Lieutenant Roland K. Lee, Lieutenant Colonel Kwoh Li, John Paton Davies Jr., Staff Sergeant Ned C. Miller, Flight Officer Harry K. Neveu, Sergeant Joseph J. Giguere, Private William Schrandt, Corporal Edward Helland, Corporal Stanley Waterbury, and Captain Duncan C. Lee. *Kneeling:* Sergeant Richard Passey, Lieutenant Colonel Don D. Flickinger, and Corporal William G. McKenzie. *In front on stretcher:* Sergeant Walter R. Oswalt. (*Photo by Frank Cancellare, War Pool Photographer for Acme News Pictures*)

AMONG THE HEADHUNTERS

AN EXTRAORDINARY WORLD WAR II STORY
OF SURVIVAL IN THE BURMESE JUNGLE

ROBERT LYMAN

DA CAPO PRESS

A Member of the Perseus Books Group

Library of Congress Cataloging-in-Publication Data
Names: Lyman, Robert, author.
Title: Among the headhunters : an extraordinary World War II story of survival in the Burmese jungle / Robert Lyman.
Description: Boston, MA : Da Capo Press, a member of the Perseus Books Group, [2016] | Includes bibliographical references and index.
Identifiers: LCCN 2016006387 (print) | LCCN 2016006988 (ebook) | ISBN 9780306824678 (hardcover : alk. paper) | ISBN 9780306824685 (ebook)
Subjects: LCSH: World War, 1939–1945–Burma. | World War, 1939–1945–Aerial operations, American. | World War, 1939–1945–Jungle warfare. | Naga (South Asian people)–Burma. | Burma–History–Japanese occupation, 1942–1945. | Sevareid, Eric, 1912–1992.
Classification: LCC D767.6.L953 2016 (print) | LCC D767.6 (ebook) | DDC 940.54/4973092–dc23
LC record available at http://lccn.loc.gov/2016006387

Published by Da Capo Press
A Member of the Perseus Books Group
www.dacapopress.com

Da Capo Press books are available at special discounts for bulk purchases in the U.S. by corporations, institutions, and other organizations. For more information, please contact the Special Markets Department at the Perseus Books Group, 2300 Chestnut Street, Suite 200, Philadelphia, PA 19103, or call (800) 810-4145, ext. 5000, or e-mail special.markets@perseusbooks.com.

Design by Jane Raese
Set in 11-point New Baskerville

10 9 8 7 6 5 4 3 2 1

THIS BOOK IS DEDICATED
TO THE MEMORY OF GORDON GRAHAM,
1920–2015.

CONTENTS

Preface   ix

Abbreviations and Glossary   xi

Dramatis Personae   xv

1   "Dumbastapur"   1

2   Burmese Days   16

3   Banzai!   27

4   The Crash   35

5   Vinegar Joe   43

6   The Passengers   58

7   Dr. Sevareid, I Presume?   74

8   Taming the Nagas   82

9   The 1936 Punitive Expedition   107

10   The Battle of Pangsha   127

11   Return to Mokokchung   143

12   Eric and the Headhunters   159

13   Mongsen   174

14   The Sahib of Mokokchung   186

15   The Long Walk Home   196

16   Back to Chabua   208

17 Blackie's Gang 215

      Epilogue 231

Map 1: The Administered Area 237

Map 2: Routes Between Mokokchung and Pangsha 238

Appendix A: Weapons of the Patkoi Nagas 239

Appendix B: 1936 Expedition Diary 240

Appendix C: 1943 Crash Diary 241

Selected Bibliography 242

Acknowledgments 247

Index 249

PREFACE

In 1943 a Soviet spy, a celebrated American journalist, a top-ranking political adviser, and eighteen others—American and Chinese—survived an air crash on the mountainous and remote border between India and Burma. It was, and remains, the largest evacuation of an aircraft by parachute, and, given the fact that even the crew had never been trained in the technique, it was a miracle that so many survived. They fell with their crippled plane from the frying pan into the fire. On disentangling themselves from their parachutes, the twenty shocked survivors soon found that they had arrived in wild country dominated by a tribe that had an especial reason to hate white men. The Nagas of the Patkoi Hills on their remote and unsurveyed land were notorious headhunters, who continued—despite the feeble wrath of distant British imperial authority—to practice both slavery and human sacrifice. Their specialty was the removal of the heads of their enemies—often women and children—achieved with a swipe of ugly, razor-sharp *dao*s. On two occasions in recent years their village, or parts of it, had been burned to the ground and their warriors killed in running battles with sepoys sent to teach the villagers a lesson and to exert the authority of the Raj.

Nevertheless, and against all the odds, all but one of the twenty-one passengers and crew on the doomed aircraft survived. This is the story of the extraordinary adventure of those men among the Nagas of Pangsha and of their rescue by the young representative of the distant imperial power, the British deputy commissioner who arrived wearing "Bombay bloomers" and stout leather walking shoes, carrying a bamboo cane, and leading an armed party of "friendly" Nagas. In their meeting in some of the world's most inaccessible and previously unmapped terrain, three very different worlds collided. The young, exuberant apostles of the vast industrial democracy of the United States came face-to-face with members of an ancient mongoloid race, uncomprehending of the extent of modernity that existed beyond the remote hills in which they lived and determined to preserve their local power, based on ancient head-hunting and slaving prerogatives. Both groups met— not for the first time for the Nagas, whose village had been burned twice, in 1936 and 1939, because of persistent head-hunting—the vestiges of British authority in India, disintegrating as the Japanese tsunami washed up at its gate.

—Robert Lyman

ABBREVIATIONS AND GLOSSARY

ADMINISTERED AREA An area under the legal jurisdiction of the government of Assam and therefore the responsibility of a British deputy commissioner.

ASSAM RIFLES The local militia of the state of Assam, which began life as the Naga Hills Military Police. Many of its sepoys (soldiers) were ex-Gurkhas of the British-Indian Army who now lived in Assam.

ATC The Air Transport Command of the US Army Air Forces (USAAF) in the China-Burma-India (CBI) theater.

AVG The American Volunteer Group, or Flying Tigers, American mercenaries recruited to fly for the Chinese government immediately before the war.

BASHA The Indian Army term for a temporary shelter made out of canvas or local materials/vegetation.

CBI China-Burma-India theater, the US war command in the Far East.

C-46 The Curtiss-Wright airliner rushed into service in the CBI theater in mid-1946 and designated the "Commando."

C-47 SKYTRAIN The military version of the Douglas DC3 airliner, known as the Dakota by the RAF and nicknamed the "Gooney Bird" by Americans.

CONTROL AREA An area outside the directly administered British territory in the Naga Hills in which the Raj claimed political influence. The territory was not formally administered by the government of Assam, but anything untoward that happened in it was considered to be of interest to the British deputy commissioner in Kohima and his assistant in Mokokchung.

DACOIT The Burmese word for a marauding bandit.

DAO The Assamese word for a machete.

DETACHMENT 101 A unit of the OSS in northern Burma with responsibility for taking guerrilla warfare to the Japanese using local Kachin tribespeople.

DOBASHI A British-appointed Naga interpreter. Each Naga tribe spoke its own language (not merely a different dialect), which made intertribal communication extremely difficult, although a form of Naga creole (called "Nagamese") based on Assamese did develop as a kind of linguistic glue to facilitate communication among the separate tribes. A *dobashi* was provided with a red blanket to denote his appointment.

DUMBASTAPUR Nickname, a derivation of "dumb bastard," given by men of the ATC to Chabua Air Base, Assam.

EAST INDIA COMPANY The London-based trading organization, known colloquially as "John Company," which through a process of commercially inspired expansion (supported by British military power) ruled much of India from the eighteenth to the mid–nineteenth century. It was dissolved following the mutiny of 1857 and replaced by direct rule by the British government, known as the "Raj."

FDR Franklin Delano Roosevelt, the thirty-second president of the United States, who died in April 1945.

GAONBURA Headman of a Naga village, appointed by the British and provided with a distinctive red blanket, shawl, or waistcoat as a badge of office.

HUMP The nickname given to the air ferry route established in 1942 across the mountains between northeastern India and Kunming in China. The Japanese capture of Burma in 1942 and closure of the Burma Road that ran from Rangoon to Lashio necessitated an alternative means of supplying the Kuomintang.

ICS The Indian Civil Service, the elite administrative arm of the British Raj, which between its inception in 1858 (after the mutiny, when the British government took over the governance of India from the East India Company) and 1947 numbered never more than 1,200 civil servants appointed through competitive examination.

KET The Kohima Educational Trust, a UK-based charity established in 2003 (www.kohimaeducationaltrust.net). Its purpose is to provide educational assistance to the young people of Nagaland, India, in order to repay the debt of honor owed to the Nagas for their un-stinting help given to the Second Division and other British Army units during the battles to stem the Japanese invasion of India in 1944. The KET's parallel organization in Nagaland is the Kohima Educational Society (KES).

KHEL A subset (or colony) of a Naga village, similar to a suburb within a Western town. Each village is divided into several *khel*s, primarily on the basis of geography and clan. Often *khel*s have their own assistant *gaonburas*.

KUOMINTANG The Chinese nationalist party led by Chiang Kai-shek, which governed most of China beginning in 1928. This power was contingent upon the support of many hundreds of warlords who had sprung up following the demise of the Qing Empire in 1911.

LEE-ENFIELD The British Army's standard service rifle, with a caliber of 0.303 inch. The weapon used by the Assam Rifles was the short-magazine (SMLE) Mark III version.

LEWIS GUN The British Army's World War I–era light machine gun. With a caliber of 0.303 inch, it was fed by a drum holding forty-seven rounds.

MAHSEER A large freshwater fish common to the streams and rivers of Assam.

MITHAN A domesticated form of the gaur, these animals browsed through foliage rather than grazing on grass. Never milked, they were grown for their meat and were the standard Naga source of beef.

MORUNG The young persons' dormitory in a Naga village, where teenagers (from about the age of ten) would live communally and learn the rites of the tribe.

OSS Office of Special Services, the forerunner of the CIA.

PANJI STICK A sharpened bamboo spike left in the ground as a trap for the unwary, often placed in large numbers. It could easily penetrate the unprotected sole of the foot and was often poisoned.

PITT RIVERS MUSEUM An anthropological and archaeological museum in Oxford, part of the University of Oxford.

RAJ The common name given to British rule in India (Raj means "rule" in Hindi) between the end of the mutiny in 1858 and independence in 1947. It included areas administered directly by the United Kingdom ("British India") as well as the princely states ruled by individual rulers under the "paramountcy" of the British Crown. The region was less commonly also called the "Indian Empire," the "Federation of India," and the "Empire of India."

SACO Sino-American Cooperative Organization.

SEPOY An Indian soldier. The sepoys in this story were soldiers in the Assam Rifles.

SUBEDAR A native Indian Army rank between a noncommissioned and commissioned officer, equivalent to a US lieutenant.

USAAF US Army Air Forces, a component of the US Army that was the military aviation service of the United States during and immediately after World War II and the direct predecessor of the US Air Force, which came into being in 1947.

ZU Naga beer. Where it was plentiful, it was made from rice. In the eastern territories, such as Chingmei, where rice was scarce and extremely expensive, it was made from millet.

DRAMATIS PERSONAE

Persons of Historical Interest

SIR JOSEPH BAMPFYLDE FULLER Governor of East Bengal and Assam, 1905–1906.

MAJOR GENERAL SIR JAMES JOHNSTONE The political agent to the maharajah of Manipur, who launched the rescue expedition to Kohima from Imphal in 1880.

SIR ROBERT NEIL REID Governor of Assam, 1937–1942.

Persons in the Indian Civil Service

PHILIP FRANCIS ADAMS Leader of the rescue party in 1943, Adams, whom the Patkoi Nagas called the "sahib of Mokokchung," joined the Indian Civil Service in 1937 (undertaking the journey from England by car) and was posted to Mokokchung as the subdivisional officer under Charles Pawsey in Kohima. He was twenty-nine at the time of the rescue.

WILLIAM "BILL" ARCHER The subdivisional officer in Mokokchung after Adams, Archer stayed until independence in 1947.

J. P. MILLS James Philip ("J. P.") Mills was born in 1890 and entered the Indian Civil Service in 1913. He was subdivisional officer at Mokokchung in the Naga Hills of Assam from 1917 to 1924 and deputy commissioner, based at Kohima, during the 1930s. In 1930 he married Pamela Vesey-FitzGerald. In 1930 he was appointed the honorary director of ethnography for Assam. He published well-received monographs on native peoples in 1922, 1926, and 1937. He became secretary to the government of Assam in 1932.

SIR CHARLES RIDLEY PAWSEY Born in 1894, Pawsey resigned from the British Army after World War I to join the Indian Civil Service. He was appointed assistant commissioner in Assam in 1919 at the age of twenty-five and became director of land records in 1932. He was made a deputy commissioner in 1935. He undertook a punitive expedition to Noklu in 1937 and was deputy commissioner in Kohima during the siege of 1944. He was a recipient of the Military Cross, a British award for gallantry.

G. W. J. SMITH The subdivisional officer at Mokokchung and in command of the 360 Naga carriers during the first expedition to Pangsha in 1936.

Persons in the Assam Rifles

MAJOR W. R. B. WILLIAMS Born in 1896, Major W. R. B. ("Bill") Williams was the commandant (commanding officer) of the Third Battalion, Assam Rifles (on secondment from the Seventh Gurkhas), taking personal command of the two and a half platoons (150 sepoys) involved in the first expedition to Pangsha in November–December 1936.

Anthropologists

URSULA GRAHAM BOWER A pioneer anthropologist in the Naga Hills between 1937 and 1946 and a guerrilla fighter against the Japanese in Burma from 1942 to 1945, Bower was a good friend of Philip Mills, Bill Archer, and Christoph von Fürer-Haimendorf. She became so familiar with Naga culture that she was known as the "Naga Queen."

G. H. DAMANT The British officiating political agent for Manipur and an ethnologist of note who was killed by the Nagas of Khonoma (near Kohima) on October 4, 1879.

DR. CHRISTOPH VON FÜRER-HAIMENDORF   A renowned Austrian anthropologist who accompanied the 1936 expedition to Pangsha in the company of his good friend Philip Mills. Mills referred to him in his letters to his wife as "the Baron."

DR. JOHN HENRY ("J. H.") HUTTON   A colonial administrator in the Naga Hills who arrived in 1912 and became an eminent anthropologist.

COLONEL LESLIE SHAKESPEAR   Shakespear (1863–1933) was the deputy commander of the Assam Rifles during World War I and was involved in the suppression of the Kuki Rising, 1917–1919. He wrote a history of the Lushai-Kuki people in 1912.

Passengers and Crew of C-46 Number 41-12420, August 2, 1943

STAFF SERGEANT JOSEPH E. CLAY   USAAF, Air Transport Command.

JOHN PATON ("JACK") DAVIES JR.   Davies joined the US Foreign Service on graduation from Columbia University and was posted to China in 1933. He, like Lee, had been born in China, the son of American missionaries. He became political attaché to General Joseph Stilwell in March 1942, serving under "Vinegar Joe" until the latter's recall from China in 1944.

SECOND LIEUTENANT CHARLES FELIX   USAAF, Air Transport Command. Felix, the copilot, was the only fatality of the crash.

STAFF SERGEANT JOSEPH "JIGGS" GIGUERE   USAAF, Air Transport Command. A chef by training, he was being posted to Kunming.

CORPORAL EDWARD HELLAND   USAAF, Air Transport Command.

SERGEANT GLEN A. KITTLESON   USAAF, Air Transport Command.

LIEUTENANT COLONEL KWOH LI   Chinese Army. A young but hard-bitten soldier whom the Americans admired, he had marched out of Burma with Stilwell during the retreat of 1942.

CAPTAIN DUNCAN C. LEE A prewar lawyer, Lee was confidential assistant to Major General William Donovan in his legal chambers. The son of American missionaries to China and a Rhodes scholar, Lee was the head of the China section of the Secret Intelligence (SI) branch in 1943 and 1944. From 1942 on he was a Soviet double agent operating under the cover name "Koch," making him possibly the most senior source the Soviet Union ever had inside US intelligence.

SECOND LIEUTENANT ROLAND K. LEE USAAF, Air Transport Command.

CORPORAL BASIL M. LEMMON USAAF, Air Transport Command. He was the last parachutist to join the survivors at Wenshoyl colony after struggling alone in the bush for four days.

STAFF SERGEANT NED C. MILLER Aerial engineer and crew chief and, at forty, by far the oldest of the US servicemen on Flight 12420.

FLIGHT OFFICER HARRY KENNETH NEVEU A twenty-year-old pilot in the USAAF, Air Transport Command, Tenth Air Force. "Flight officer" was the most junior warrant officer rank in the USAAF.

SERGEANT WALTER K. OSWALT Oswalt, the radio operator, broke his leg on landing and was the direct cause of the rescue jump undertaken by Don Flickinger, Richard Passey, and William McKenzie.

PRIVATE WILLIAM SCHRANDT USAAF, headquarters, Services of Supply, Delhi.

ERIC SEVAREID Sevareid was one of a group of elite war correspondents hired by pioneering CBS news journalist Edward Murrow at the outset of the war in Europe. He was the first to report the fall of Paris when it was captured by the Germans in 1940.

CORPORAL LLOYD J. SHERRILL USAAF, Air Transport Command.

SERGEANT FRANCIS W. SIGNER USAAF, Air Transport Command.

WILLIAM ("BILL") T. STANTON A representative in the CBI theater of the Board of Economic Warfare, which collected and analyzed economic information about the enemy. A banker in Hong Kong before the war, he was in his forties at the time of the crash.

COLONEL WANG PAE CHAE   Chinese Army.

CORPORAL STANLEY WATERBURY   USAAF, Air Transport Command.

TECHNICAL SERGEANT EVAN WILDER   USAAF, headquarters, Twelfth Air Force.

Persons of the Kuomintang

CHIANG KAI-SHEK   The Kuomintang warlord who effectively governed the Republic of China beginning in 1928 (succeeding Sun Yat-sen) and led its military endeavors against both Japan and the Communist Party under Mao Zedong.

MADAME KAI-SHEK   Soong Mei-ling, the American-educated wife of Chiang Kai-shek.

GENERAL DAI (TAI) LI   The Kuomintang's secretive spy chief.

T. V. SOONG   The Harvard-educated brother of Madame Kai-shek.

Persons of the US Government and Military

BRIGADIER GENERAL EDWARD ALEXANDER   Alexander, Stilwell's air commander, was appointed head of the Air Transport Command, based at Chabua, in December 1942.

MAJOR GENERAL CLAIRE LEE CHENNAULT   Born in 1893, Chennault was a military pilot who, retiring from the US Army in 1937, began to work as an aviation adviser and trainer in China. He started in early 1941 with funding and control by the US government. He commanded the First American Volunteer Group (known as the Flying Tigers) before being given command of the US Army Air Forces in the CBI. He feuded constantly with General Joseph Stilwell and helped Chiang Kai-shek to convince FDR to remove Stilwell in 1944.

MAJOR GENERAL WILLIAM ("WILD BILL") DONOVAN   A World War I soldier of some repute, postwar lawyer, and founder and director of the Office of Strategic Services (OSS), the predecessor of the CIA, during 1942–1946.

CAPTAIN MILTON "MARY" MILES USN   US Navy; the de facto commander of SACO and deputy to Dai Li.

GENERAL "VINEGAR JOE" STILWELL   General Marshall's representative to Chiang Kai-shek, to which post he was appointed in January 1942. He was also Chiang Kai-shek's chief of staff and, in due course, the deputy supreme allied commander of the South East Asia Command (SEAC).

Persons of the US Rescue Group

STAFF SERGEANT JOHN LEE DECHAINE   A member of the air warning scheme in the Naga Hills overlooking the Chindwin farther south (100 miles southeast of Kohima), DeChaine marched from Mokokchung with the rescue party led by Philip Adams in 1943.

LIEUTENANT COLONEL DON FLICKINGER   The thirty-six-year-old ATC wing surgeon who parachuted into Pangsha after the crash to tend to Oswalt's injuries. He had been duty medical officer at Pearl Harbor during the Japanese attack on December 7, 1941.

CAPTAIN GEORGE E. KATZMAN   One of the two pilots of the Chabua-based C-47 that found the wreckage of Flight 12420 and provided immediate support to the survivors. Katzman was an experienced rescue pilot, having conducted dozens of searches for downed aircraft in the region since late 1942.

COLONEL RICHARD KNIGHT   The ATC wing operations officer who used Oswalt's radio signals to determine the approximate site of the crash, enabling Hugh Wild to find the downed aircraft.

FIRST LIEUTENANT ANDREW "BUDDY" LABONTE   Leader of the Air Warning Station, LaBonte—a radio operator—marched from Mokokchung with the rescue party led by Philip Adams in 1943. He was awarded the Legion of Merit for his part in the rescue.

MAJOR ST. CLAIR MCKELWAY The ATC wing intelligence officer based at Chabua, McKelway was a well-known journalist for the *New Yorker* who knew Sevareid well. It was he who contacted Philip Adams at the first news of the air crash and warned the survivors of the dangers they faced from the Nagas.

CORPORAL WILLIAM G. MCKENZIE A member of the rescue team who parachuted into Pangsha with Don Flickinger after the crash.

SERGEANT RICHARD PASSEY A member of the rescue team who parachuted into Pangsha with Don Flickinger after the crash. A fine athlete, he nearly defeated the Pangsha Nagas at their own game in a spear-throwing contest.

CAPTAIN JOHN ("BLACKIE") PORTER Porter set up a nascent air-rescue team at Chabua after the loss of Flight 12420. After a very successful series of rescues, he was killed on December 10, 1943, when his B-25 and another rescue plane were lost to enemy action.

CAPTAIN HUGH ELDON WILD One of the two pilots of the Chabua-based C-47 that found the wreckage of Flight 12420 and provided immediate support to the survivors.

Persons of the Nagas

CHINGMAK (OF CHINGMEI) *Gaonbura* of the Chang village of Chingmei and great friend of Philip Mills. His two sons were Sangbah and Tangbang. Mills had a photograph of Chingmak at Mokokchung as early as 1920, which demonstrated the longevity of their friendship.

EMLONG (OF MOKOKCHUNG) A *gaonbura* and noted tiger hunter who accompanied the 1936 expedition and acted as Philip Adams's factotum during the 1943 rescue.

MATCHE (OF YIMPANG) A Kalyo-Kengyu from Yimpang, ally of Pangsha, who fled to Chingmei in 1936 for fear of his life after falling afoul of his erstwhile comrades. Chingmak urged that he provide information to the British to allow Pangsha and its allies to be punished for their constant raiding, and he became Mills and Williams's chief scout. Fürer-Haimendorf believed that without Matche, success against Pangsha would have been impossible.

MONGSEN (OF PANGSHA) A famous warrior and leader of one of Pangsha's three *khel*s who'd taken fourteen heads in the recent sacking of Saochu village, Mongsen led the counterattack against Major Williams at Wenshoyl on November 28, 1936, attacking repeatedly with spears against the disciplined Lee-Enfield fire of the Assam Rifles despite suffering from a badly burned foot. He negotiated a settlement with Mills at Chingmei a few days after this deadly skirmish. The survivors of Flight 12420 in 1943 called him "Moon-face" and recorded his calm acceptance of their presence in his village. Colonel Flickinger saved his baby's life by giving him antibiotics for an abscess that would otherwise have killed the child.

MONGU (OF PANGSHA) A notorious local bully and slaver, he and Mongsen were the two headmen of Pangsha in 1936.

NATCHE (AO GAONBURA) A noted *gaonbura* who accompanied the 1936 expedition. Well known for his skill at languages, he acted as an elder statesman and interpreter for Philip Mills.

SANGBAH (OF CHINGMEI) Chingmak's son and friend of Philip Mills, Sangbah attended school in Mokokchung. He accompanied Mills and Williams in the 1936 attack on Pangsha. In 1943 he provided immediate protection for the survivors of Flight 12420 by positioning himself with them in Pangsha and thus asserting vicarious British protection over them.

SANTING (OF PANGSHA) One of Pangsha's most famous warriors, he and Mongsen led the Pangsha raid against Saochu, the two men rivaling each other in the taking of heads. Santing was killed by rifle fire from British sepoys during the battle of Wenshoyl on November 28, 1936.

TANGBANG (OF CHINGMEI) Chingmak's son and Sangbah's brother, who arranged the unseen Chingmei "security detail" for the survivors at Pangsha, placing his warriors in the hills around Pangsha as protection, as much from the predatory Nagas as from the Japanese. Tangbang wore a leopard skin, had seventeen heads to his credit, and clearly impressed the survivors of Flight 12420 by demonstrating his prowess with the cross-bow. He too had accompanied his father and brother into battle with Mills and Williams on November 27–28, 1936, against their mortal enemies at Pangsha during the first punitive expedition.

WANG-DO (OF CHINGMEI) A *khel* leader from Chingmei and friend of Sangbah and Tangbang who assisted in the protection of the survivors in 1943. Sevareid believed that Wang-do had supplanted Chingmak as *gaonbura* of Chingmei.

AMONG THE HEADHUNTERS

1

"DUMBASTAPUR"

Harry Neveu looked up at the vast silver bird above him. It was dawn on Monday, August 2, 1943. The ramshackle US Army Air Forces (USAAF) air base at Chabua in northeastern India prepared for another busy day of activity. About eighty aircraft of various types, including C-47 Skytrains (nicknamed "Gooney Bird"), C-87 Liberators, C-54 Skymasters, B-25 Mitchells, and new C-46 Commandos, crowded the dirty concrete apron. Aircraft of the China National Aviation Corporation (CNAC) mixed with those of the USAAF and a few of the Royal Air Force (RAF), although for the most part the CNAC and RAF operated from Dinjan, a few miles farther up the Brahmaputra Valley. As the preflight bustle readied the Curtiss-Wright "Commando" transport, the young pilot walked methodically around the huge plane, checking that everything was in order before climbing into the hold. Making his way forward, Flight Officer Harry Neveu, pilot that morning of Air Transport Command (ATC) Flight 12420, adjusted his parachute before carefully placing it just behind the cockpit. This was where the crew always placed parachutes, ready to be grabbed if they were needed.

Following flying training in America, the draft for India had put the twenty-year-old as far from Coleman, Wisconsin, as he could imagine. Early morning at Chabua was always cold, but the fur-lined flying jacket warmed him as he surveyed his checklist. He would need the jacket when he was flying at 15,000 feet later in the day on his way to China. The only way to combat the cold was layering: "Underwear, wool work pants and shirt, issue sweater, zippered flight coverall and leather A-2 flight jacket," recalled Hump veteran Peyton Walmsley, "with the 'blood chit' sewn on the back, later transferred inside, left side." A blood chit was a square piece of cloth on which was printed the nationalist flag of the Republic of China together with, in Mandarin Chinese characters, promises of a reward for downed air crew to proffer to anyone who found them and kept them alive.

Neveu, who had flown the route several times, worked his way through the checklist automatically—crossover valve (down), emergency brake valve (down), wing flaps (up), glider release (down), tail wheel (locked)—on and on they went. The checks seemed endless. There were thirty-one in all before he was allowed to start the C-46's twin engines. Beside him copilot First Lieutenant Charles Felix tested the ailerons, throttle, and steering yoke while radio operator Sergeant Walter Oswalt worked the frequencies and established contact with Chabua tower.

Across the vast concrete taxiway ground crew examined the engine cowlings, oil and fuel caps, propellers, and external fittings of scores of C-46's– 'he USAAF's most modern, but insufficiently tested, transport aircraft. Rows of them stretched out beside the apron, awaiting duty in the dangerous skies of the Assam-to-Yunnan air-ferry route, known to everyone as the "Hump."

The "deuce-and-a-half" truck raised a dusty wake as it ferried the C-46's passengers from their canvas billets a mile away. The air crew were billeted in dormitories built of the ubiquitous bamboo, with walls made of woven nipa mats and a roof constructed from bamboo fronds. The floors were made of dirt. Showering took place quite satisfactorily underneath a fifty-five-gallon drum sitting atop a bamboo tower and heated by a wood-burning stove. They had breakfasted on fried eggs flown in on planes returning from China along with fried potatoes, ketchup, and coffee.

Today was unusual. They rarely carried passengers nowadays: "Most loads to China were gasoline only," recalled Walmsley. "Fifty-five gallon drums, standing on end in a row starboard side each lashed with 3/8 inch sisal [rope] to ring bolts recessed in the floor.

Boarding inspection verified the manifest, satisfactory tie-down and absence of leaks or vapor. 'Leakers' were removed. Then we queued for takeoff, the first plane down the strip, west to east, as soon as it was light enough to 'recognize' the runway."

Separated by piles of luggage and parachutes, the two rows of men in the truck remained lost in thought. It was too noisy, and too early, to talk anyway. The truck backed up to the fuselage, and each man stood up, collected his hand gear, and stepped directly into the belly of the plane, with Staff Sergeant Ned Miller, from Ottumwa, Iowa, directing them to their seats. Ground staff chucked the eighteen passenger parachutes into the craft, and Miller laid them between the rows of aluminum seats running along each side of the fuselage. Calling for the passengers' attention, the forty-year-old crew chief demonstrated how to don a parachute. The passengers watched him, but hardly alertly. Surely they would never have cause to use the ungainly canvas-wrapped packs? They didn't check the contents of the survival pouches on the parachute packs, assuming that everything was present and correct. Each pouch should have contained a range of items that would be helpful during the first few hours or days of survival in an alien environment: fishhooks and line; pocketknife with can opener; Hershey bar; vitamin capsules; iodine to purify drinking water taken from jungle streams; polished-metal signaling mirror; maps; pocket compass; waterproof matches; atabrine tablets to ward off malaria; a clip of .45-caliber ammunition; and several messages written in Urdu, Hindustani, and Burmese asking for help from friendly natives. Don Downie recalled the advice he was given soon after arrival at Chabua: "A ground officer spent perhaps thirty minutes explaining what we might expect following a bail-out. In a capsule: walk downhill, downstream, find friendly natives, follow them to the nearest village, and expect a hand-off to more friendly natives who would see that you were eventually returned to a military outpost. That was, unless they turned you over to Jap patrols for a higher reward of rice, cocaine, or money."

Within two hours the temperature would climb to 88 degrees. August was the wet season in the upper reaches of Assam—106 inches of rain fell there every year, three times more than the average US rainfall. On either side of the broad valley created by the Brahmaputra River, hills rose in the first stages of their relentless climb toward the sky. *Chabua* was a combination of two words: "Cha'a" from the Chinese name for tea and "bua"—Assamese for plantation. The British East India Company had been growing tea here since 1826, and, seventy years later, Assam was the world's leading tea producer. Now Chabua was a concrete megalith, the sprawling air base sustaining massive aerial operations into China, with eighty heavy transports calling it home. Its sister base at Jorhat lay a hundred miles down the Brahmaputra, and similar airfields were dotted across the remote region at various stages of construction, all built on old tea plantations. But only Chabua and Jorhat had the hard, all-weather runways usable during the monsoon.

Existence at Chabua for those who had to work and fly from there was primitive. In early 1942 the difficult job of keeping in touch with China had been achieved by flying over the toughest mountain ranges in the world, day in, day out. The men who flew this route were pioneers of a new age, their work reminiscent of the old '49ers, or those who had opened up the West, requiring gallon loads of pluck, grit, and personal sacrifice. A legend of their exploits began to build. They sang a ballad about themselves that was self-consciously based on the legend of railway hero Casey Jones:

It was Sunday morning and it looked like rain,
Around the mountain came an airplane,
Her carburetor busted and her manifold split,
The copilot gulped and the captain spit.
Cockpit Joe was comin' round the mountain,
Cockpit Joe was goin' to town,
Cockpit Joe was comin' round the mountain
When the starboard engine she done let him down.

In an article in *LIFE* magazine the journalist Theodore White recorded that in the early days the ferry pilots flew without weather reports, navigation aids, adequate fields, ground transportation or radio. They took off on instruments, flew by compass, let down by calculated flying time. . . . The officers and men ate together in one mud *basha* with a dirt floor; there were no lights, native cooks served bully beef and British biscuits. [The days began at 3:30 each morning.] There was just one shift—a 16-hour shift—broken only by sandwiches and hot drinks. The Japs were in the air constantly. The only protection the Hump had was two P-40s loaned by Chennault and two P-43s loaned by the Chinese Air Force.

Chabua got the nickname "Dumbastapur" because on one occasion in 1943, during a Japanese air raid, the men stood around, hands in pockets, watching the spectacle. The shouted encouragement to take cover—from Colonel Gerry Mason—was "Take cover, you dumb bastards!" From that moment the name stuck.

The flight that morning was not one of Neveu's usual jaunts across the roof of the world. In the first place it was carrying passengers rather than gas, and there were lots of them—eighteen. In addition to nine members of the ATC traveling to join the Tenth Air Force in Kunming were two officers of the Chinese Army returning home after training at the Indian Army training center at Ramgargh. Also on board were four senior figures. John ("Jack") Paton Davies Jr., Lieutenant General Joe Stilwell's political adviser from the State Department, was charged with ensuring that political relationships were maintained between Stilwell's headquarters across the China, Burma, and India (CBI) theater. Eric Sevareid, the hugely popular Columbia Broadcasting Service (CBS) journalist who had broken the news of the German occupation of Paris in June 1940 via live broadcast, had been sent by the White House to take a firsthand look at the issue of China. The third VIP was Bill Stanton, a senior civil servant from the Board of Economic Warfare (described by Sevareid as a "tall American of forty with close-cropped hair and a lilting British accent" picked up during long years spent in Hong Kong) whose task in the CBI theater was to analyze economic information as part of the war effort against the Japanese. The fourth VIP to climb aboard that morning was Captain Duncan C. Lee from the Office of Strategic Services (OSS). A distant descendant of General Robert E. Lee, he was also—unknown to his fellow passengers—the most senior Soviet spy to penetrate this predecessor to the Central Intelligence Agency (CIA). Jack Davies was later to record that Lee was "the son of missionary parents in China. He had been a Rhodes Scholar, then one of the bright young lawyers recruited by General 'Wild Bill' Donovan for his Office of Strategic Services. Duncan belonged to OSS headquarters in Washington. . . . We had travelled together from Washington via London, Algiers and Cairo, to the CBI Theater where he was now on an inspection tour." One of Lee's tasks was to interrogate General Dai Li, Chiang Kai-shek's secretive intelligence chief, about the paucity of usable intelligence reaching the OSS from China despite the cornucopia of hard-won supplies America was lavishing on the Kuomintang.

Sevareid had first encountered Lee and Davies at Khartoum Airport. Under the burning sun he had spotted Davies squatting "in the narrow shaft of shade under the wing of the waiting plane," at peace with the world and with himself:

> He was a man of medium size, with thinning, sandy hair, an obvious civilian, hatless, and dressed in khaki trousers and a cotton army shirt open at the neck. With complete self-possession he continued to sit there, reading a book, oblivious to the activity around him. Here, I thought, is a superior man, who has mastered this nerve-shredding business of doing a civilian job under army routines. I noticed that the book was Laski's *Reflections*, and then I recognized the face. He was John Davies of the State Department, political advisor to General Stilwell. . . . I was traveling in good company. . . . A time was coming when Davies's intelligence, humor, and coolheadedness were to be important factors for personal salvation in a common crisis.

When he first set eyes on Dumbastapur, Eric Sevareid was appalled—it was hardly a fit place for young Americans to live and work, particularly when they were sacrificing so much to support the unscrupulous Kuomintang. The bodies of young American air crew scattered across the roof of the world testified to that.

Save for a few officers who could enjoy the comfort of tea-garden bungalows, they were living in shocking conditions. There were at this time absolutely no amenities of life—no lounging places, no Red Cross girls, nothing cool and refreshing to eat and drink, no near-by rest resort to visit on leave. It was a dread and dismal place where dysentery was frequent and malaria certain, where haggard, sweating men dragged their feverish bodies through the day, ate execrable food, and shivered on cramped cots through nights often made unbearable by the mosquitoes. Men collapsed under the strain, and officers were frequently broken by distant superiors when the statistics of their performance fell short.

Sevareid was keen to leave India. At Dumbastapur he had had the comfort of a tea planter's bungalow but been irritated by the complacency of an imperial system in which British administrators would spend their lives "in lonely and correct preparation for a lonely and correct death." His frustration at the apparent British nonchalance toward the US war effort would have been tempered if he had known that the training of the Chinese Army at Ramgargh had actually been funded by Britain. Ignorant of the finer points of the combined Allied war effort but incisive in his judgments about crumbling imperial edifices, Eric Sevareid was relieved that morning to be climbing aboard the C-46 and getting out of the place. Declining British global power was contrasted with the energy of young Americans taking on the world. He wrote in lyrical terms of the youthful men of the ATC who daily sustained the Hump:

They measured the far horizons and calculated the heavens with their stubby schoolroom pencils. They peered through the majestic avenues of castellated cloud and wiped their dime-store colored spectacles. Their young eyes looked into the depths of mysterious seas and regarded the unfolding of the vast continents which showed on their faces the laboring of God's time and the hands of men, while they munched a wad of Wrigley's Spearmint, fingered the newly sprouted mustache, and wondered about its effect in Lauterbach's drugstore back in Des Moines. They knew the lines and corrugations of the ancient earth as they knew the palm of their hands, and took them equally for granted.

Theodore White agreed, observing that these youngsters were doing a man's job but did not have the experience to "qualify them for a co-pilot's job on an American airline."

Low cloud had been forecast in the upper reaches of the Brahmaputra Valley that morning but was due to disperse as the day warmed up. Importantly, no higher formations of cumulus were predicted. Despite this, Harry Neveu had carefully studied the sky before boarding, trying to spot telltale signs of the towering white accumulations that could shear the wings off an aircraft. There had been enough pilots' stories of terrifying journeys over the Hump and the 8,000 square miles of green mountains stretching deep into Manipur and beyond to make crews acutely cloud conscious—not just at the start of the three-and-a-half-hour flight but throughout the perilous 700-mile journey across northern Burma into Kunming. Aircraft caught in clouds that could rise from 2,000 to 40,000 feet had been violently tossed around and sometimes destroyed. Pilots exited cloud formations to find themselves flying upside down; others entered at one altitude to emerge facing completely different directions at wildly differing heights. For pilot Eric Forsdike, flying twin-engine transport aircraft through these monstrous cloud formations was an occupational hazard: "If we could not find a way between the cumuli-nimbus clouds, developing into huge mushroom shapes we reduced speed, sunglasses on to reduce the glare of the lightning flashes which were almost continuous, and hoped for the best." And if the weather didn't get them,

Japanese Zeros flying from Myitkyina in north-central Burma routinely fell on the transports as they lumbered toward China.

From Chabua's runway it was impossible to see beyond the mountains reaching high into the sky to the east, north, and west, the dark mass of tangled green hills providing a formidable barrier to the endless Burmese jungle beyond. This remote terrain offered sanctuary to the scattered Naga population, whose exposure to Westerners had increased since the Japanese war had lapped against their shores in 1942. Only those Nagas who had come down from the hills to live in the river valley maintained any contact with the new influx of foreigners—primarily Chinese and Americans who were there to sustain the US support to China over the Hump and, later, via the tortuous land route over the Burma Road from Ledo. Few visitors were allowed to venture into the remote territories that ran east for 200 miles down to the Chindwin and Burma. After subduing Naga head-hunting raids into the Assamese tea plantations in the 1880s, the British had applied a light dusting of imperial paternalism across most of the Naga territories, trying to protect the ethnological purity of the region by controlling visitors through an "inner line" system: only those with a legitimate reason to visit the hills could secure a restricted-area permit from the deputy commissioner in Kohima.*

To the west the hills rose sharply from the wide river valley, the lower reaches of massive mountain ranges originating right up to the roof of the world. Like a great bottleneck, the valley floor to the northeast was hemmed in on three sides by mountains that seemed to punch into the sky. To reach Kunming in China's Yunnan Province, the standard route was across the 10,000-foot-high Patkoi Hills immediately to the east of Chabua, then over the northernmost reaches of Burma—first the Hukawng Valley, followed by Fort Hertz, then the 15,000-foot-high Kaolikung Range, then the Salween River, after which the massive range separating the Salween from the Mekong, with some peaks over 20,000 feet high,

---

*A process that didn't end until 2010.

appeared—before dropping to the Yunnanese plateau, 6,000 feet above sea level.

Flying the Hump was one of the scariest things a pilot ever had to do. It repeatedly exposed men to very high levels of risk, as the journey, crossing the upper reaches of Burma, was one of the most dangerous imaginable. This was partly because of the extreme heights at which the unpressurized aircraft had to fly above the complex tangle of snow-covered Himalayan peaks on Burma's northern and eastern borders. It was also because the Japanese were close by, with fighter planes based in the northern Burmese town of Myitkyina sweeping out daily in pursuit of the lumbering American transport planes making their way to and from China. The word *Hump* was one "that made men afraid," observed the Australian journalist Ronald McKie, who visited India in 1943. It was also because so little was known about much of the unmapped green vastness that stretched for hundreds of miles far beneath the thin aluminum air frames making their bumpy way to China. What fierce tribesmen inhabited the wastelands below, far from the comforting certainties of Western civilization?

The first question every pilot involuntarily asked himself when setting out on a journey over the Hump was "What are my chances of getting to Kunming?" The second was "What are my chances of survival if I have to bail out?" There were hundreds of hazards for pilots to face. White listed a few:

> Ice can build up so rapidly on the wings that within five minutes a plane loses all flying capacity and drops like a rock into the jungle. In summer there are monsoons—black, solid masses of rain and wind that flick a plane about as if it were a feather. There are convection and thermal currents that send the instruments into crazy spins. The indicated rate of descent may be 1,500 feet a minute going down when the altitude meter shows 1,500 feet going up. A pilot may be putting his plane down as hard as he can and the wind and clouds will be sending it up twice as fast as he is descending; or vice versa, which is worse.

The luggage lay in piles between the passengers, dispersed along the fuselage to ensure that the center of gravity remained just forward of the wing main spar and secured by rope netting to the floor. The men had been searched (a "severe examination," according to Sevareid) for the alcohol and cigarettes that servicemen routinely smuggled into China, though the searchers missed the bottle of gin that Lee had secreted on his person. Such was Davies's authority that the rare cognac he carried was deemed a "gift" and waved through. The C-46's hold luggage weight amounted to less than 7,000 pounds, but when added to the twenty-one passengers and crew (3,150 pounds) it was the maximum that could be carried by the twin-engine plane. Neveu's primary concern was that the weight of the aircraft be accurately calculated and carefully distributed so that the plane was neutrally balanced, that is, neither front- nor rear-heavy. "If you had something heavy towards the back it could be dangerous, you had to keep the center of gravity," he recalled. "And as you use your fuel up, your center of gravity changes too, so you had to be concerned with that too. Although with passengers you could move them around too to adjust for it."

It is almost certain that none of the passengers were aware that they were embarking in an aircraft that had had its license to carry passengers temporarily revoked. The demands of war had resulted in its rushed introduction into service long before all its testing was complete. It therefore arrived in the theater full of niggling faults that gave it a poor reputation for reliability. The first thirty aircraft arrived at Chabua in April 1943, and the crews—inherently suspicious of military equipment produced for the lowest tender—quickly dubbed them "the Curtiss Calamity," "the Plumber's Nightmare," and "the Flying Coffin." Stilwell—the American whom Roosevelt had loaned to Chiang Kai-shek, leader of the nationalist Kuomintang—testily noted in his diary that "the C-46 is full of bugs. Carburetor ices up. We have lost six over the Hump and the boys' morale is lower and lower." Theodore White described the problem of the C-46 in *LIFE* magazine when reporting that restrictions on ATC operations across the Hump had been lifted in 1945:

The early runs had been made in DC-3s, whose normal ceiling was 12,000 feet and which had to be flown at 17,000 and 18,000. The C-87 had trouble with icing, and maintenance of its four engines was a drain on limited repair facilities. [Brigadier General] Alexander [ATC commander] chose as his ship the new Curtiss C-46—a twin-engine, big-bellied, ugly work-ship. It was just beginning to come from the assembly lines in the U.S., but the need for it was so great that it was rushed to Assam before the bugs had been taken out. There was no time for routine test flying to build up a backlog of pilot experience and knowledge of spare part requirements. The planes came out factory-fresh and were test flown in actual operation under conditions no other plane in aviation history has had to meet. They were subjected to all the climatic conditions of India and the Hump—dust, excessive heat, flight with maximum loads at higher than maximum serviceable altitudes, at maximum rates of climb, through turbulent winds and storms. . . . Critical parts began to give way all at once, at rates which no previous experience could have forecast. Men died in the air and on the ground learning about the ship, ironing out its weaknesses, beating out a body of experience in the presence of overpowering military emergency.

When they arrived in India the C-46's had been accompanied by Curtiss-Wright test crews, including Chief Test Pilot Herbert Fisher, who completed ninety-six missions into China to remove bugs. Sevareid knew of the aircraft's reputation—nearly refusing to enter when it dawned on him that this was a C-46—but admitted that he lacked the moral courage to protest. "That's something one just doesn't do," he later observed. With a journalist's instinct he had discovered that the aircraft had arrived in theater "with 196 alterations still to be made" to make it airworthy.

Like Sevareid, most passengers would have been all too aware of the dreadful attrition rate of the aircraft flying the Hump. Between June and December 1943 the official history of the ATC recorded "135 major aircraft accidents on the Hump route" with 168 fatalities.

ATC officials at Washington, New Delhi, and Chabua regretted the casualties but felt obliged "to push the job for all it is worth." As ATC chief of staff General Cyrus Smith put it, "We are paying for it in men and airplanes. The kids here are flying over their head at night and in daytime and they bust them up for reasons that sometimes seem silly. They are not silly, however, for we are asking boys to do what would be most difficult for men to accomplish; with the experience level here we are going to pay dearly for the tonnage moved across the Hump. . . . With the men available, there is nothing else to do." The USAAF described the route between India and Yunnan Province as "the most dangerous ever assigned to air transport." During the second half of 1943, 155 aircraft came down, a rate of nearly one a day.

Since leaving the States in July Sevareid had been at the mercy of the USAAF, flying on hard, aluminum-framed seats across the world—from Washington to Ascension Island, the Gold Coast to Khartoum, Eritrea to Aden, and finally New Delhi to Ramgargh—to the point where, arriving in India, he and his colleagues had reached the limits of their endurance. They swore to draw up a charter for "The American Society of Airplane-Haters—under the rules no one would be eligible unless he had spent so many hours on 'bucket seats' with extra points for those who had passed their hours over Africa or Asia in midsummer."

But if the passengers hated it, air crews were all too aware of the risks they ran in flying each day. From what Sevareid could deduce, they knew they were doing far too much with far too little:

Pilots were overworked, and when they had made the perilous flight to China and back the same day, having fought storm and fog and ice, they simply fell into their cots as they were, unshaved and unwashed, to catch a few hours of unrefreshing sleep before repeating the venture next day. Hardly a day passed that the operations radio did not hear the distress signal of a crew going down in the jungle valleys or among the forbidding peaks. Few at that time were ever found again, and there was a saying among the pilots that they could plot their course to China by the line of smoking wrecks upon the hillsides. It is not often that one sees fear in the faces of fliers, but I saw it here. Each one reckoned that it was only a matter of time before his turn would come; they had the feeling of men who know they have been condemned.

The CBS journalist had arrived at Chabua at a point when the ATC was in crisis. Massive pressure on a limited number of aircraft to increase the tonnage of war materiel flown over the Hump; poor facilities at the airfield for air crews, passengers, and ground crews; the inexperience of pilots, mechanics, and navigators; the limited availability of spare parts for the C-46's; and a paucity of radio and navigation aids made the high attrition rates a simple though depressing fact of life.

With passengers and baggage safely stowed, the crew chief poked his head through the cockpit door and announced, "Ready to go." Harry Neveu nodded his thanks and flicked the starter switches for the two Pratt & Whitney "Double Wasp" 2800s, throttling back to warm them before receiving permission—a flashing red light—from Chabua Tower for takeoff. They were slightly late, probably because of the time it had taken to marshal the passengers and parachutes on board, but at 8 he was able to taxi to the runway and take off. As he gradually increased the throttle, the plane rapidly gained speed and, with tail rising off the ground, hurtled down the runway. Neveu gently drew back the wheel, and the plane became airborne.

Circling the airfield, Neveu climbed gradually before setting a course for 115 degrees, taking them east to the new Burma Road being built from Ledo into China before turning southeast on the Burmese side of the Patkois for a hundred miles, then banking left across northern Burma, avoiding the Chinese border's worst mountains. ATC pilots were allowed some route discretion but had to file flight plans with air traffic control at Chabua before departure so that their journey could be retraced in the event of the loss of the aircraft. Harry Neveu had often flown into Kunming, and with the C-46's operating ceiling of 24,500 feet his route avoided the highest mountains and allowed the greatest distance from the Japanese combat patrols at Myitkyina. If he met one of the deadly Zeros, he knew that his only defense "was to climb and jump into the clouds. And then you had to worry about the mountains digging up into the clouds and running into them. It was pretty much a seat-of-the-pants navigational flight."

The morning was beautiful. The mist over the Naga Hills rolled westward like a waterfall. Climbing east through a thin layer of haze, the twin Pratt & Whitney radials drummed serenely away, the mist changing color from white to pink as the tops of the Patkois were reached and turning to gold as the sun appeared over the horizon. The vibrations through the aircraft made it too noisy for talk, and many passengers dropped off to sleep.

Jack Davies was aware of problems afflicting C-46's but had been satisfied by the powerful surge of the aircraft as it took off; he made himself as comfortable as he could. Sevareid stared out the window as Neveu took them through wisps of cloud before turning south. When the plane tilted to turn he caught a glimpse of the majestic, snow-capped Himalayas, sunshine streaming through the windows and illuminating the cabin like a klieg light. As the plane gathered height Davies was struck by the intense green far below, the acres of tea gardens marching in regiments across the hills. Beside him Duncan C. Lee settled into his book as Sevareid scribbled down his thoughts. Colonel Wang Pae Chae and Lieutenant Colonel Kwoh Li looked less comfortable, turning green with each movement of the C-46. As they headed out over the vast green wilderness everything seemed to be working perfectly.

Exactly one hour later the C-46 was above the Patkoi Hills, whose highest peak, Mount Saramati, lies at 12,500 feet. As Neveu began turning the aircraft due east Sevareid, who had been lost in thought, was startled by Corporal Stanley Waterbury tripping over his outstretched legs as he rushed down the fuselage.

"Know what?" the young man yelled in his ear. "The left engine has gone."

2

BURMESE DAYS

Thirty minutes after leaving Chabua and climbing over the northern reaches of the Patkoi Range, Harry Neveu entered Burmese airspace. His plan was to fly just on the eastern edge of the Patkois for a hundred miles or so before turning left and heading over the Chindwin River and the lower reaches of the Hukawng Valley in an easterly direction toward China. The hills of the Patkois were populated by Nagas. Once the jagged mountains had flattened out into the hills and river valleys of northern Burma, the area became the territory of the Kachins, whose largest settlement was Myitkyina, lying in the center of north Burma.

Burma's 261,200 square miles is the size of Texas.* The distance between its border with northern Malaysia (then Malaya) and the Pangsau Pass, which traverses the northern edge of the Patkoi Range into India, is about 1,750 miles (2,800 kilometers) by road, a distance comparable to that between Paris and Moscow or New York and Phoenix, Arizona. The country is surrounded on its northern and eastern sides by rugged mountains and is bordered on the western side by sea. The Himalayas guard its northern extremities and then flow deep into the heart of the country, petering out into a thick belt of high, precipitous, and tangled hills. Of these, the Naga Hills in the northwest and the Chin Hills in the center boast heights of between 8,000 and 12,000 feet, and the Arakan Yomas in the south form a natural barrier between central Burma and the coastal strip to the north and south of Akyab. In the east,

---

*The country has been called Myanmar since 1989.

bordering Yunnan, the mountains reach double that height. The Chinese name for the Naga Hills, in a hint of their distant fearsomeness, translates as "Savage Mountains."

Wide, prairielike plains in the center of the country offer sharp contrast to the tropical jungle in the south and east. Vast rivers—the Irrawaddy, Chindwin, Sittang, and Salween—split the country like giant wedges. The Irrawaddy flows more than 1,300 miles from the northernmost reaches of the country and the Salween even farther. The Chindwin starts in the far northwest, meandering from its watershed in the Himalayas south through the vast river valley with the green, mist-shrouded mountains that separate Burma from India reaching into the sky on its western flank. The huge distances of this country were made even more formidable by the paucity of roads or railways. In 1941 most inland trade and communications were conducted largely on the great rivers. The few roads and railways that did exist in Burma tended to run north–south with the grain of the country, following the line of the rivers. Only one road of significance ran into China, the 1,500-mile-long Burma Road. The few tracks that existed were not suitable for all-weather use, particularly by vehicles, and were liable to interruption by floods and landslides during the monsoon. The best way of getting around was by airplane.

The British had been rulers of this ancient country since their defeat of the last Burmese king, Thibaw Min, in 1885. In early 1942 this period of colonial rule came to an ignominious end when the Japanese occupied the country following an extraordinarily successful invasion, driving out and defeating the humiliated British in a lightning advance that mirrored the German blitzkrieg in France in 1940. Japanese generals had visited France, escorted by their exultant German hosts, to learn the secret of the Wehrmacht's success. The Japanese invasion was designed to protect the "back door" of its advance on Singapore and to sever the famous Burma Road that ran American supplies 1,500 miles from Rangoon into Yunnan. The Burma Road was the lifeline for Chiang Kai-shek's beleaguered nationalist Chinese, who had been fighting the Japanese since the start of the Sino-Japanese War in 1937. The Chinese were at the time tying down twenty Japanese divisions, about half of the fighting formations of the Imperial Army. By the end of 1940 the Burma Road was the only external source of supplies for the Chinese and a considerable hindrance to Japanese ambitions, even though, because of theft and corruption, only a third of all the American lend-lease supplies arriving in Rangoon ever reached Chungking. The most effective way for the Japanese to halt US support to the Chinese would be to seize Rangoon and thus close the Burma Road. Until late 1940, however, British assessments of the threat limited Japanese action to the occasional air raid on Burma's capital city. The British did not consider a Japanese invasion possible, or probable.

In 1941 the forty-two-year-old Connecticut-born, Pulitzer Prize–winning journalist Leland Stowe was in Burma's capital city. He had been something akin to an Old Testament prophet in his warnings about the enemies that threatened American somnolence in the years leading up to World War II. Even from the perspective of 1941, his prescience was remarkable. He had argued to an uncomprehending West for nearly a decade that the world was an ugly place—and about to get much uglier if those countries that had the wherewithal to control the bullies in the European playground did nothing about it. A hostile, militaristic state lay like a dangerous cancer in the heart of Europe, intent on both domestic political subjugation and territorial expansion and driven by a grotesque and racist ideology. However, this state—Fascist Germany—was surrounded on all sides by democracies that were intent on keeping their heads resolutely in the sand. At best they refused to accept the political realities staring them in the face; at worst they wanted to guarantee their security through a policy of appeasement, whatever the risk to their principles. Shocked by the rampant militarism of the Germany he had observed firsthand during a visit in 1933, Stowe attempted to awaken the West to the danger it faced. He was rebuffed by a solid wall of complacency on both sides of the Atlantic. He wrote newspaper articles warning of German militarism, but they were ignored by editors unwilling to be labeled alarmist—or to upset the Germans—and even the book Stowe wrote on the subject, *Nazi Germany Means War*, was a flop. People didn't want to spend money on a book persuading them, after the recent trauma of the Western Front, that war was once more imminent. After observing firsthand the German invasion of Norway in April 1940 and the role played by Quisling's Fifth Columnists in the bloodless capture of Oslo, Stowe found himself in Rangoon at the end of 1941, reporting for the *Chicago Daily News* on what he was later to describe as "the greatest racket in the Far East": the Burma Road.

Two days before Christmas 1941 he heard the approaching sound of massed aircraft. The noise brought last-minute Christmas shoppers onto the streets, despite the midday heat (it was an almost unbearable 111°F) to observe this unusual sight. There were few aircraft of any type, civilian or military, based in Rangoon at the time, although they included fourteen American P40 Tomahawk fighters, with their distinctive tiger teeth painted on the engine cowlings, flown by the mercenaries of the American Volunteer Group (AVG) who called themselves the "Flying Tigers" and operated on behalf of the Chinese Army. Alongside these the British possessed a mere sixteen fighters, obsolete Brewster Buffaloes. There were no bombers. "They must be British reinforcements," thought some as they watched the slow-moving, high-flying aircraft arrive overhead in a tight, disciplined formation. It had been two weeks since the shocking news had arrived that the Japanese had attacked Pearl Harbor and simultaneously launched invasions of Hong Kong, Malaya, Borneo, and the Philippines. The Japanese had even occupied a point on the distant southern tip of Burma. The British governor, Sir Reginald Dorman-Smith (known irreverently to some as "Dormouse-Smith"), had assured the population that the country was well protected; after all, Burma was part of the British Empire, over which the sun never set. The great fortress of Singapore was nearby and would provide military aid in the unlikely event that it was required. In the next few moments the sound of whistling filled the air before loud explosions began to reverberate across the city of half a million inhabitants. The aircraft were Japanese.

At Mingaladon Airfield, to the north of the city, Chuck Baisden, an armament technician in the AVG, stood watching the oncoming aircraft high in the sky while one of his colleagues started counting them. When he got to twenty-seven he shouted, "Hell they are not ours, we don't have that many."

There was an immediate mad dash for some slit trenches a few feet from where we had been standing. One group of the bombers targeted our field and laid their pattern precisely down the runway and through our dispersal area. I remember those black dots getting larger and larger accompanied by a whoose-whoose sound and thought they were all aimed directly at me. It was nothing compared to the shock of the bombs as they walked up the field with the noise getting louder and louder. The concussion bounced us around in the trench and from the smell someone had voided in his trousers. I know one 21 year old that grew up in a hurry.

In the city large numbers of native workers stood looking in wonder at the silvery flight of aircraft far above them and became tragic casualties of unheralded aggression. With no expectation of attack, a grotesque complacency by the authorities and no public air-raid shelters (although Dorman-Smith had one for his own family and staff, recently completed at considerable cost to public funds) caused some 3,000 casualties and the mass panic of the population. It was not merely the docks, where some 85,000 tons of American lend-lease supplies awaited transport to China along the Burma Road, that were targeted, but both residential and city-center locations. By the end of the day vast numbers—perhaps the bulk of the population—were clogging the roads northward in an attempt to escape the horror. A second attack was launched the following day, Christmas Day. Many vital civil and administrative functions ceased, and a paralysis in government and administration set in. Public hysteria was followed by widespread lawlessness. At a stroke the city lost its entire labor force. All essential services ceased. Some staggered on for the next few months before the Japanese arrived at the gates of the city in early March, whereas others stopped completely. The railways and buses; electricity, telephones, water, and sanitation; post; and mortuaries as well as private enterprise, especially food supply, never recovered from those two first devastating air raids. Scores of thousands fled north, perhaps three-quarters of the entire population, with whatever possessions they could carry to what they believed to be the safety of central Burma. The US war correspondent Alfred Wragg watched Rangoon empty like a bathtub of dirty water after that first attack: "It was an exodus on foot. Men, women and children. Pitiful in their terror, their lack of food supplies and equipment. Pathetic in their urgency to escape. Their sudden determination to walk home [to India], to walk a thousand miles—two thousand miles! That night, Rangoon was a city of the dead."

These attacks and the invasion that followed precipitated a human disaster for hundreds of thousands of men, women, and children for whom the end of British protection meant extreme danger. Colonial Burma had been populated for decades by many scores of thousands of low-paid Indian workers fulfilling menial but essential jobs in an economy dependent on large-scale manual labor. They had followed the British in the good times as the empire had expanded. These foreigners had helped maintain British rule and repress nationalist ambitions among the subjugated Burmese. In any case, Burma in 1941 was divided along ethnic and tribal lines. Little love was lost between the ten million or so indigenous Burmese, who populated the coastline and the lowland plains, and the seven million people of the tribes who occupied the hill country away from the river valleys: the Shans, Karens, Chins, Kachins, and Nagas. Many Burmese were strongly nationalistic; a significant minority actively opposed the British (and what they regarded as the colonial rulers' Indian lackeys) and, when war came, openly sided with the Japanese against their hated colonial overseers. The people of the hills, by contrast, tended to be anti-Burmese and, consequently, pro-British. Unsurprisingly, until 1937, when Burma received its independence from India (it remained a British colony, with a governor reporting to London), the local Burma Army re-cruited almost exclusively from the tribespeople and those Indians and Gurkhas who were domiciled in Burma.

Try as they might, no correspondents could get the magnitude of the disaster past the British government censors, so the world remained largely unaware of Burma's predicament. "Damage was slight and casualties few," reported those newspapers across Amer-ica on January 1, 1942, that even bothered to run the story of the bombing of Rangoon on Christmas Eve. The attack had an imme-diate impact, however, on at least two American families. The *Corsi-cana Daily Sun* in Texas reported that the secretary of state—Cordell Hull—had informed the family of Neil G. Martin, a former football star of the University of Arkansas and a pilot in the AVG, that he was missing following the attack, but that no further information was available. His father refused to believe he was dead. "We can only hope for the best until we receive further word," he told the newspaper. Martin's death was confirmed within days, however. He had been shot down in his fighter plane. Another American, twenty-one-year-old Henry Gilbert, died in aerial combat with the invaders on that fateful Christmas Eve. Like Neil Martin's aircraft, his P40 was destroyed as he engaged the overwhelmingly superior Japanese force.

Journalist O. D. Gallagher estimated that by the end of Christ-mas Day, 300,000 men, women, and children had fled the smoke-shrouded capital. The exodus became dramatically magnified when news began to seep through that the Japanese were advancing from the south and that nothing seemed able to stop them. It has been estimated that nearly a million people were on the move in Burma during the first five months of 1942, most of whom were heading north with little more than what they could carry in an attempt to escape the advancing Japanese. Numbers remain hard to ascertain, but perhaps half a million or more attempted to walk all the way into India, with as many as 20 percent of these pitiful refugees dy-ing in the attempt. No one really knows, but it was a humanitarian disaster of epic proportions. News of the barbarity with which it treated anyone whom it considered to be its enemy had long gone before the Japanese Army, fanning the flames of panic. In mid-February 1942 the government had ordered the compulsory evacuation of Europeans and selected Asians: those who had worked for the colonial power and would be vulnerable if left behind. Fear fueled their every step. Stephen Brookes, who was eleven years old at the time, described the sight as people attempted to escape from Myitkyina, the sound of gunfire in the distance:

> The road we followed was a wide cart-track cut out of the thick jungle, which rose on either side like a green curtain fifty feet high. Within this gloomy corridor moved a stream of refugees, thousands of them as far as the eye could see—Indians, British, Chinese, Eurasians; troops, civilians, government officials; parents and children, the sick and the dying. There were families pushing barrows laden with children and heavy sacks of food and bedding; bullock carts swaying with the weight of people crowded on their flimsy frames; lorries, cars, bicycles, army trucks, jeeps, cattle and the occasional elephant—all loaded to breaking point with people and belongings. And entwined in this curious procession were thousands more on foot: plodding, sleeping, cooking, giving birth and dying in the jungle. Our family was a mere grain of sand in this dust-storm.

If they couldn't get out by sea or upcountry by the now thoroughly disorganized train service (which went as far as Myitkyina, 750 miles north in Kachin territory) or by road transport, they had no choice but to walk. The prospect was a terrible one. The journey from Rangoon to Imphal, in the eastern state of Manipur, was 750 miles, but for much of this route the refugees would be at the mercy of indifferent roads (there was no formal road between Burma and India), the vagaries of the weather (the monsoon season arrives in late April each year and runs until October), disease (malaria was rampant), and lack of food. Even worse was the fact that law and order had broken down in many parts of the country—including much of Rangoon, and the hostility of the Burmese population and marauding companies of *dacoit*s (bandits) who plagued the countryside during times of disorder proved a danger to those making their way to safety. For those unable to take the route to the Burmese border at Tamu on the Chindwin, the alternative was to travel north from Mandalay to Myitkyina and from there to attempt to make their way through the Hukawng Valley, a dangerously malarial stretch of remote country in the extreme north of the country. If hostile Burmese didn't get them, disease, exhaustion, or starvation would. Alfred Wragg called his book—referring to all who died across southeast Asia as a result of the Japanese invasion—*A Million Died!* It seems as reasonable an assessment as any.

The last inhabited area on the Burmese side of the Hukawng Valley was the Naga village of Shingbwiyang, 160 miles northwest from Myitkyina. From there traders' tracks extended a further sixty miles into India, crossing the 3,727-foot-high Pangsau Pass on the way. This was to be the point from which the new Burma Road would in due course be built, but in 1942 Shingbwiyang was where the innocent detritus of Burma washed up, many never to leave, their mortal remains rotting along pathways in the remote jungles. Stephen Brookes, who reached there on June 19, described it as "the gateway to India for about 45,000 refugees and Chinese soldiers. Most of them died in the village, others on the track to India, but no one cares any more. It was merely a side-show in the great scheme of things."

Beth Bootland was lucky enough to escape through Tamu into India with a party of families from Maymyo. It took a Japanese air raid to persuade her husband, Alan, to organize his family's flight. He gave Beth a revolver with instructions to shoot the children and then herself if the Japanese managed to catch up with them. He told her, "They raped the nurses in Hong Kong and Singapore, and killed them afterwards. You might as well kill yourself straight away. Shoot Ian first, then Keith, Lotte and yourself." Beth had no doubt that she would have done. "I didn't fancy being raped by the Japanese," she thought.

They were lucky. Their small party made it to Imphal in three weeks in a group of women and children escorted by a couple of Indian policemen. Countless others were not so fortunate. Survivors' narratives are replete with stories of starving refugees littering the hundreds of miles of trails stretching into India. Stephen Brookes saw things that still haunted him when he was persuaded to write his memoirs sixty years later: "During the weeks and months ahead I was to see hundreds of dead and dying people. I walked over them and sometimes, too exhausted to move, I slept next to them. I saw the dead in grotesque postures, rotting in the mud, the rivers and the jungle. I saw them in ones and piled up in dozens; in family groups and in whole camps. In the end, I became inured to the process of death."

Captain Geoffrey Tyson described one of many tragic scenes he saw along the road of death, coming across a slash-and-burn cultivation clearing (*jhum*) in the jungle:

The clearing was littered with tumble-down huts, where often whole families stayed and died together. I found the bodies of a mother and child locked in each other's arms. In another hut, were the remains of another mother who'd died in childbirth, with the child only half-born. In the one jhum more than fifty people had died. Sometimes pious Christians placed little wooden crucifixes in the ground before they died. Others had figures of the Virgin Mary still clutched in their skeleton hands. A soldier had expired wearing his side cap, all his cotton clothing had rotted away, but the woolen cap sat smartly on his grinning skull. Already the ever-destroying jungle had overgrown some of the older huts, covering up the skeletons and reducing them to dust and mold.

It could have been a metaphor for the death of an old regime and the onset of a new. By the end of May 1942 the Japanese were the new rulers of Burma. When in May 1942 the British and Chinese had been forced back to India, their tails very firmly between their legs, the commander of the British troops, Lieutenant General Bill Slim, had asserted, "We, the Allies, had been outmaneuvered, outfought and outgeneraled." In Lieutenant General "Vinegar Joe" Stilwell, who found himself commanding a ragbag of Chinese troops during the retreat, likewise observed in his no-nonsense way, "I claim we got a hell of a beating. We got run out of Burma and it is humiliating as hell."

3

BANZAI!

Far below Neveu's plane as it began its journey over Burma were the feared Japanese, specifically Lieutenant General Shinichi Tanaka's Eighteenth (Chrysanthemum) Division, the same outfit that had successfully captured Singapore in February 1942. The fighting ability of the Japanese soldier came as a profound shock to American and European troops in late 1941 and 1942. Although there had been many reports over the preceding decades of these troops' discipline, hardiness, and courage, their brutal professionalism came as an unwelcome surprise when combat was first joined at the start of Japan's offensive against the American and European colonial possessions in Asia in December 1941. The Japanese troops who invaded Burma were experienced, hardy, and well prepared. The Japanese soldier fought aggressively with a single-minded determination to succeed, repeatedly shaming his less persistent opponents. He tended to despise an enemy who gave up after halfhearted resistance as an unworthy adversary. Every individual Japanese soldier owed allegiance directly to the emperor, whom they believed to be directly descended from the ancient sun goddess. Disobedience, disloyalty, or failure were inconceivable, no matter how bad the situation or hard the circumstances. His daily routine included obeisance to the emperor through a ritual and energetic exclamation of "*Banzai!*" ("May the emperor live for 10,000 years!") together with bowing in prayer in the direction of Tokyo. The troops were intensely motivated. The war was widely perceived as a new dawn for Japan. There was a very real sense, sustained over many years by effective militarist propaganda, that the invasion forces were the divine instruments for securing Japan's destiny. The spiritual purpose and motivation for the troops were overwhelming.

Although the Japanese were arguably the toughest opponents that American troops—and British, Dutch, and Australian forces, for that matter—have ever had to fight, the almost universal attitude among the Western armies across southeast Asia in 1941 and 1942 was that the Japanese would be a poor enemy, easy to beat. Racism—and thoughtless lies that Western governments told their people about the military defenses and readiness of the region—bred profound ignorance. It was inconceivable to most Americans and Europeans in the Philippines, Malaya, Burma, Dutch East Indies, and Singapore that the Japanese Army represented a real threat to them in a stand-up fight. Most Europeans in the Far East, before the events of late 1941 and early 1942, regarded the Japanese, in the words of one Gurkha, John Cross, as "second-rate soldiers—short sighted, bad shots, afraid of the dark, so short-legged that they could not easily walk over rough ground and whose almond-shaped eyes could not see through bomb sights," even when there was considerable evidence of something very different from countless army-to-army exchanges over recent years. "We were arrogant about the Japs, we regarded them as coolies," said another young officer, John Randle. "We thought of them as third rate. My goodness me, we soon changed our tune." The US military observer in Singapore at the time of the invasion of Malaya described Japanese tactics:

> The Japs show great physical endurance and ability to cross difficult terrain including streams, swamps and jungle. In encounter, leading elements immediately fan out right and left to locate flanks, and attack simultaneously with the main body when it comes up. Their attitude is consistently aggressive and they infiltrate rapidly round any resistance met. . . . A company column is usually preceded by an advanced patrol split up into groups of

one or two men with tommy guns, who allow any British counter-attack to pass through them and then open fire on them from the rear. . . . They show great stamina and move through under-growth, climbing trees to avoid or ambush hostile patrols, and may lie hidden in bush or padi for hours waiting for a chance to advance or join up.

The Japanese overran Burma in an offensive that began shortly after the surprise attack on the US Pacific Fleet at Pearl Harbor in early December 1941. These operations began almost simulta-neously with attacks against the American-run Philippines; Brit-ish-run Hong Kong, Malaya, and Borneo; and Dutch-run Sumatra and Java. In Burma the Japanese were able to achieve complete and decisive victory in only five months.

During the relentless advance of the Japanese through Burma their method of war and their single-minded determination to win, together with their savagery and wanton disregard for life, their own or their enemies', came as a brutal shock to those en-trenched in the European military tradition and its deeply rooted codes of military conduct and chivalry. To ordinary fighting men the Japanese soldier quickly gained fame as a fearsome fighting beast for which none of their training had prepared them. Lieu-tenant James Lunt remembered the "speed with which they seized the fleeting chance; the exploitation of every weakness; the ruth-lessness with which they drove forward across terrain considered impassable; the skillful handling of their mortars; their stamina and, let it be said, their courage." Gallagher reported on "their fanaticism—their complete indifference to death, or rather their anxiety to die for the sake of Japan." The long years of occupa-tion in Manchuria and China had allowed a racist virus to perme-ate the ranks of the Japanese Army, and its rapid moral decline could be seen in the way it treated its victims. This attitude al-lowed the murder—indiscriminate and often brutal—of noncom-batants and prisoners of war to flourish. Terror was an intimate part of the fighting philosophy of the Imperial Japanese Army, as was retribution, and both were applied without distinction to civilians and soldiers. Shocked at what he had seen, Gallagher wrote in 1942, "What other so-called civilized nation could produce soldiers who pose for their pictures, proudly smiling, with bayonets dug deep into the backs of stripped, Chinese peasants? Where else could you find an Army officer grinning into the eye of the camera, his right hand holding a bloody sword, his left the hair of a severed, sightless but staring head? What they did in Hong Kong, Malaya, New Britain, is also known."

The ferocity of their onslaught gave the Japanese an immediate psychological advantage over their more pedestrian enemies and allowed them to dominate the battlefield, creating a legend of the invincible Japanese "superman" that would take at least two years to erase. Flyers such as Harry Neveu had a very real fear of falling into the hands of "the Japs." Pilot Lucien Ercolani told historian Henry Probert that the "thought of coming down among the Japanese was a constant anxiety, coupled with the fear of engine failure over the jungle or in the Bay of Bengal, and the fright all too often occasioned when flying in monsoon conditions—especially by night." Much had already been learned by 1943, from escapees and military intelligence seeping back from occupied areas, of the casual brutality handed out as a matter of course to prisoners of the Japanese. Captured fliers were especially hated. Men who had managed to escape from Hong Kong told of the bayoneting of the wounded in their hospital beds and of the repeated rape of nurses, followed by their murder. During the advance down the Malay Peninsula wounded prisoners were routinely bayoneted to death, and several hundred Australian and Indian prisoners had been bound and systematically murdered at Parit Sulong. In Singapore the patients in the Alexandra Hospital, including one on the operating table, had been murdered. From the Philippines came rumors of the Bataan Death March, during which 7,000 men, American and Filipino, of 76,000 who had surrendered had been butchered as they were harried on the forty-mile march from Manila to San Fernando. This news served to reinforce years of horror stories emanating from Japanese-occupied China during the previous decade, especially the rape of Nanking in 1937 and 1938. Japanese militarism had for many years inculcated in the minds of its people, especially its military personnel, a loathing of foreigners. Under the banner of "Asia for the Asiatics" this hatred was focused especially on Anglo-Saxons. No humiliation was sufficient for those pathetic specimens of European humanity, male or female, who surrendered to the Japanese Army. In the context of the interpretation of Bushido in play during the 1930s, surrender was the worst kind of humiliation, to which the Japanese samurai (soldier) was duty-bound to respond by suicide (often by means of ritual disemboweling, known as hara-kiri).

The extent in both type and scale of such extraordinary abuses had been reported in the American press, but the trauma that these events represented was too far away to have any direct consequence for American readers; in any case, many regarded the stories as exaggerations. "China tried to tell the world the truth about the . . . Japanese during her long war with them," observed Gallagher, who visited Shanghai in 1937. "Few of us were interested enough to listen carefully." The retreat north from Rangoon between March and May 1942 had already provided a substantial collection of accounts of Japanese battlefield brutality. A clear pattern emerged of not merely an apparent disregard for the rules of war but also a distinct stream of sadism that ran throughout the psyche of the entire Japanese Armed Forces. Summary beheadings and the mass execution of prisoners by bayonet for seemingly no reason except the satiation of martial pleasure were the least of these accounts. Claims of worse atrocities, such as crucifixion and deliberate cruelty to helpless captives, were widespread. Air crew, especially those of bomber aircraft, were regarded by the Japanese as especially pernicious because they dealt random death from the sky. The American newspapers in particular had begun to report horror stories from the war in the Far East as 1942 progressed, and these issues were well known to men such as Harry Neveu and his crew. Survivors from Bataan shocked American readers with the

stories of barely believable atrocities perpetrated on large numbers of weakened men following their surrender. Most newspapers
across the United States reported on April 22, 1942, the news that
three of the eight airmen who had been captured following the first
bombing raid on Tokyo (the "Doolittle Raid") had been executed
as war criminals in violation of all the accepted rules of war. Inter-
estingly, most articles appeared to contextualize Japanese brutality
and disregard for the humanitarian principles at the heart of the
Geneva Conventions of 1929 by referring to the Nanking Massacre.
The reporters didn't yet know that on August 13, 1942, the military
government of Japan had promulgated the death sentence for all
captured fliers in its "Regulations for Punishment of Enemy Air
Crews": "Enemy flyers who have raided Japanese territories, Man-
chukuo, or our operational areas, come within our jurisdiction, and
violated wartime international law shall be tried by court martial
and sentenced to death or heavy punishment as important war
criminals."

Later in the year, on October 5, 1942, American newspapers
widely reported the news of the discovery of the diary of a Japanese soldier that described the beheading of an American pilot. In
Burma Japanese mistreatment of captured flyers was routine. In
but one example a Liberator bomber on radar-detection duties was
shot down by a Japanese fighter forty miles southeast of Rangoon
on January 31, 1945. All six crewmen managed to bail out but were
handed over to the notorious military police, the Kempetai. The
Japanese were furious that the Allies were using radio-detection
techniques in their war effort and were desperate to gain any intelligence they could gather from the crew. They focused their at-
tentions not on the pilot and copilot, who survived, but on the four
noncommissioned officers, including the radio operator, twenty-
three-year-old Stanley Woodbridge. Hours of torture failed to elicit
any information from the four men. Forced at bayonet point to
march ten miles into the jungle on February 7, they were made
to kneel before a large pit. There they were blindfolded and their
heads taken off, one by one, by a Japanese officer with his sword.

Their bodies were kicked into the grave, and the jungle was allowed to swallow up the evidence.

|||

The Japanese invasion of Burma in 1942 swamped the country like a tsunami. Yet, as these destructive waters flowed into Burma's hilly periphery, especially in the north—which was the territory from Myitkyina and above of the pro-British Kachins—Japanese influence, due to the wide spread of their resources, became weaker. However, this weakening did not matter to the Japanese Army. Its primary task—were it ever to be necessary—was to protect Burma from counterattack by the British from India to the east and from the Chinese in Yunnan to the west as well as to suppress any hint of local rebellion by the hill people of the mountainous peripheries of the country: the Chin, Lushai, Kuki, Naga, Kachin, Karen, and Shan.

In the north this rebellion began almost immediately, with British-led Kachin rebels laying ambushes, killing small groups of soldiers, and taking on enemy patrols, although for much of 1943 these actions caused less harm to the Japanese than did casualties from tiger attacks and malaria. Tanaka, commander of the Eighteenth Division, placed two of his regiments (each containing three battalions), the 55th and 56th, in the Hukawng Valley and the 114th at Myitkyina.* At the time of Neveu's flight into Burma in August 1943 Tanaka's forces were spread thinly across this vast terrain. As they had advanced through Burma in 1942 they had enjoyed the support of large numbers of anti-British nationalists who did what they could to assist the Japanese, even to the extent of taking up arms against the hated British and harrying the exodus of soldiers and civilians as it made its difficult way to sanctuary in India. The leadership of the anti-British movement was held by Aung San, a

---

*His third regiment, the 124th, together with the 35th Brigade, had been detached for duty in the Pacific theater in late 1942.

student leader who had thrown in his lot with the Japanese in 1940 and who is best remembered outside Burma today for his Nobel Peace Prize–winning daughter, Aung San Suu Kyi. However, as the Japanese moved into the hill country that made up almost the entirety of Burma's periphery, the situation changed. The people of the hills generally held much less animus against the British colonialists and their Indian lackeys than did the Burmese of the plains; many in fact preferred them to the Japanese. Aung San's Burma Independence Army made limited, if any, progress in the Kachin Hills of north Burma despite the fact that in the early months of the invasion its numbers swelled as the Japanese fanned out across the country and excited nationalists and young hotheads alike joined the movement. In the east the hostility of the ethnic Burmese movement to the pro-British Karens resulted in widespread bloodshed. Indeed, the war that erupted between the Buddhist pro-Japanese ethnic Burmans and the pro-British Christian Karens precipitated a civil war that continues to this day. In the north the Japanese were harried from the start by the Kachins, who in due course flocked in large numbers to British and American anti-Japanese guerrilla units, not least of which was Detachment 101 of the OSS. The primary Kachin-led insurgency against the Japanese was farther to the east, in the Hukawng Valley, through which thousands of hapless refugees had streamed in 1942.

The men of the Hump airlift daily defied the threat of falling into the hands of the Japanese. To do so would mean a death sentence.

4

THE CRASH

Eric Sevareid hadn't detected any change in tone from the engine or the aircraft's smooth vibration as it made its way through the still blue skies. Perhaps the young corporal was mistaken? Looking around, he saw the two Chinese officers sitting with their eyes closed. A few months earlier American crews had dubbed the airlift of 14,000 Chinese troops from Kunming to Ramgargh the "vomit trail," as virtually all of the passengers, taking their first flight, had been airsick during the journey. The journalist contemplated the pilots' backs through the cockpit door—which periodically opened and closed—reflecting that he hadn't even seen their faces, let alone heard their names. He wrote, "I was on the left side of the plane, and I squeezed my cheek against the window to look at the engine. I rather expected to see the propeller blades hanging motionless. They seemed to be going around all right, though I knew that didn't mean anything. Sunlight flashed in from another angle, and I realized that we had turned, which must mean that the pilot was making back for India. A day wasted, at least, and I was already long overdue in Chungking."

In the cockpit the first sign that anything was amiss was an oscillating oil-pressure gauge for the port engine. The needle was moving rapidly from full to zero and back again. Neveu and Felix initially thought it might be a faulty dial but kept a wary eye on it. If an engine ran out of oil, a lockup could wrench it from its mounting and send the aircraft plummeting to earth. Minutes went by while the dial danced manically. Then Neveu noticed further evidence of a problem with the engine. Slowly, inexorably, the temperature gauge was rising. The two pilots quickly agreed that the port engine must be shut down to avoid disaster. With half of the power of the heavily laden C-46 gone, they now had no prospect of rising above their current height of 12,000 feet and zero chance of making it to Kunming. Their only option was to bank right and head for home.

At this point they were 200 miles from Chabua, over territory dominated in the sky by Japanese Zeros and on the ground by the Japanese Army. The natural escape route was to turn due west and fly back over the Patkois toward Chabua's sister air base at Jorhat, farther down the Brahmaputra. The altitude they would need to maintain was slightly lower than the route flown that morning. Neveu and Felix quickly decided to make for this emergency destination. As Neveu turned the aircraft slowly onto its western course, however, he struggled to maintain altitude. It was clear that the C-46 was too heavily laden for a single engine, and the altimeter needle continued moving counterclockwise. Every minute was costing them a hundred feet. The C-46 needed at least 10,000 feet to clear the mountains blocking the route to Jorhat. If their descent continued, it was only a matter of time before they collided with the hills separating them from safety. The truth began to dawn on them: the Curtiss-Wright was sinking as the remaining engine strained to keep the plane aloft. Even worse, they were entering the cloud base on top of the mountains. The situation looked grim as they had to navigate solely with instruments; Neveu later admitted that he was "expecting the side of a mountain to come into the windshield at any second."

The young pilot's primary task was to keep the plane flying straight, preventing it from corkscrewing into the ground. His mind racing, desperately thinking of ways to stave off catastrophe, Neveu realized that they had to jettison baggage—and as quickly as possible. Fifteen minutes had now passed, and Neveu gave instructions to Staff Sergeant Miller to chuck the cargo. Miller rushed down the fuselage, co-opting passengers to throw out luggage. "I watched my flight bag go over the side with some regret," recalled Jack Davies, "for it contained an assortment of presents for Chinese friends and acquaintances, including for Madame Sun Yat-sen a bottle of fine cognac and a couple of bottles of the brown ink she fancied."

It was now that calamity nearly struck. In his eagerness Miller had forgotten the basic premise that to remain airborne and flying forward—especially now that it had only one engine—the C-46 needed to maintain its center of gravity. With the crowd of panicked men clustering around the open rear cargo door, the C-46 began falling onto its tail, nose rising, the one good engine clawing the thin air. No power from the single remaining engine would be able to overcome this. Neveu desperately worked to control the aircraft as, in slow motion, the C-46 tilted upward. A fatal stall seemed inevitable.

Realizing what was happening, Miller screamed at the passengers to get away from the rear of the plane, and, by a miracle, disaster was averted. The reluctant aircraft was persuaded to slip sideways, allowing the nose to regain level flight. The sweating Neveu was amazed—he had never heard of a fully laden aircraft recovering from a near stall—and later recalled it as "one of the most frightening experiences I think I ever had."

But the struggle to regain control of the C-46 had cost them irrecoverable altitude. At 7,000 feet the crew confirmed that they were heading on a westerly track but were horrified to realize that they had no chance of rising above the mountain barrier blocking the route to Jorhat. A crash into the green void below was now inevitable, and Oswalt began sending distress signals on the emergency frequency, giving estimates of their position. Their intense fear was that they would collide with a mountain as they flew in dense cloud, but the Curtiss-Wright suddenly broke free from the cloud layer, and at 6,500 feet they saw, to their relief, that they were in the middle of a wide valley, bisected by a river far below. Neveu followed the line of the valley floor, which ended at a V-shaped ridge five miles ahead. He knew he couldn't rise above the ridge because the C-46 was still losing height and had no space to turn around. The decision was made: they would have to bail out. Both pilots agreed that they had only a few minutes before hitting the ridge.

In the meantime Davies had walked forward into the cockpit to see what was going on. He could see Oswalt working the radio, sending emergency calls to Chabua; Neveu and Felix were "staring at their instruments with blanched, silent concentration. I got no reply to my questions as to where we were." The pilots' headphones prevented them from hearing Davies behind them, and the din from the open cargo door made conversation impossible. Davies ran back to the fuselage, convinced that the only thing to do was parachute. He had never jumped before in his life—no one on this plane had—but it was obvious that the aircraft was doomed.

Men struggled to move through the crowded cabin while others remained fixed to their seats in mute horror. Neveu commanded Miller to tell everyone to jump, but the noise made it difficult to understand what had to be done. To make things worse, no instructions had been given as to how to parachute safely. Davies stared around him:

> Each of us aboard the stricken aircraft was preoccupied with his own little preparations for disaster, his own private terrors. We were a distracted, atomized group; no one took command to pull us together. Word was babbled down from the pilot that we should jump, depart the plane without further ado. Loath to leave the cold aluminum womb of the C-46 and plunge into the steaming primordial jungle some 3,000 feet below, I hesitated to venture forth. But no one else stepped forward and out the door, and as time was wasting, I decided to get the inevitable over with. In a letter to my wife days later, I wrote, "I stood in the open door of that miserable Commando and declared, 'Well, if nobody else is going to jump, I'll jump. Somebody has to break the ice.'" Clutching my dispatch case and kukri* to my chest and with my

---

*The famous Gurkha fighting knife.

right hand grasping the parachute release ring, I waddled out
into the wild blue yonder.

Eric Sevareid was also in shock, the whole experience surreal.
He watched as Jack Davies "crouched by the door staring down
into space. There was a curious half-smile on his face just before he
leaped, froglike, and vanished with a whistling sound." He couldn't
rationalize what was happening; his mind rebelled against what
his eyes were telling him. *The C-46 was still flying; this was all a bad
dream.* He remembered thinking that at least they were flying away
from the Japanese and that every mile placed between them and
the enemy was good. Sevareid looked at the other passengers:

> Two or three were pale. The younger Chinese was staring at the
> door, his jaw muscles puking rapidly. Several minutes passed,
> and the plane seemed to be flying much lower. I thought we were
> following a valley, but then a peak or ridge would pass very close
> beneath. More minutes went by, and the suspense was unbear-
> able. I found myself opening the notebook again and absurdly
> scrawling sentences: "Nine fifteen a.m. Baggage out. Left engine
> not working," etc. I closed the notebook, carefully inserted it in
> the brief case, snapped it shut—and threw it out of the door. Then
> I realized that I had not buckled my 'chute.

A further five men jumped in sequence just after Jack Davies,
lightening the aircraft and slightly reducing the rate of descent. But
the inexorable downward direction continued. Despite this, several
men still lingered, paralyzed by fear. It was only when Neveu and
Oswalt rushed from the cockpit, looking for their parachutes—with
Felix bravely remaining at the controls—that a final panicked exodus from the stricken plane began. Harry Neveu could not find his
parachute:

> My first reaction was just stark fear that somebody had thrown
> my chute out. In their confusion I thought they had thrown it

out with the cargo. I couldn't find it anywhere. The cabin was completely bare: about all there was on the floor was a couple of candy wrappers. And the doorway was jammed with passengers that still hadn't jumped. And I yelled at them to jump, to get going and I asked where my chute was—where in the hell was my chute—got no response from anybody—so I started searching around and I spotted a chute under the navigator's table.... With a sigh of relief I grabbed it and started putting it on.

Unable to pluck up courage to jump, Sevareid remained on board. The sheer injustice of losing his life and family horrified him—it was as if a disembodied self were watching his human form hurtling toward oblivion: "Blood was pounding in my head and it was hard to breathe. For a moment there was utter suspension of thought, and I existed in a vacuum. There were no articulated thoughts, only emotional protest 'Oh, no, no! Oh, no! This can't happen to me, not to me!' The mind did not accept it, but the numb body moved toward the door. There was a jam of bodies around the door, and somebody was shoving from behind." He watched as Bill Stanton galvanized himself, barging his way to the door, shouting above the din of the rushing air, "For Christ's sake, if you're not going to jump, get out of the way!"

Parachute secured, Neveu returned to the cockpit to make one final check to see if he could save the aircraft, but he was turned around by Oswalt, who yelled that their remaining engine was on fire. Seconds remained before they would be incinerated. Oswalt hoped that Felix would be able to follow him from the cockpit. Returning to the cabin, he was appalled to see men still clinging to the plane: "I headed to the door and they were jammed in there, hesitating, afraid to jump, some of them clinging to the side—had to pry their hand loose—hands loose—I shoved one out . . . and about this time the plane started to go into its death roll—started to roll into its dive and the cargo door rolled down facing the earth."

As Neveu ran toward him, Sevareid finally staggered to the cargo door, crouching on the right side of the opening. As he did so, a dark green mountain peak passed close by. They were now just above 500 feet, seconds from death, the last point when anyone could jump. Sevareid felt his "knees buckle slightly as the plane tipped abruptly to the left. There was no interval between the realization that the pilotless plane was going into a dive and the action of my body. I closed my eyes and leapt head first into space." Neveu and the others jumped almost simultaneously as the C-46 began its death roll, Felix sprinting back to jump last. The aircraft seemed to roll over them. "It was damn near," said Neveu. "Two more seconds and anybody in front of the door would have gone out whether they wanted to or not."

For Eric Sevareid, eyes closed tight, the noise of the wind and sudden jolt of the parachute were followed by the realization that he was safe. Somehow he had had the wit to pull the ripcord. He heard someone yell, "My God, I'm going to live!" and realized it was his own voice. Swinging under the silk canopy, he saw the C-46 plow into the mountainside terrifyingly close below and three hours' worth of aviation fuel erupt into a fireball. He realized that he was frighteningly close to the burning wreck as a sea of trees and scrub rushed up to meet him. Three other parachutes were coming down nearby. "Dear God, don't let the fire get me. Please!" Sevareid heard himself shout before he crashed through foliage into the bushes of a steep incline, sliding until the parachute caught the undergrowth, arresting his descent.

Harry Neveu's jump, likewise, was a new and frightening experience. He felt a rush of air, "a sensation like a violent windstorm," and immediately pulled his ripcord. Suddenly the noise stopped, and he was swinging in the quiet stillness of the sky. It seemed as though someone had just "turned a strong fan off. Just real quiet."

> I realized my chute had opened—it was such a relief to know that, as far as I was concerned, I had made it. . . . Then I was halfway anxious over the fact that I was drifting toward the plane, I was afraid I was going to land in it. So I oscillated—really only oscillated once or twice and I started to try to control my 'chute cords

to make me drift away from the burning wreckage. Though I didn't want to do that too much, I figured I'd overdo it and be in danger of spilling the chute, but by this time I was almost to the ground.

Sevareid stood up, struggling to get his bearings. He was surrounded by dense jungle, panicked by a near-death experience. Hysteria threatened to overwhelm him. But he was alive.

5

VINEGAR JOE

Jack Davies was the State Department's representative to the CBI theater and hence Lieutenant General "Vinegar Joe" Stilwell's political adviser. The American presence in the upper reaches of Assam in 1943 came about in the first instance because officials in Washington had been persuaded by virtue of sophisticated and relentless lobbying by Chiang Kai-shek (through his plausible, American-educated wife and her brother, T. V. Soong, a banker and the Kuomintang's smooth-talking ambassador to Washington) that the United States had a significant role to play in supporting Chinese efforts to engage and perhaps restrain Japanese ambitions in the region. American support of the Chinese, which had begun in 1941, had become formal Allied policy following the conference of Allied leaders at Tehran in May 1943. The conference decided on a strategy of supporting China through air supply while a new land route was built to replace the one that had been lost when Rangoon had fallen to the Japanese the previous year. This road would be pushed through from Ledo, in the upper reaches of the Brahmaputra Valley, 1,125 miles to Kunming. It was a masterpiece of civil engineering that was eventually completed in January 1945. In the meantime, logistical support would be provided to the Chinese by means of an unparalleled airlift of supplies across the daunting range of mountains, a dangerous route quickly dubbed the "Hump" by the pilots of the ATC.

Stilwell was a Chinese-speaking infantryman whose clear-sightedness with regard to China's future was ultimately undermined by a profound inability to influence and convince those in Washington (and Delhi) of the merit of his pronounced views. For most of 1943 China was a political battleground between Chiang Kai-shek, Britain, and the United States, and the struggle was almost as intense and protracted as that between these so-called Allies and the Japanese. Indeed, the very reason that Eric Sevareid was a passenger on Flight 12420 on August 2, 1943, was because Roosevelt's White House team wanted an objective and hopefully unbiased view of what was going on in Chungking. Amid the fog of competing claims and prejudices, clarity was essential. Until now there had been conflicting reports and opinions of Kuomintang intentions and policies and the best strategies to deploy to maximize Chinese strengths in the common defeat of the Japanese. On one side was the sophisticated politicking by T. V. Soong, peddling half-truths in Washington to often-gullible politicians willing to believe that China's single-minded focus was the defeat of the Japanese rather than the defeat of Mao Tse-tung's communist insurgency or the propping up of the Kuomintang. Likewise, media moguls and pundits sought to distill the complexity of China into simplistic conceptions of black and white, "cowboy and Indian"–type explanations of who was "good" and who was "bad." On the other side were the alarming reports from Stilwell that China was duping America, that the nationalist Chinese were not willing to do what they promised, and that American blood and treasure were being expended in a vast logistical effort that in actuality was keeping a bunch of corrupt clowns in power. Through the middle of all this came an ego-driven, single-minded American airman by the name of Claire Chennault, who believed that the best expenditure of American resources in this already fractious region was not on training Chinese peasants to fight in Burma under Stilwell but on building an air bridge into China in order to prosecute an aerial bombing campaign directly against Japan.

Stilwell had in fact spent many years of his military service in China and knew the country, its people, and its politics better than perhaps any other American serviceman. A two-year posting in

Shanghai starting in 1911 was followed by a second three-year tour beginning in 1920 and a further three years between 1926 and 1929, during which time he observed China's breakup under the stresses of revolution. He served a further four years in China as the American military attaché between 1935 and 1939. A gifted linguist, he had traveled extensively and independently before the onset of war while observing the warlords of the Kuomintang coming to power and seeing at first hand the devastation wrought by the Japanese invasion with the consequences of internal revolution. He was thus ideally placed to serve as General George Marshall's (the chief of staff of the US Army) representative to Chiang Kai-shek, to which post he was appointed in January 1942. The United States had agreed to dispatch lend-lease supplies to China through Burma in early 1941 to bolster Chinese defense efforts against the Japanese. Materiel was shipped into Rangoon port and traveled into the Chinese province of Yunnan by rail from Rangoon to Mandalay to Lashio, and thence by the famous Burma Road, which had been completed in 1938 and ran for 726 miles to Kunming. The road had been scratched, as one American engineer observed, by Chinese villagers along the route "out of the mountain with their fingernails."* Stilwell was to serve both as Chiang Kai-shek's chief of staff, with direct responsibility for training the Chinese Army for war, and as commander of all American forces in the CBI theater. He was expected simultaneously to serve the interests of the United States and China. But with the two sides following diametrically divergent strategies, it was not possible for him to find a way to serve two masters. Both Marshall and Stilwell believed that the Chinese should be forced to commit troops to fight the Japanese in Burma in exchange for US largesse, but until April 1944 Roosevelt refused to tie aid to any specific military demands, allowing Chiang Kai-shek to do what he willed with the thousands of tons of American supplies pouring in across the Hump and along the Burma Road. It didn't help that with British and American grand strategy

---

*Quoted in Stowe, *They Shall Not Sleep.*

from 1942 focused primarily on the defeat of Germany, Stilwell would always be short of necessary supplies and adequate forces.

For the straight-talking, no-nonsense American, these command arrangements were a daily frustration that very nearly sent him mad. Indeed, to understand China, as few statesiders truly did in 1942 and 1943, one needed to understand—as did Stilwell—a system of command that reflected the reality that Chiang Kai-shek himself didn't possess the unequivocal support of his own warlords. They supported him so long as he remained successful in generating and protecting their wealth. Their armies constituted a significant part of that capital and were not to be frittered away in needless offensives that didn't contribute to the perpetuation of their own positions and status. The long and protracted war against the Japanese during the past decade had forced them to develop an approach that conserved forces and avoided pitched battles. Large-scale actions and offensives were sought only when the Chinese, not possessing artillery or air support, otherwise enjoyed overwhelming odds over the Japanese. Chiang Kai-shek also sought to retain his authority by means of the principle of divide and rule: if he allowed a degree of confusion to exist amongst his army and divisional commanders, it would ensure that they would never be organized enough to band together to depose him. As Jack Davies was presciently to observe in late July 1942, Chiang Kai-shek's two objectives were first to ensure the perpetuation of the Kuomintang and its domestic supremacy and second to come to the peace talks at the end of the war as militarily powerful as possible.

After little more than a month of campaigning in Burma during 1942, Stilwell concluded that all the command problems he had encountered in the Chinese Army were the fault of Chiang Kai-shek. He would never change this view. By April 1942 he already regarded the Chinese leader as mentally unstable, two-faced, and surrounded by parasitic sycophants. Frustrated that he was being asked to command the Chinese armies in the field against a ferociously competent and disciplined enemy while being constantly undermined by the Chinese system of command, Stilwell complained bitterly to anyone who would listen. Unfortunately, his complaints were countered by effective messaging to the contrary and by the fact that Stilwell was well known for his misanthropic language and racist attitudes, not to mention his aversion to the British.

When the final evacuation from Burma had taken place in May 1942, Stilwell had wasted no time in making plans to rebuild his Chinese forces and retake Burma. To do this he proposed a new Chinese Army of 100,000 men, trained in India (at Ramgargh in Bihar, 230 miles northwest of Calcutta), equipped with American supplies, and commanded by American divisional and corps commanders. Once training had been completed, which he estimated would take six months, Burma could be attacked from the north and east. The essence of these plans was accepted by both Chiang Kai-shek and Washington (although Stilwell's request for a full American infantry division was turned down), but Stilwell was now entering the dangerous waters of Chinese politics, which turned especially treacherous when they touched on relations with outside powers. As Stilwell was to realize in time, things were not always as they seemed. His purpose was to create an effective fighting army. It needed clear and unambiguous structures of command, the modernization of administration and supply, and the concentration of scarce US equipment in an elite thirty divisions.

Simple as these plans were in concept, they foundered repeatedly on the rocks of international politics and the domestic struggles for power in a divided China. The cutting of the Burma Road from Rangoon in 1942 as a result of the Japanese invasion had reduced the delivery of lend-lease supplies to a trickle, although T. V. Soong complained bitterly that the United States was failing to keep its end of the bargain and vociferously campaigned, cajoled, and threatened Roosevelt and Churchill to ensure that supplies kept coming through, by airlift if necessary.

Chiang Kai-shek's policy toward the Allies was based largely on the argument that China played a critical role in Asia because it tied down large Japanese forces that would otherwise be directed against the Allies in southeast Asia and the Pacific. He used this bargaining chip ruthlessly for his own advantage, going so far as to threaten to withdraw from the fight and to strike terms with the Japanese if the Allies didn't meet all his demands. Stilwell bore the brunt of Chiang Kai-shek's politicking, finding himself unwillingly caught between a demanding and ungrateful China on the one hand and an uncomprehending United States on the other. He struggled to hold to a position of benign neutrality, insisting that his task was not to broker deals between Chiang Kai-shek and Roosevelt but to prosecute the war against the Japanese. Chiang Kai-shek undoubtedly wanted Stilwell to become a mouthpiece for Chinese demands and saw his appointment merely as the key that unlocked the American piggy bank. Stilwell, in refusing to kowtow to Chinese demands and insisting on remaining concerned merely about military affairs, raised Chiang Kai-shek's ire. Within months of Stilwell's appointment, Chiang Kai-shek was calling for his dismissal. This response is hardly surprising. Stilwell refused to support Chinese demands for US supplies (which he constantly reminded the Chinese were "the gift of the hard-working American taxpayer") for their own sake; he supported them only within the context of the military reconstruction of Chiang Kai-shek's armies *for the purpose of invading Burma.* Stilwell recognized, as did most officials in Washington by mid-1942, that Chiang Kai-shek was interested in acquiring US resources as much to fight off the threat to his hegemony by the communists as to fight the Japanese. Because he refused to change his position, Stilwell was of no use to Chiang Kai-shek, who worked thereafter to engineer his removal. He was eventually to succeed.

For his part, Stilwell quickly came to despise Chiang Kai-shek with an antipathy that he found hard to disguise and that ultimately served to undermine his position. To his diary, in letters home, and even in public, Stilwell referred to the Chinese leader as the "Peanut," "coolie-class," and "incompetent" and to the Chinese government in Chungking as the "Manure Pile." Given the pungency of Chungking's atmosphere, Stilwell tried hard to avoid the place. His focus was on preparing the Chinese to fight, and his natural orbit was Ramgargh, where 9,000 of his Chinese soldiers were being trained and equipped.

One of the first disputes that arose and that he could not avoid hinged on the role of airpower in the region. The Chinese had always urged the United States to commit significant air resources to the country, and the inability to deliver on promises during 1942 because of the pressures of the war in Europe caused anger in Chungking. Stilwell found himself caught up in lobbying from Chungking as well as from American air sources led by Colonel (soon to be Major General) Chennault. Chennault, commander of the AVG (the famous Flying Tigers) before being given command of the US Army Air Forces in the region, believed that Allied strategy in southeast Asia would best be served by building up an offensive air capability in China so that they could strike from there at Japan.

This idea clearly ran counter to the original mission, which was to use the aircraft flying over the Himalayas to build up supplies so that the Chinese land forces could take the war to the Japanese. Stilwell remained an advocate of this policy throughout the war and strongly rejected the arguments put forward by Chennault and his supporters. There were times when it appeared as if outright war had broken out between the two factions, one supporting Stilwell and the land policy and the other supporting Chennault's air strategy.

Stilwell argued that it would be Chinese land forces that in due course of time would need to reconquer territory, something that could not be achieved by airpower alone. Indeed, the danger of using airpower was that the bases required to launch the aircraft would themselves become targets for Japanese attack and would also consume vast quantities of aviation fuel that would have to be flown in from India. The dispute, acrimonious at times, rumbled on at least until 1944 and caused a near breakdown in the relationship between Stilwell and Chennault, who had much to achieve in working closely and harmoniously together.

In late 1942, so as better to coordinate his wide responsibilities, Stilwell created the CBI theater with its main headquarters in Chungking. He built a rear headquarters in New Delhi and attempted to provide structure, purpose, and energy in a command that stretched from Karachi in the west to Chungking in the east.

In early 1943 Stilwell despaired of getting the Chinese leadership to achieve anything more than self-gratification and of getting Washington to comprehend the true nature of Chiang Kai-shek's corrupt and self-serving regime. Though he thought much of the individual Chinese soldier when well trained and equipped, he thundered against the regime and its leaders like a medieval reformer, speaking contemptuously of "the Chinese cesspool. A gang of thugs with the one idea of perpetuating themselves. Money, influence, and position the only considerations of the leaders. Intrigue, double-crossing, lying reports. Hands out for everything they can get; their only idea to let someone else do the fighting; false propaganda on their 'heroic struggle'; indifference of 'leaders' to their men. Cowardice rampant, squeeze paramount, smuggling above duty, colossal ignorance and stupidity of staff, total inability to control factions and cliques, continued oppression of masses."

In the midst of what he regarded as widespread graft, Stilwell continued to try to improve the combat effectiveness of Chiang Kai-shek's US-supported divisions. His view was that the supply and maintenance of these forces could be achieved only by building a new Burma Road to China, this time from Ledo in India across northern Burma. Building this road would necessitate British/Indian and American/Chinese combat operations to push the Japanese back far enough to prevent them from interfering with the project. The objective Stilwell had in his mind was the capture of the airfield and town of Myitkyina. In Allied hands, the town would greatly assist the air route to China by adding a staging post far from the dangerous mountains over which the Hump aircraft otherwise had to fly. Henceforth Stilwell's single-minded focus lay on recovering those parts of northern Burma that had been

captured by the Japanese in 1942 and were essential to the maintenance of a land supply route to China from Ledo.

Discussions with General Archibald Wavell (the British commander in chief in India) in New Delhi on October 18, 1942, regarding the possibility of operations in Burma the following spring
using the newly trained Chinese divisions concluded with an agreement to mount an offensive down the Hukawng Valley to capture
the airfield at Myitkyina. This operation would take place in conjunction with a British offensive against Arakan and a further Chinese offensive into the Shan states from Yunnan. Chiang Kai-shek
eventually agreed to prepare a force of fifteen divisions, known as
the Yoke Force, for the Yunnan offensive.

With these agreements secured, things were looking up for
Stilwell. It appeared that both Wavell and Chiang Kai-shek were
committed to operations in which the retrained and reorganized
Chinese would play a significant part, and the hostility toward Stilwell in Chungking had abated. But by December the situation had
quickly begun to unravel, and Stilwell's plans were being assailed
on all sides. Chiang Kai-shek had agreed to the creation of the
Yoke Force only on condition that the Allies mount massive air
and amphibious operations in the Bay of Bengal to prevent the
Japanese from using Rangoon as a port. Stilwell knew this was impossible, although he promised to make the appropriate represen-
tations to Washington. However, the US War Department refused
to underwrite Stilwell's request for extra supplies to ensure the success of these plans. He responded angrily to Washington that US
pusillanimity threatened to undo everything he was trying to do in
China and Burma.

Also at this time in 1943 the proponents of Major General
Chennault's airpower strategy began pressing his ideas of aerial
bombing against the Japanese from inside China instead of a land
campaign in Burma and to voice public criticisms of Stilwell's plans
for an advance to Myitkyina. Chennault worked hard to persuade
Roosevelt with a plan to win the war in six months by launching a
bombing campaign from China with him in command. His plan

was to provide 147 fighters and bombers on Chinese air bases to fly long-distance missions against the Japanese homeland in the sure and certain hope that such aerial bombardment would quickly bring Japan to its knees. Chennault's ideas resonated positively in Chungking, as such a strategy would not entail any greater Chinese commitment to the war effort than the provision of air bases, and Stilwell's plans for an expensive land campaign, with the expenditure of blood and treasure that it would inevitably entail, could be shelved.

Stilwell rejected the idea of an air-only campaign. He realized precisely what Chennault had failed to learn from experience of air campaigning elsewhere in the war, namely, that air forces alone could not retake lost ground. He was angered as much by Chennault's failure to comprehend this fact as he was by Chennault's disloyalty in proposing alternative plans to Washington behind his back. More in exasperation than anger, he wrote in his diary that this was just the excuse that Wavell and Chiang Kai-shek (although for different reasons) were seeking in order to halt offensive operations into Burma. He believed that the British would do anything possible to avoid a commitment to a land offensive into Burma and saw the difficulties with which he was faced as a vindication of his fears: "What a break for the Limeys. Just what they wanted. Now they will quit, and the Chinese will quit, and the goddam Americans can go ahead and fight. Chennault's blatting has put us in a spot, he's talked so much about what he can do that now they're going to let him do it." To reinforce Stilwell's fear of British perfidy, Wavell, a month after his agreement to support an advance to Myitkyina, suggested that he might not have the air supply resources available after all.

In truth there were a series of competing strategies for defeating the Japanese through China, one of which was Stillwell's and another Chennault's. As is so often the case in these matters, the debate between Stilwell and Chennault was driven down party lines, the army supporting Stilwell and the air force Chennault. The fact that Stilwell had been appointed by the War Department (i.e., the army) under General Marshall and not the Joint Chiefs of Staff didn't help his cause, despite Marshall's consistent loyalty to him.

In theater Stilwell found it difficult to confide fully in peers, superiors, or subordinates (although he wrote regularly to Marshall), with the result that there was little effective dialogue in the CBI headquarters, and the group processes that existed in other headquarters to weigh and decide on issues of military strategy (and even, on occasion, grand strategy) were nonexistent. Stilwell's unhelpful habit was to bottle up his frustrations and express himself freely only to his diary. He was a poor communicator and was not able to press his ideas with the dispassionate vigor needed to ensure that his voice was heard in a reasoned and winning argument. The situation was not helped by the fact that Chennault's powerful personality gave considerable impetus to his grandiose, ill-formed plans for the aerial bombardment of Japan from airfields in China and allowed little room for disagreement.

The clamor around Chennault's ideas intensified during 1943. The basic problem Stilwell faced was that US military strategy remained undecided. The grand strategy of US policy was support to China; the military strategy, however, remained an issue of dispute between the War Department and Chennault's airpower supporters. Disregarding the fact that in Europe the impact of aerial bombardment had already been shown to be grossly exaggerated, Marshall and Stilwell were concerned that such a plan would provoke the Japanese to launch strong counteroffensives against Chennault's air bases in China and that without effective land forces these bases would quickly fall.

Chennault's plan, and the support it rapidly acquired from Madame Kai-shek and T. V. Soong, made Chungking's agreement to Stilwell's requirements increasingly difficult. The fact that Stilwell was ultimately to be proved right in 1944 didn't help him to fight the argument in 1943. On January 2, 1943, Chiang Kai-shek proposed the Chennault plan to Roosevelt and added the rider that the Yoke Force could be used from Yunnan only in conjunction with a wider Allied attack—by sea and air—in Burma. Without these

commitments, the Chinese leader insisted, Stilwell's spring offensive could not be countenanced. The battle with Chennault for
strategic dominance raged throughout 1943 and was one that Stilwell, loyally supported by Marshall, lost in the face of Chennault's
successful lobbying of Roosevelt and the American press, combined with the vociferous support given to Chennault by Chiang
Kai-shek.

Stilwell found himself struggling against the enemy within–
Chinese ignorance, selfishness, and greed dangerously combined
with American political naïveté–as much as he was fighting the
Japanese. In preparation for the Trident Conference in Tehran in
May 1943, he summarized the strategic dilemmas he faced and the
consequences of not keeping a close rein on Chinese demands:

1. President has no idea of Chiang's character, intentions,
   authority or ability.
2. British and Chinese ready to shift burden on to US.
3. Chiang's air plans will stop formation of effective ground
   forces.
4. Air activity could cause Japanese to overrun whole of Yunnan.
5. Chiang would make fantastic strategic decisions.
6. Chiang will seek control of US troops.
7. Chiang will get rid of me and have a "yes" man.
8. Chinese will grab supplies for post war purposes.

In many of these accusations and prophecies Stilwell was to
be proved right. His logic remained compelling to the War Department in Washington, but he failed completely to ensure that
his views had the political impact they needed to survive. He was
preeminently a fighting soldier, unable to deal with the complex
nuances of the political environment in which he was forced to
operate. The Australian journalist Ronald McKie described him as
"small and sinewy. A cannibal would have rejected him. His face was
slashed with age lines, his brown eyes were humorous even behind
thick steel spectacles, and his cropped hair, grey at the temples,

stood to attention on top and gave him a startled 'little-boy' look.
. . . He had been born in 1883 and looked old and frail, far too old
to be commanding a couple of Chinese divisions and some Americans, particularly in the middle of the monsoon. He was, however,
about as frail as a steel girder and, to many people, as unbending."
Watching him closely in Chungking, General Adrian Carton de
Wiart put his finger on the problem, describing Stilwell as having
"strong and definite ideas of what he wanted, but no facility in putting them forward."

Chennault, by contrast, fought to gain direct access to Roosevelt,
bypassing Marshall altogether, and in these overtures he was assisted in Washington by T. V. Soong. Stilwell's wholly admirable
though ineffectual approach was to state what he believed, and
state it loudly so that all could hear, but his failure was to believe
that this was all that was necessary for him to do. The Chinese,
seeing their strategies potentially undermined by this American
Mr. Valiant-for-Truth, applied every devious political pressure they
could to undermine Stilwell's views, and in the end—in a clear win
for the Mr. Facing-Both-Ways and his neighbors in Chungking's
decadent Vanity Fair, Stilwell lost the argument. Roosevelt had admonished him a year earlier for speaking sternly to Chiang Kai-
shek (and he was to do so again at Cairo in November 1943 when
Stilwell called Chiang Kai-shek "Peanut" in the president's hearing), and the sharpness of his tongue, whatever the prescience of
his observations, served to whittle away what political capital he
retained in Chungking, New Delhi, London, and Washington.

Under the ill-informed pressure of the aerial strategists, the Trident Conference in May 1943 endorsed increasing the quantity of
air resources to China, and agreement was reached in principle
later in the year for a strategic bombing offensive to be launched
from new bases in eastern China against Japan once the war in
Italy and Europe had been successfully concluded. This outcome
encouraged renewed opposition in Chungking to land-based operations in Burma and continued the difficulties that Stilwell faced
in preparing Chinese troops for war. As supplies to Chennault

burgeoned, the road building from Ledo almost stopped, the training of the Yoke Force became halfhearted, and plans for the attack
on Burma received renewed criticism from Chungking.

Chiang Kai-shek repeated his demand that any Chinese commitment of ground forces be accompanied by overwhelming Allied amphibious and aerial attacks on Burma. Stilwell was furious
that Chiang Kai-shek had the nerve to demand more resources
from the Allies while offering little in return. In circumstances like
these Stilwell was at his most eloquent: "This insect, this stink in the
nostrils, superciliously inquires what we will do, who are breaking
our backs to help him, supplying everything—troops, equipment,
planes, medical, signal, motor services . . . training his lousy troops,
bucking his bastardly Chief of Staff, and he the Jovian Dictator who
starves his troops and who is the world's greatest ignoramus, picks
flaws in our preparations, and hems and haws about the Navy, God
save us." When, finally, Chiang Kai-shek appended his signature
on July 12, 1943, to the plan for an offensive down the Hukawng
Valley, Stilwell exclaimed with relief as much as fury at the pain
he had had to go through to win even this concession: "What corruption, intrigue, obstruction, delay, double crossing, hate, jealousy
and skullduggery we have had to wade through. What a cesspool.
. . . What bigotry and ignorance and black ingratitude. Holy Christ,
I was just about at the end of my rope."

It was in this context—confusion, recrimination, partisanship,
and relentless propaganda—that Eric Sevareid's trip to China was
conceived. What was going on in China? Who was right? One day
Sevareid was invited to meet a man whom he knew to be close to
the president. Would Sevareid be happy to employ his talents as
an investigative journalist by travelling to Kuomintang-run China
and offering an unbiased view for the benefit of the White House?
The American population, at the hands of a deeply partisan media,
believed the propaganda that China was America's staunch Chur-
chillian ally in the region and that every American dollar spent on
Chiang Kai-shek was money spent on Chinese bullets to be fired at
their common enemy. The truth—that American lives were being

sacrificed to line the pockets of graft-ridden Kuomintang generals and keep them in power—was too unpalatable to consider, and
those responsible for signing the checks had a habit of keeping
their heads in the sand on the issue. The American public had been
fed a diet of half-truths about China for so long that only the fresh
objectivity of someone like Sevareid could do anything to break
the stranglehold that this mythologizing had on popular feelings
about Chiang Kai-shek. Sevareid's biographer, Raymond Schroth,
observed:

> The Roosevelt circle's gamble in promoting a Sevareid mission
> was that a dose of Sevareid-delivered truth—even bad news—
> would either soften the greater shock of a later Chinese collapse
> or strengthen the president's hand by making public opinion de-
> mand more of the generalissimo. It is easy to see why Sevareid
> accepted. The assignment got him back into the action; he re-
> vered Roosevelt: and he did believe that a hard dose of the truth
> is often the best medicine for an ailing democracy.

So it was that Sevareid kitted himself out in a war correspondent's uniform and an expensive "war zone" ensemble that took
him a good deal of effort to acquire in Washington and climbed
aboard one of a succession of indifferent and deeply uncomfortable
aircraft for the long journey across the South Atlantic to Africa, India, and China. Little did he know that one of the men who would
accompany him on the flight into Kunming, Jack Davies—who saw
clearly the true state of this latter-day Heart of Darkness—would
himself, in a later decade, have his career destroyed under Sena-
tor Joseph McCarthy for suggesting that the Communists would
win the long struggle for the creation of a new China and that the
much-lauded Kuomintang was a busted flush.

6

THE PASSENGERS

Harry Neveu knew nothing about the eighteen men who had boarded his plane that morning: they were merely names on a manifest, part of the C-46's payload. His job was to transport them through these dangerous skies to their destination. He would have been surprised had he paid the list any attention, for it boasted an eclectic cross-section of America. Eleven were noncommissioned officers and enlisted men of the USAAF, nine of whom worked for the ATC. They were traveling to their place of duty in Kunming, there to work at the China end of the Hump operation. They were Staff Sergeant Joseph "Jiggs" Giguere, Staff Sergeant Joseph Clay, Sergeant Francis Signer, Corporal Edward Helland, Corporal Basil Lemmon, Sergeant Glen Kittleson, Corporal Lloyd Sherrill, Corporal Stanley Waterbury, Private William Schrandt, Technical Sergeant Evan Wilder, and Second Lieutenant Roland Lee. Two were officers of the Kuomintang: Colonel Wang Pae Chae, of whom little is known, and Lieutenant Colonel Kwoh Li, who had marched out of Burma with Stilwell. A young but hard-bitten man, he was much admired by the Americans. Of the four remaining Americans, one was William ("Bill") Stanton, a representative in Stilwell's CBI theater of the Board of Economic Warfare, which collected and analyzed enemies' economic information. A banker in Hong Kong before the war, he was in his forties at the time of the crash. The final three were Eric Sevareid, Captain Duncan Lee, and Jack Davies.

Eric Sevareid was born in November 1912, an American of Norwegian ancestry. He grew up in the rural town of Velva, North

Dakota, harboring a boyhood ambition to become a newspaper-man. He was to succeed in this dream. Indeed, he was eventually to become one of the most prominent radio journalists of his age. His rise to prominence came with the start of the war in Europe in 1939 when he went to work for CBS (joining the likes of William Shirer, who was to write, among others, *Berlin Diary* and *The Rise and Fall of the Third Reich*) and began to report to listeners across America on events in France. Sevareid and his fellows became known as "Murrow's boys" after the well-known reporter Edward Murrow. At a time before television, when immediacy in journalism came from the radio, with the newspapers several days behind, Sevareid and others brought the meaning of war to millions of Americans through the power of their voices and the currency and pertinence of their observations. They were also increasingly partisan in favor of ordinary Britons' resistance to the threat of Nazi bullying and of Britain's herculean struggle against the fascist jackboots striding contemptuously across Europe, trampling all in their path (to use the rhetoric of the day). For all his intellectual abhorrence of the concept of the British Empire (he had adopted radical politics and pacifism at the University of Minnesota in the early 1930s), Sevareid was, in 1940, to align himself completely with the citizens of London, who suffered the nightly bombardments.

Sevareid had met Murrow in 1937, when both were print journalists for American news organizations in Europe, Murrow in London with CBS and Sevareid in Paris for the *Paris Herald* and United Press International (UPI). With war came a phone call from Murrow, and Sevareid joined a band of journalists Murrow had been pulling together to report on the coming conflict. As the Wehrmacht rolled into France in May 1940 Sevareid quickly became a critical part of CBS's live broadcasts from the front. He reported the occupation of Paris and the capitulation of France some weeks later. It could be said that in those months he made his career. His reports were interesting, accurate, and full of the pathos engendered by war. Despite the battles within CBS in the United States about the requirements for objectivity in reporting at a time when

America was still neutral, "Murrow's boys" defined what it meant to be a radio journalist rather than merely a reader of news. By selecting, presenting, and interpreting the news, they effectively commented and analyzed at the same time. They found that they could not separate themselves from the war and increasingly observed its rights and wrongs from a personal and a moral perspective. For millions of ordinary Americans, these news reports brought the reality of war to life in kitchens and living rooms across the nation, and the full moral horror of the Nazi subjugation of Europe became known to a gradually comprehending and increasingly angry American audience. As the historians Cloud and Olson observed, this was a new sort of conversation between the reporter and the listener thousands of miles away back home: "What Murrow wanted was for the Boys to imagine themselves standing before a fireplace back home, explaining to the local editor or college professor or dentist or shopkeeper what was going on. But imagine, too, he said, that a maid and her truck-driver husband are listening at the door. Use language and images that are as informative and compelling to them as to the guests around the fireplace. Avoid high-flown rhetoric and frenetic delivery."

Sevareid covered the war for CBS from the outset until he managed to escape on one of the last boats leaving Bordeaux in June 1940 for the relative safety of London. In the first few months of what British soldiers called the "Bore War," he observed the deep-seated hostility of the French people to the idea of renewed hostility with Germany. They, and the French Armed Forces, remained superficially dutiful but not passionate about fighting yet another war against the Boche. In any case it was confidently and conveniently believed that the eighty-nine miles of Maginot Line would stop a German attack in its tracks. When the Phony War* ended

---

*The period between the declaration of war on September 3, 1939, and the German invasion of France in May 1940 was called the "Phony War" in Western Europe because, unlike other wars in recent human experience, in this one nothing seemed to happen.

after eight months, the full horror of real war shocked Sevareid. Caught in a house at Cambrai, shaken by the repeated concussions of close-landing artillery shells, he wondered whether he was brave enough to face the dangers of battle close up, even though he was far from being a combatant. "And God!" he recalled. "The terrifying violence of bombs nearby, how they stunned the mind, ripped the nerves, and turned one's limbs to water!" What he saw with his own eyes he felt deeply, and he struggled to compose himself when reporting the sight of a train packed with refugees that had been devastated by Luftwaffe machine guns. Unable formally to take sides, he was able nonetheless to make plain his moral indignation at the deliberate, wholesale slaughter of innocent civilians by a ruthless German war machine: "To a pilot, I suppose, a freight train is a freight train. It may carry women and children; it may carry troops. But even a pilot can tell what direction it's moving, and troops are not moving south." Sevareid, having managed to ensure the evacuation of his wife, Lois, and newborn twin sons on a ship to the United States, left a collapsing Paris only after the escape from the city of the country's panic-stricken leaders. His last broadcast from Paris warned America that his next would not be under the control of the French government. Making his way by stages first to Tours and then to Bordeaux, Sevareid managed to travel by freighter to Liverpool and thence to London. He broadcast the imminent collapse of France from Bordeaux and was the first to announce the capitulation to the world.

During the long, hot, violent summer of 1940, Eric Sevareid was one of the voices of CBS—orchestrated by Edward Murrow—that nightly told Americans of the calm stoicism of ordinary Britons in London under repeated and terrifying aerial bombardment. His recordings became part of the established narrative of the Blitz, which stretched from September 7 to the end of October. In the midst of this period of relentless attack, CBS agreed to repatriate an exhausted Sevareid to the United States. Just before he left for home he broadcast his farewell to a London that he had come to believe personified resistance to the brutal ugliness of totalitarianism:

Paris died like a beautiful woman, in a coma, without struggle, without knowing or even asking why. One left Paris with a feeling almost of relief. London one leaves with regret. Of all the great cities of Europe, London alone behaves with pride and battered but stubborn dignity. . . .

London fights down her fears every night, takes her blows and gets up again every morning. You feel yourself an embattled member of this embattled corps. The attraction of courage is irresistible. Parting from London, you clearly see what she is and what she means. London may not be England, but she is Britain and she is the incubator of America and the West. Should she collapse, the explosion in history would never stop its echoing. Besieged, London is a city-state in the old Greek sense.

Someone wrote the other day, "When this is all over, in years to come, men will speak of this war and say, 'I was a soldier,' 'I was a sailor.' Or 'I was a pilot.' Others will say with equal pride, 'I was a citizen of London.'"

Sevareid had arrived in London with many of the Anglophobic prejudices of the time. He left a convert to its bellicose spirit and stubborn refusal to give in to tyranny, something that he had not seen in France and that seemed to him to characterize more than anything else the British spirit of indomitable pluck. It was a lesson for his compatriots back home to learn: "During those bright days and livid nights of 1940, the spirit of the British called up from despair the spirit of other men. . . . It was this spirit and example which overbore the defeatists in the United States. . . . Americans thought they were saving Britain—and they were. But the spirit and example of Britain also were saving America."

|||

At the time of the crash Duncan Lee had been a Soviet spy for over a year. A lawyer in the peacetime chambers of William "Wild Bill" Donovan, head of the OSS, he had followed his boss and mentor into this new organization, designed to lead the coordination of American intelligence operations abroad. No one thought to do an exhaustive background check on the bespectacled twenty-eight-year-old lawyer; he seemed to be just the right sort of person for this sort of secret work. That he had been educated at Yale and had been a Rhodes Scholar between 1935 and 1938, with a privileged education and impeccable American credentials—General Robert E. Lee was one of his ancestors—seemed perfect reasons to welcome Lee into the fold of the spy organization that would one day become the CIA. The massive expansion of the US military also meant that the checks on Lee's associations, to test his loyalty, were perfunctory. Unfortunately, his credentials masked the fact that he had been a member of the Communist Party for three years and believed passionately that only communism could rescue the world from the poverty and social inequality that had been rampant in the wake of the Great Depression.

The threat of fascism, which Lee, like many others, naively believed to be the polar opposite of communism rather than its twin, only fueled his desire to help the Soviet Union—the only bastion of true equality in the world—in its life-and-death struggle against the forces of Nazi evil. There was no contradiction in his mind between fighting for America in its war against Nazi Germany and totalitarian Japan and his support for the social paradise established by the proletariat across the "old" Russian Empire. As his biographer Mark Bradley demonstrated, a combination of his mother's intense Christian socialism and his immersion in the politically radicalized Oxford University of the mid-1930s made him easy pickings for Soviet intelligence. Bradley concluded that his experience of revolutionary ideas while a student in England "transformed him from a mild, mostly apolitical socialist into a future communist willing to spy against his own country." His time at Oxford coincided with the rise of the fascist right in Europe, crystallized by the Spanish Civil War. Soviet support for the democratically elected Republican government in the face of a rebellion by Franco's right made Stalin a hero to many thousands of people in the West who were disillusioned by the failure of capitalism during the Great Depression and of the Western democracies to stand up to fascism. As news seeped out about the purges and terror, they were conveniently excused by most Western communist-leaning intellectuals as necessary evils to restrain opposition within the Soviet Union to communist principles—collectivization, a planned economy, and public ownership of the means of production.

Lee was one of these intellectuals. His personal epiphany occurred at Oxford when he met the woman who would become his first wife, the radically inclined Isabella ("Ishbel") Gibb. The daughter of a British colonial civil servant, she had rebelled against the lazy assumptions of imperialism in the India of her upbringing. Together they went on an Intourist package holiday to Leningrad (St. Petersburg) and Moscow in August 1937 and fell hook, line, and sinker for the carefully packaged propaganda of the tour. These excursions were as notorious as the Red Cross tours for happy vacationers at Nazi concentration camps, but at the time they persuaded many thousands of Western visitors that a vast worker's paradise had been created out of serfdom. If only, these converts believed, the means of production in the West were also collectivized, then workers in the West would enjoy the same fruits of the dramatic social change they thought they had seen on their closely guarded and carefully chaperoned tours of Russia. As Mark Bradley explained, Lee's conversion came as the culmination of a lifetime of struggle to understand his own mind and the direction of his life—as distinct from his parents' strongly held Christian beliefs—and to determine his role in saving both himself and the world. He believed that "the great Soviet experiment, with its promise to usher in a new kingdom on earth, was fighting for its very life. Chance and ability had brought Lee into the OSS. He could not pass on this stunning opportunity to help what he deemed the best hope for the future of mankind. The red star had replaced the Christian cross."

At the time that Lee clambered aboard Flight 12420, he had been passing material to Mary Price, his Soviet handler, since August 1942, only a month after he had joined the OSS. He was granted a military commission with the rank of lieutenant within a few days of joining, despite never having spent a day in military training of any kind. By September Moscow was jubilantly reporting that "Koch" would memorize secret OSS documents and feed them to Price for onward transmission. By February 1943 Lee had become the assistant chief in the secretariat, the very heart of the OSS. In this position he would see every signal, letter, paper, and other intelligence relating to the entire suite of OSS activities across the globe. He met Mary Price regularly, memorizing key documents and passing them to her verbatim at her flat. Ever careful, he refused to allow her to take notes; she had to learn his information by heart. The information, in abbreviated form, made its way to Moscow. Bradley recorded the import of these exchanges from the notes of Lee's Moscow handler, which became available after the fall of the Soviet Union, revealing the full extent of Lee's perfidy: "It ranged from Chinese Nationalist leader Chiang Kai-shek's plans to meet with Chinese Communist Party leaders to a report from the US ambassador in Moscow about rumors circulating there that Churchill had told Stalin that the allies would not open a second front against Germany until the USSR declared war on Japan."

Duncan Lee had two reasons to be a passenger on Harry Neveu's plane that day. In the first place he had been tasked by Wild Bill Donovan himself, his peacetime boss in the legal chambers of Donovan, Leisure, Newton & Irvine and now his wartime boss in the OSS,* with reporting on some of the complex intelligence-related politics that had been allowed to develop in the region. One of these, a major part of his trip, had arisen as a consequence of the arrival in the theater of Captain Milton "Mary" Miles of the US Navy and the subsequent April 1943 Sino-American Cooperative Organization (SACO) agreement. The agreement was an unusual treaty, driven by Miles's advocacy and supported fully by the US Department of the Navy in Washington, authorizing the establishment

---

*Donovan was appointed coordinator of information (COI) on July 11, 1941. This agency became the OSS the following year.

of a US-funded and -supplied armed militia in China under the effective command of Dai Li, Chiang Kai-shek's head of intelligence.

Miles had originally been sent to China in early 1942 by the Navy Department to secure Chinese agreement to establish a series of meteorological stations that would allow the navy to predict weather patterns across the Pacific and to secure intelligence about Japanese shipping movements along the Chinese coast. By the time a year had passed, the SACO mission had grown significantly, driven by Miles in close collaboration with Dai Li and excluding any other branch of American policy, including the CBI (in the form of Stilwell), the State Department (in the form of the US Embassy in Chungking), or the OSS. In exchange for US support, supplies, and training Dai Li promised Miles unparalleled access and cooperation within China in order to create a guerrilla army of 50,000 men. Miles leaped at this opportunity and persuaded the Navy Department to place its imprimatur on the venture. It became the means by which a formidable Chinese intelligence apparatus was built up, financed, trained, and supported by SACO. In all this, Miles was the willing subordinate to Dai Li. From the moment of his arrival in Chungking, it is clear that Miles's priorities and allegiance were to his own mission—as he interpreted it—and to the new organization he began building up with Dai Li, above US military or political policy in the region. By the time the agreement was signed in April 1943 its aim was "by common effort, employing American equipment and technical training and utilizing the Chinese war zones as bases to attack effectively the Japanese navy, the Japanese merchant marine and the Japanese air forces in different territories of the Far East, and to attack the mines, factories, warehouses, depots and other military establishments in areas under Japanese occupation." These offensive operations included provision for substantial armed units of guerrilla forces.

It was clear to Jack Davies that Dai Li was taking Miles for a ride, securing for the secretive Chinese official the promise of vast US resources for an unaccountable Chinese secret army. William Donovan also looked on at this dangerously anomalous situation with

anxiety. The OSS was being deliberately kept at arm's length by
Miles, who seemed to want to take control of all guerrilla activity—
and intelligence gathering—against the Japanese. Under Miles, the
Americans and US interests were entirely subordinate to Dai Li, at
least within the geographical confines of China. SACO allowed an
OSS presence in China, but only under Dai Li's strict control. Miles
entirely concurred with this and pressured Donovan in late 1943 to
make him OSS head of station in Chungking. Miles began to develop Kurtzlike tendencies early on. He eschewed direct control by
the State Department, American Embassy, CBI theater officials, or
OSS—though he was attached to the embassy and as a US serviceman should have reported directly to Stilwell—and began to work
directly with Dai Li to create a Kuomintang guerrilla force. In June
1943 Donovan instructed Lee and another OSS officer, Lieutenant
Colonel Richard Heppner, to travel to China to meet General Dai
Li and to attempt to negotiate a better deal for the United States.
On June 29 Lee climbed aboard a USAAF aircraft bound for Lon-
don, the first stop on a journey that would take him on to Cairo,
New Delhi, Chabua, and then Kunming.

At the same time the OSS was attempting—in the teeth of opposition from Stilwell, who never saw the need for irregular forces,
and from Miles, who saw the OSS as competition—to create its
own guerrilla force to harry the Japanese across northern Burma.
Donovan was keen to demonstrate that his newly formed organization—Detachment 101—could contribute to the war against Japan.
Even before Stilwell had walked out of Burma in May 1942, Donovan had established a team to lead an insurgency-style campaign
against the Japanese, building on the natural antipathy of the Naga
and Kachin hill people. At the outset neither Donovan, Stilwell,
nor Colonel Carl Eifler, whom Donovan had placed in charge of
Detachment 101, had much idea of what the unit could or should
achieve, apart from the general goal of building up an intelligence
picture of the Japanese and perhaps harrying their forward patrols
and bases. But as 1943 went on, and as Eifler built up his Kachin
forces, it became clear that Detachment 101 could both engage in

sabotage work against the Japanese garrisoning northern Burma in conjunction with indigenous Kachin tribespeople and gain tactical-level intelligence about Japanese operations and plans. It could also coordinate the rescue of downed air crews. A pattern began to emerge. Before any operations could be conducted in a particular territory, intelligence about Japanese strengths, movements, and intentions was required. After that, selected sabotage operations could take place. If these went well, sabotage was a natural segue into guerrilla warfare.

The presence of two competing guerrilla organizations—SACO and Detachment 101—was the outcome of competing political imperatives. Nevertheless, given the prickly relationship between US officials on the ground in China and the Kuomintang, Stilwell considered the strong relationship between Miles and Dai Li to be one of the positives in the Sino-US relationship and advocated a policy of leaving well enough alone on the basis that he could ill afford another debilitating internal battle with the vested interests in Washington. However, Miles's position rankled with Donovan, especially when it became clear that for the OSS to have any influence with China, Miles would need to be appointed the local (that is, CBI) OSS chief. But he had no choice, even though the official SACO agreement meant that Donovan never really controlled anything in China: US intelligence operations existed by sufferance, in effect, of Miles and the Navy Department.

Miles's imperious politicking at the expense of wider US interests irritated Jack Davies. Few Americans in the theater really knew what Miles was up to—even his protectors back in Washington—enabling him to make promises and commitments on behalf of the United States only because Stilwell refused to pick an argument with the Navy Department. But Davies regarded Miles's alliance with Dai Li as stupendously naive.* "Dai Li's function was the familiar one of secret police chief in an authoritarian regime threatened by domestic dissent," he argued. "It was surveillance, spying and

---

*Miles's approach is described in his book *A Different Kind of War*.

repression. His primary concern was internal enemies, not the external foe." Miles seemed entirely unaware, or disbelieving of, the possibility that Dai Li was using him—and the US government—on a grand scale to prop up Chiang Kai-shek's government by providing the instruments of a police state. The only intelligence Miles ever received from Dai Li was given in exchange for the provision of war materiel—tommy guns, for instance, and signals equipment. "Support" eventually extended to FBI-trained experts in police work, skills that Davies observed were not required for fighting the Japanese. Miles never appeared to appreciate that the intelligence exchange was one-way and in Jack Davies's estimation rather enjoyed and boasted of the association he had created with the head of Chiang Kai-shek's gestapo. Here was a senior navy officer, also appointed to a senior rank in the Kuomintang, not merely running a guerrilla force in competition with Donovan but also indulging in political work to the exclusion of the US Embassy in Chungking and secret intelligence work also to the detriment of Washington. It was this fundamental dysfunction at the heart of US policy regarding the management of intelligence in China that infuriated Donovan, and he tasked Lee with reporting back on the situation as best he could. Even Donovan knew that Lee would not be able to rein in Miles, but understanding what he was up to was the first step in attempting to exert a measure of control over the wayward sailor.

Lee also had another task. Reports arriving in Washington in mid-1943 indicated that Detachment 101 was failing to secure any of the secret intelligence work expected of it. Donovan, desperate for the OSS's first venture to be a success, tasked Lee with reporting back on the situation. Donovan should not have been surprised that Detachment 101 seemed to have created many enemies in Burma other than just the Japanese, with an ambivalent Stilwell at the helm and an antagonistic Miles sniping at it from Chungking. When Stilwell had first given Eifler his orders, they had been to disrupt "Japanese communications, shipping, and to bring about Japanese reprisals on the native population which will result in discouraging native aid to the Japanese." In particular, Eifler was to "deny the use of the Myitkyina aerodrome to the Japanese" and in "the vicinity of the aerodrome [to] destroy the railroad cars, and sink river vessels carrying fuel." By the end of 1943 the groundwork had been effectively laid by the small OSS team, using locally recruited Kachin helpers, and valuable lessons had been learned:

> By the end of the year six base camps had been established behind the lines in northern Burma, three east of the Irrawaddy River and three to the west. Each of these had recruited and trained a small group of indigenous Kachin personnel for local protection and to perform limited operations, principally simple sabotage and small ambushes. Each also trained a few native personnel as low-level intelligence agents, who reported their information by means of runners or via the bamboo grapevine. From the field bases this information was forwarded to the base camp in India by radio. By the end of the year it was possible to assemble a fairly comprehensive picture of Japanese strengths and dispositions in northern Burma.

However, none of the limited operations conducted that year could be considered a success. Perhaps Eifler was trying to secure success too early in order to vindicate the trust placed in him, and indeed in the entire Detachment 101, and as such the fact that some operations went off half-cocked was understandable. It was reports of these failures getting back to Washington that prompted Donovan to tell Lee to pack his bags and travel to the war zone. Lee's conclusion—after he had survived the crash and returned to work—was that "the criticism of Eifler's SI [Secret Intelligence] reports is well founded." He believed the trouble was due to the fact that "[Eifler] does not have on his staff either trained SI staff officers or trained instructors" and that he had started out to "run a [Special Operations] show and is now being called upon by General Stilwell for principally SI work."* Keen to ensure that these apparent

---

*Quoted in Brown, *Wild Bill Donovan*, pp. 173, 413.

failings didn't lead to the entire operation shutting down, Donovan determined to visit Burma and China personally; he arrived in December 1943. Eifler was replaced. Donovan also met Dai Li in Chungking but found to his chagrin that there was nothing he could do to wrest control of SACO from Miles. He had to accept that, in China at least, because of the political groundwork established by Miles in Washington and Stilwell's reluctance to fight this particular battle, the OSS would play second fiddle to Miles's and Dai Li's private—US-funded—army.

Jack Davies's role was to ensure that effective political relationships were maintained between Stilwell's headquarters and the vast array of political and ambassadorial relationships across the CBI. It helped that he liked and admired his boss, although he recognized the other man's weaknesses only too clearly. More importantly, he could see with the same clear-sightedness as Stilwell the political and military issues at stake in the region, and he concurred with Stilwell on every one of them. Davies did as much as he could to articulate Stilwell's evaluation of the Chinese situation for consumption within the State Department in order to counter the insidious effects of pronationalist propaganda evident from the White House to the media in the United States. In a briefing note for Clarence Gauss, the US ambassador to Chiang Kai-shek, in early 1943, he observed that the Chinese "have a more highly developed political sense than we. Political considerations loom larger in their evaluation of situations (including the military situation) than they do for even the Russians and the British." In other words, short-term military imperatives were of less importance to the Kuomintang than the long-term preservation of its political situation. Stilwell's role was to enable the Chinese to utilize US lend-lease supplies for the purpose of defeating the immediate threat posed by the Japanese, but most Chinese officers, Davies suggested, had no great interest in fighting the Japanese:

> Venality in the Chinese Army goes along naturally with the apathy. Chinese troops have traditionally had to shift for themselves.

Most units have lived off the localities in which they have been stationed. This situation has further deteriorated in most regions bordering Japan-occupied territory. Chinese commanders in these areas have settled down with their wives and families and gone into trade. They control and profit enormously from the contraband traffic across the "fighting" line. . . . The Japanese are as corrupt as the Chinese. The difference, however, is that the Japanese can be depended upon to fight when the orders come from the top. Corruption has not yet enervated them.

Commenting specifically on Stilwell's position, he observed that "it would be naïve in the extreme to suggest that all he has to do to make China an aggressive factor in the war against Japan is to place lend-lease arms in Chinese hands and in consultation with the Generalissimo issue orders for the attack."

All he can do, in fact, is argue, plead and bargain, with lend-lease material and the Ramgargh project as the inducement to follow his lead. It follows that the intemperate eulogies of the Chinese Army which appear in the American press and over the American air (largely inspired by the Chinese pressure groups in the United States and uninformed American sinophiles) only play into the hands of the Chinese factions wishing to obtain lend-lease equipment without restriction to its use (or non-use). It is scarcely necessary to note that anyone whom the Chinese might suggest as a replacement of General Stilwell could likely be a man whom the group in power in Chungking believe they could use to their own advantage. In feeling this way the Chinese are neither contemptible nor vicious—merely political.

But Stilwell was always going to play a losing battle when, as Davies noted, FDR's "fictional view" was that Chiang had "unified China under his undisputed leadership." The pro-Chiang lobbyists had clearly won the battle for the ear of the president. The blindness of Roosevelt to the reality of the situation in China led Davies repeatedly to urge Stilwell to allow Davies and one of his senior staff—either Colonel Haydon Boatner or Brigadier General Frank Merrill—to travel to Washington to tell his side of the story. Reluctantly, Stilwell agreed, although he told Davies that he grieved that he had to "play politics" in this way. Once Davies had arrived in Washington, however, General Marshall ordered Stilwell to the capital too.

In mid-1943 Chiang Kai-shek had asked Roosevelt to allow Chennault to present the "Chiang-Chennault" plan for an air offensive from China against Japan. In order for him to be able to tell his side of the story, Marshall instructed Stilwell to be in Washington at the same time to state his case. Davies accompanied him, using the opportunity to introduce his boss to a range of influential men in the capital, including journalists accustomed to hearing only pro-Chiang propaganda and politicians who continued to believe that the nationalist leader held the key to the defeat of the Japanese. It was on his return from Washington to Chungking that Davies climbed aboard Flight 12420 on the early morning of August 2, 1943.

7

DR. SEVAREID, I PRESUME?

Davies had been the first to jump into space. Now standing on a steep hillside, his crumpled parachute around his legs, he looked up and saw Flight 12420 disappearing over the ridge in the distance, seemingly hightailing it to safety in India now that it had been relieved of its extraneous weight. "Damnation," he thought, "they have unloaded us and now they are light enough to make it back to base." He had leaped into the unknown, eyes tightly closed, with both hands locked on the pin that would pull the ripcord. Counting to ten—because he had read in novels that this is what parachutists did—he had pulled hard and after an enormous jolt found himself swinging gently under a mass of silk, the blue sky above and the green hillside below. He landed on the side of the hill without much finesse, and Captain Duncan Lee, Sergeant Evan Wilder, Staff Sergeant Joseph "Jiggs" Giguere, and Lieutenant Colonel Kwoh Li landed close by. They were none the worse for their ordeal, apart from a few bruises and strains. Duncan Lee had stuffed a bottle of Carew's gin into his shirt before he jumped, and it had survived intact. But they were shocked, psychologically dislocated by the experience they had just been through. The time that had passed between realizing that they had to jump and standing here on a silent hillside could be measured in minutes. One moment they were safely dozing on a quiet passenger flight to Kunming, and the next minute they were, well, who knew where?

Each man stood and looked around to get a measure of their surroundings. They were high on the side of a mountain with a river running through the deep valley far below. The terrain was

covered with scrub rather than jungle, with tall trees massed in
clumps across the slopes. It was silent, without even the rustling
of the leaves in the trees or the chirping of birds to share their
shocked contemplation. Duncan, at least, admitted that he was
"scared fairly stiff." Where had they landed? Were they in Burma?
Where were the nearest Japanese? Were there any natives? If so,
would they be friendly? And what of any wild animals? Did tigers,
leopards, and wild buffalo inhabit this wilderness? All they had to
defend themselves was a Colt .45 automatic pistol that Duncan Lee
had in a holster strapped to his waist.

A small stream gathered itself in a pool a little way down the hill,
and, suddenly feeling the dryness of their mouths, the five men
clambered down the slope to slake their thirst. Pushing their way
through the bushes, they knelt down and began to drink. According to Davies's memoirs, it was while quenching his thirst that he
looked up toward the opposite side of the pool, and his eyes con-
nected with those of another human being who was watching him
intently. Looking around, he saw other faces and was relieved to
record that they reflected curiosity rather than hostility. He smiled,
and six or so men, virtually naked, stepped out from the bushes on
the other side of the pool. "They were superb physical specimens
in loin cloths and saucer-sized brass disks shielding their genitals,
bearing red tasseled spears and carrying long machete-like knives
strapped on their backs." The two groups of men stood there,
sizing each other up. With no nefarious intent apparent, the first
challenge was that of communication. The silence was broken by
Kwoh Li blurting out, in Chinese, "Where are we?" The question
elicited not even a flicker of a response. The nearly naked, spear-
wielding warriors a few feet away appeared not even to have heard
the words, let alone understood them. The impasse was broken
when Davies noticed a leech on his arm. One of the tribesmen
reached over and with a tug removed it, an act that Davies interpreted as friendly. He had in one of his pockets a small notebook.
He now drew it out and, standing next to the native, began to draw
sketches of those quotidian things that might create a link between

the two groups.* Did the natives recognize them? A rough drawing of a train—shown with the attendant sounds—was followed by both Japanese and British flags. Blank incomprehension. The drawing of a rifle and the sounds of gunfire didn't trigger any signs of recognition or understanding either. They looked at each other in silence. They appeared to have nothing in common, these white men in crumpled khaki who had dropped from the sky and these near-naked warriors who had emerged silently from the undergrowth in the midst of a vast green wilderness. Then the tribesmen gestured for Davies and his colleagues to come with them. Looking at each other, they shrugged their shoulders in acquiescence. There was little else they could do, and the natives didn't appear unfriendly. Slowly they began to ascend the hill. Alarmingly, one of the natives looked at Davies and, grinning, drew his hand across his throat. Were they being led to their slaughter after all? What could they do about it, with a single .45 automatic among them? But at the same time the natives appeared concerned for the well-being of their visitors. The track went directly up the hill, and, noticing their visitors' inability to move at their pace, the natives slowed down and waited patiently for them to clamber up. Davies thought quickly. They didn't appear to be in danger, and they needed to adopt a calm and measured attitude toward their newfound friends. Weakness, Davies thought, or fear would be exploited and could be dangerous.

After about thirty minutes they crested a ridge, and there on its peak they saw a village, its back resting comfortably against the hillside. A cluster of houses, all built of palm thatch, were grouped together, the fronts elevated on stilts to compensate for the slope of the ground, verandas reaching across the front of each. What views of the valley below! It was a verdant paradise. But those same magnificent views would allow the villagers plenty of time to prepare if an enemy decided to attack. In this respect the village was

---

*These drawings are now with the Davies Papers in the Truman Library, Independence, Missouri.

no different from countless others across the region, where families protected themselves from the depredations of their enemies by perching their villages on the peaks of the hills rather than in the more sensible but less secure valleys. On the verandas of the houses, Davies noticed, were the village's womenfolk, "a diverting sight with their bare bosoms festooned over the balustrades."

At the heart of the village was what appeared to be a large communal house with a distinctive frontage—like an inverted V with elaborately carved uprights—which the men were encouraged to enter. From the veranda at its front they caught their first sight of a column of smoke rising into the sky across the neighboring mountain. With a sudden shock they realized that the fire came from the remains of Flight 12420, which had clearly been unable to make its way back to India. What had happened to everyone else? Davies hadn't seen any parachutes other than those of the four men with him. Presumably many might now be dead, but others would have been able to get out of the plane alive. Not knowing what to think, he scribbled a message in his notebook, ripped out the page, and handed it to the man whom he had now judged to be the most senior. Pointing to the distant smoke, he pressed the page into his hands. A flicker of understanding crossed the other man's face. The native men talked among themselves before one of the warriors was handed the paper and went off at a trot, disappearing into the bush at the end of the ridge. Davies had written, "Those who bailed out this morning should join the rest of the party at the village. The bearer will lead you. This means you, too, Eric."

The ice now having been broken, the natives of the Naga village of Ponyo, just inside the border in Burma, lost some of their earlier inhibitions and clustered around the men, fascinated by everything they saw, fingering their clothes, boots, and items of equipment. Duncan Lee had emptied the Colt .45 of its cartridges, and the natives touched it in awe, allowing their hands to run over the machined metal. The other villagers had by this time also overcome their shyness and crowded around the men from the plane. A man whom Davies judged to be the leader approached him—singling Davies out as the head of the small group of aliens who had dropped from the sky—and with both hands outstretched offered him a sword, the handle prominent, with much careful ceremony. It was immediately understood by Davies to be a sign of peace. The sword looked to be British, which meant that some kind of contact clearly existed between the village and the outside world. It was clear to him that the natives were friendly and intended them no harm, although he knew nothing of their history or reputation. On reflection, he realized that the tribespeople must have become used to the almost daily sight of the strange machines flying high over their homes but had never seen who was in them or had the opportunity to reach out and touch these godlike beings who could travel so high in the sky—the province, it was thought before these noisy creatures were first seen, of the birds and of the gods.

In Angami territory (around Kohima), when the first aircraft had been seen only a year or two before, it had caused both consternation and awe. Noumvüo Khruomo was twenty when he saw his first aircraft. He was working with his family in the fields when he saw the airplane, and they exclaimed in astonishment at how amazing it was that they had witnessed something so spectacular in their lifetime. Neilao, a young man of the same age, first saw a plane flying above Khonoma village. He stared at it in wonder: "The others with me shouted '*Lei, Lei, Lei, kepruo lei*' (look, look, look, a plane, look). We were so filled with awe at seeing that flying object in the sky. I thought to myself, so that is what a *kepruo* is. The second time we saw aircraft was when four or five planes flew over Khonoma." On first seeing an aircraft, the villagers of Chakhesang ran outside to watch, the elders calling out, "Come, come out and see, there is a strange bird in the sky!" The "bird" then proceeded to open its belly and drop bombs into the valley below. The villagers were shocked, some calling out in surprise, "Look out! It's defecating!" before the bombs exploded deafeningly, sending them running back in terror to their huts. The next day was declared a taboo day, a no-work day to purify the village of any ill consequences from the sighting of the strange bird and its terrifying excrement.*

With as much dignity as he could muster, Davies took the proffered weapon. What could he offer in exchange? The four men had gathered up their parachutes and harnesses and brought them with them to the village—they might come in handy, they thought—and after handing back the sword as reverently as he could, with plenty of head bowing, Davies offered the man the great bundle of white silk from his 'chute. Taking off his watch, he offered that too, attempting briefly to explain the purpose of the strange instrument. He gave up. The headman had accepted these gifts impassively. Then the headman—who certainly looked much older than the others—dipped his hand into a native haversack attached by a strap to his shoulder and solemnly brought out a silver Indian rupee for each of the downed men, yet more evidence of the village's contact with "civilization" and of the friendly intent of their hosts.

These ceremonies over, the five men were led to a circular seating area in the center of the village in front of the large building, which Davies assumed was some sort of guesthouse, where a fire had been lit and preparations were being made for a feast of some kind. It was for the men only, the women and children disappearing quietly from view. Rows of bamboo mugs had been prepared, filled with some unknown concoction that they would later understand to be *zu*, beer that was made in these parts with millet. Then, pulled by a rope, into the village struggled a scrawny goat, bleating pitifully. In a flash of understanding Davies realized now what that sinister throat-cutting motion had meant earlier: it was the sign that an animal was to be sacrificed to celebrate the arrival among these unknown people of their guests from the sky. There is no doubt that if these five men had known among whom they had fallen that day—the Nagas of Ponyo village, close allies of Pangsha—their terror would have been real and justified. But on

---

*Quotations from Lyman, *Japan's Last Bid for Victory*.

this occasion, ignorance was bliss. Davies, as befitted the leader of the heavenly visitors, was offered a large *dao*: it was evident that he was expected to remove the head from the nervous, bleating ruminant. He demurred and nodded instead to Evan Wilder. "With a visible lack of enthusiasm," Davies recalled, "the Texan grasped the knife and, as three braves held the uncooperative goat, hacked off the beast's head." Then, head removed and blood spurting from the stump, the body was passed from man to man for each to take a mouthful of the warm liquid. They did so for the sake of fraternity, unwilling to upset their hosts, for whom this ceremony was clearly of some significance. It wasn't the most pleasant experience of his life, Davies thought—the warm blood tasting "rather bland, something like unchilled tomato juice without Worcestershire sauce and lemon"—but the day was now accumulating a long series of new experiences, and there seemed plenty of time for more. The blood-drained carcass was then thrown on the fire, without being skinned or gutted, and slowly cooked, innards and all.

Whatever ceremony was then planned Davies could not say, for at that moment in the far distance could be heard the distinctive and miraculous sound of a twin-engined C-47 Skytrain, the military version of the famous DC3 Douglas airliner, known in British usage as the Dakota, flying low. Some of the tribesmen rushed to the outskirts of the village, gesturing excitedly at the sky. Sure enough, lumbering majestically across the valley a few miles away was the most comforting sight the five men had ever seen. Excitement overcame them, and they began jumping and shouting somewhat foolishly, Davies later admitted, vainly hoping to attract the attention of their colleagues several miles away. The aircraft turned out of sight at the end of the valley without any indication that their village had been seen. Nevertheless, they continued to hear it for some time to come. The smoke from the crash site had disappeared by now, but the C-47 was apparently searching the ground, as it circled among the hills in the neighboring valley. Eventually, however, the sound of aircraft engines disappeared, and the party settled down around the fire to tear strips from the now-roasted goat. The morale of the four men had risen dramatically as a result of the welcome apparition they had just witnessed.

The party was well under way with the sun into its decline nearly three hours later when up to the circle came running the messenger they had sent earlier with Davies's scrap of paper. The man solemnly handed Davies another piece of paper in return. It was a note from Eric Sevareid and read, "Dear John—Eleven men here—two have bad legs— supplies dropped here, plane will return here—rescue party on way—please come here—we are about one mile south of wreck. Eric." The decision was made: they would join Sevareid's party and to do so would need to set out before it got dark. Somehow this plan was understood by their hosts, and with much bowing and exchange of felicitations the five men set off, accompanied by the man who had carried the message and four of the spear-carrying men from the village. In normal circumstances, Davies recognized, the tribesmen would have jogged, but instead they "accommodated themselves to our stumbling gait." It was soon dark, but somehow—he could never understand exactly how— the men cut down rushes from the side of the path and lit a spark from a flint to transform the rushes into brightly burning torches. They were soaked on their way by a sudden downpour, but the rushes miraculously continued burning. Soon they were tired and stumbling, although the sure-footed natives were careful to guide them through the worst of the track. After what Davies imagined to have been four or five hours—he no longer had his watch—their guides began to call out in the darkness. They came to a wooden stockade through which they were led to a large house in the middle of a village that was a replica of the one they had left. Saturated by the rain and exhausted, they stumbled inside. There, most of them asleep, were their compatriots. Eric Sevareid was sitting up, awakened by the sudden disturbance. Davies recalled their Stanley-and-Livingstone-like meeting: "Dripping wet, I greeted him, 'Dr. Sevareid, I presume.'"

8

TAMING THE NAGAS

The rugged hills over which Harry Neveu's C-46 climbed that clear morning of August 2, 1943, were inhabited by an ancient tribal race of whom the occupants of the aircraft were entirely oblivious. They had not met a Naga before nor been briefed on the Naga culture, customs, or conventions. In any case, the origins of the people who inhabited what the British first called the Naga Hills in 1866 (parts of which were initially incorporated into the British Raj in 1881) remained then, as today, an ethnological mystery. According to the noted Edwardian gentleman scholar (and commandant of the Assam Rifles) Colonel Leslie Shakespear, the name of this scattered, warlike, Mongoloid race is a corruption of the Assamese word for "naked" and when originally coined was strongly pejorative, a fear-filled description (like that of the bogeyman) by the Assamese of the plains of the benighted savages who inhabited the vast sweep of tangled hills that separated Assam's Brahmaputra River Valley and Burma far to the east.

The lack of a written history has placed the Nagas at the mercy of every kind of speculation. The British officiating political agent for Manipur, G. H. Damant, who was killed fighting the Nagas at Khonoma (near Kohima) in 1879, believed that as a race they originated from the southeastern corner of Tibet.* The British colonial

---

*Damant's opinion is chronicled in Reid, *History of the Areas Bordering on Assam from 1883–1941.*

administrator and noted anthropologist Dr. John Henry ("J. H.") Hutton noted that connections had been made between the Nagas and the headhunters of old Malaya and Borneo, and others have traced their presence in these tangled hills to a great migration countless centuries before from northwestern China. Certainly many points of similarity exist between these people and those of other Mongoloid races scattered across Asia and the Pacific: their predilection for eating dog, for instance, for head-hunting, for practicing common types of weaving, and for the large number of highly prized seashells that bedeck their ceremonial clothing to this day. In the first quarter of the twentieth century Shakespear was especially interested to note the commonalities between the coastal-dwelling Dayak (Iban) headhunters of Borneo and the hill-dwelling Nagas, the conch shells present among the Nagas being a natural connection between the two peoples.

As in many British colonial endeavors, the growth of the Raj's engagement with the inhabitants of the hills between the Brahmaputra (in Assam) and the Chindwin (in Burma)—a population of perhaps no more than 100,000 in the 1880s—was gradual. Contrary to popular opinion, this growth was undertaken not as the result of some kind of master plan but in the teeth of opposition from administrators and politicians alike, who were combined in their objections to the untrammeled growth of their obligations. Imperialism cost money. In fact, the ink-stain effect of colonial expansion in northeastern India took place for another reason, namely, the repeated attacks by the hill people against the lowlanders in the Brahmaputra Valley. This had been a persistent problem in the long history of British engagement with this remote part of northeastern India. Looking back from the time of writing in 1924 to the inception of control in Assam by the East India Company nearly a century before, Sir Joseph Bampfylde Fuller, then governor of Assam, considered the essential security problem in northeastern India to be not the fear of transnational invasion (from Burma) but rather the clash between the growing commercial interests of the East India Company and the continuance of the warlike (and head-hunting) depredations of the Nagas.*

The raids by Nagas on the plains were meant not for seizing territory but rather for securing and consolidating local power through fear and keeping the peoples of the plains at bay. For most of the imperial period, beginning in the mid-1850s, the problem (to British colonial administrators at least) was that Naga behavior was unsuited to the progressive growth of a law-abiding, socially stable, and economically prosperous empire. The British even suspected that the Nagas enjoyed these expeditions. The language employed by Fuller—and his successor, Sir Robert Reid—was typical of the observations made of the hill people when seen through an imperial lens. Reid described them as an extremely attractive but slightly juvenile race of otherwise manly warriors:

> [They] . . . are still inspired by the ancient ideas that war is one of the most exhilarating of life's experiences, and its commemoration, in war-dress and war dances, the most enjoyable of amusements. To possess the head of an alien man, woman or child has been a treasured assurance of success and a necessary passport to good fortune in courtship. Society is organized on a war footing. . . . Peoples of the same blood have grouped themselves into clans, isolated so completely as to have developed languages that are mutually unintelligible. To ambuscade an alien village— even its women when drawing water from the stream—to burn its houses and massacre its inhabitants have been regarded as "sporting" enterprises that relieve the monotony of life. Forays into the lowlands have been still more tempting.

More than one report described their breaking of the law as behavior reminiscent of that of errant children requiring loving discipline rather than that of irredeemable criminals. Like wayward

---

*Fuller's opinion is given in Reid, *History of the Areas Bordering on Assam from 1883–1941*.

offspring in need of a firm hand, the Nagas needed only to be encouraged to obey the Christian imperialist injunctions to "love one another" and "live peaceably with all men" in order to be accepted fully into the enlightened panoply of consenting nations that made up the rich canvas of the British Empire.

The economic foundation of Assam referred to by Fuller was tea. The Treaty of Yandabo on February 24, 1826, ceded the ancient Ahom territories of Assam and Manipur—lands that included the Naga Hills—to Britain from Burma at the conclusion of the ruinous (for both sides) First Anglo-Burmese War. The result of the war meant that Britain lost its global monopoly on the Chinese tea trade, but in 1832 the British discovered the precious bush growing in Assam. As the century progressed and the East India Company gave way after the mutiny of 1857 to the Raj, cultivation of the Assamese hills increased exponentially both in terms of acreage under cultivation and profit. But the commercialization of the hills created rich targets for raiding parties from the hills. Had such despoliations by these near-naked savages not been checked, Fuller observed, "the development of the tea industry would have been impossible." Imperialism meant nothing unless it was accompanied by order; security; and the onward march of a civilization, based on loosely defined Christian values, that protected commerce. Measures were therefore undertaken during the second half of the nineteenth century to stamp out this brigandry and to impose a degree of order on the otherwise independent Naga tribes scattered across the vast greenery of their hilltop home.

This took time, however. Fighting bands of Naga warriors continued to descend from the hills to wreak havoc on the tea plantations of the plains, causing untold disruptions to the commercialization of tea, as George Barker complained in 1884:

For the benefit of those of my readers who are ignorant of the whereabouts of the Nagas, I must premise by saying that they are a warlike hill tribe, peopling the range of hills which form the southern boundary of the Assam Valley. The last Naga Expedition

(1879–80) had a disturbing effect on the communications between Calcutta and the planters. Both of the steamboat companies were requisitioned for Government service, and every
steamer that came up was laden with commissariat or military
stores. During this time very few of the civilians' stores found
their way up the river: those that did were badly treated. What
difficulties the wretched planters had to put up with during this
fearful period, arising from the uncertainty of supplies and consequent deprivation of the absolute necessaries of life that had
been reckoned upon! Even when the orders had been executed
and the packages brought up the river, the trouble of obtaining
advices as to their whereabouts made this a memorable time for
the unlucky fraternity.

The argument went that if Delhi managed to subdue these peoples' warlike instincts in order to protect the interests of capitalism in the Assamese hills, it was only fair to extend this security to
individuals and villages within the Naga Hills, if only to manage
the worst vice of the region. A common feature of life in these territories was vicious intervillage feuding, including indiscriminate
head-hunting. Establishing the king's peace was expensive, however. Certainly Delhi wasn't going to provide local security and po-
licing for free, and local taxation followed.

Until 1877, therefore, British policy was to restrain the worst ex-
cesses of the people of the hills where they were directed against
the people of the plains under the protection of the government
of Assam. Military and police actions were undertaken, beginning
in the 1840s, on an occasional basis to punish villages—especially
those of the Angami tribe, centered on Khonoma and Kohima—
for raids carried out into British-administered territory, although
they were not always successful. Khonoma and Mozema were first
encountered by the British, and burned, in 1850, and at Kohima—a
large village of 900 houses—a "bloody battle" was fought outside
the village the following year. But the Raj had no stomach for
the expenditure of money on retaining troops in these hills and

withdrew after concluding this demonstration of its power. Leslie Shakespear recorded that this policy allowed the Angami Nagas to "riot at their own free will": "Reports of those days show the jubilant Nagas when once they realized they were left alone, celebrated the new conditions by making twenty-two serious raids that year into British territory, i.e., down into the main Assam valley where the tea industry was progressing. This alone showed the impracticability of non-interference." Sir James Johnstone, onetime Manipuri political agent for the Raj, blamed the repeated snubbing of British authority by the Angami Nagas squarely on the government of India. After continued provocation a large force was sent into the hills east of Dimapur in December 1850:

Kohima, which had sent a challenge, was destroyed on February 11th, 1851. In this last engagement over three hundred Nagas were killed, and our prestige thoroughly established. We might then, with great advantage to the people and our own districts, have occupied a permanent post, and while protecting our districts that had suffered so sorely from Naga raids, have spread civilization far and wide among the hill-tribes. Of course we did nothing of the kind; on such occasions the Government of India always does the wrong thing; it was done now, and, instead of occupying a new position, we retreated, even abandoning our old post at Samagudting, and only maintaining a small body of Shan militia at Dimapur. The Nagas ascribed our retreat to fear, the periodical raids on our unfortunate villages were renewed, and unheeded by us: and finally, in 1856, we withdrew from Dimapur and abandoned the post. After that, the Nagas ran riot, and one outrage after another was committed.

| | |

Another reason for Western engagement with the Nagas was religion. It was a series of American missionaries who first brought a confident, evangelical strain of American Protestantism to the Naga

Hills in the mid-nineteenth century; within that strand of Christianity was one specifically of the Baptist variety. The influences of the Great Awakening in the late eighteenth century, together with the expansion of civilization into territories occupied until then by "Red Indians," and the march of a nascent American imperialism in Central America and southeast Asia made evangelizing missions the obvious concomitant of a new Americanism. With the destructive introversion of the Civil War now behind it, opportunities for the promulgation of a newly self-assured brand of American identity appeared widespread. The Nagas became—among many others—the targets of this imperative. New Yorker Miles Bronson first arrived in Assam in 1838 with his wife and daughter at the invitation of the East India Company. The "John Company" was not interested in evangelism per se as much as it was in civilizing the natives. If the local Nagas were to become Christian, they would cease their interference in company business. The Baptists were therefore good for business. Either way, at the time missionary work was considered good for both parties, and Bronson recorded gifts from company officials (possibly given in a private capacity) totaling 840 rupees in 1838, 250 rupees in 1839, and 300 rupees in 1840. Indeed, the true ulterior purpose of John Company largesse was laid bare in a memorandum by the local company agent in 1840 to Sir Thomas Maddock, secretary to the government of India, suggesting that the company support plans by Bronson to set up a tea plantation for local Nagas to introduce them to the discipline and rewards of cultivation: "I conceive that by a proper cooperation with that gentleman [Bronson] and the encouragement of the Nagas to cultivate the products of their hills and tea in particular, we may hope ere long to see civilization greatly advanced among these Nagas, and our supremacy gradually extend over the hills, without which, and the consequent suppression of the constant feuds amongst the tribes, there seems to be little hope of effecting any great change in the habits of the people, or of our being able to avail ourselves of the great natural resources of the fine tract of mountainous country."

Between the 1870s and the end of World War II approximately sixty American missionaries committed significant portions of their working lives to bringing the barbarous Naga tribes from darkness into light. Although most of this endeavor was concentrated in the western hills—missionary activity never reached as far, for instance, as the Patkoi Range—the results of this work by members of organizations such as the American Baptist Foreign Missionary Society was dramatic. By the time of the outbreak of war in 1939 perhaps 50 percent of Nagas—from a population now of some 200,000—called themselves Christian. Despite their quite obvious association with (British) colonialism, Nagas on the whole have consistently regarded the efforts of (American) Baptist missionaries to be "a good thing." Although the evangelizing imperative of the Baptists irritated the desires of the anthropologically minded British colonial administrators in the first decades of the twentieth century—by associating Christianity with specifically American customs and social mores (such as in clothing, personal hygiene, habits, music, and so on)—the one thing that united these cultural opposites was opposition to head-hunting. Although the swiping of the odd head or two by a village was put up with by the British—because the act was vested with deep cultural significance and it was thought that trying to stamp out the practice would provoke a violent backlash—the wholesale slaughter of villages was not, because it signaled insecurity in an area and a threat to the rule of law, however distantly applied. For the missionary, of course, nothing was more sacrosanct than life itself and nothing more heinous than its cheap destruction, especially in the name of culture or tradition.

| | |

The eventual extension of administrative control over these territories came about in the 1870s because of British reaction to attacks on the Assamese tea plantations and the internecine struggles for local power among the Naga villages. Stories of these often horrifying despoliations seeped out of the hills. A head of political steam was got up in the mid-1870s in the government of Assam when humanitarian intervention into the wildest of the western territories was advocated in order to stamp out this barbarism and to save the Nagas from themselves. The policy of preventing external raids had largely succeeded but had singularly failed to remove the local penchant for internal feuding and didn't protect British surveying expeditions into the hills. Two such expeditions were destroyed in 1874 and 1875 by Naga attacks, with most of their members killed and only a few survivors escaping. A report in 1876, for instance, blamed the Angami Nagas for the despoliation of six villages in a single month, causing the deaths of 334 men, women, and children. Continued warlike behavior resulted in a punitive expedition by the British in late 1877 that punished the two villages most at fault: Khonoma and Mozema. According to Shakespear, the punishments imposed on these large, wealthy, and powerful villages were pathetic and were a decided factor in their warriors' continuation of raiding: failing to punish the Nagas properly led only to continued impertinence.

Until the late 1870s administrative control over the eastern Naga tribes had been based in the large village Samagudting (now Chumukedima) a few miles into the hills from Dimapur. As time went by this village came to be considered too far removed from the real center of necessary influence in the hills, and an alternative site was sought. One option was Kohima, forty-six miles into the hills toward Manipur, although at the time no road ran to it from Samagudting. At about this time a new phenomenon influenced British thinking: individual Naga villages began asking for British protection, in return for which they offered to pay tribute. By 1878 seventeen villages had voluntarily come under the protection of the crown. The 1877 punitive expedition to Khonoma made the location of the district officer in these hills a sensible option in order to keep a permanent peace, and in 1878 a post was authorized for Kohima. It was established in March of the following year. The first political officer to take residence was G. H. Damant. He was not to last long, however. The nearby village of Khonoma (twelve

miles away), which had supposedly been pacified after the 1877 expedition, together with the village of Mozema, rose against the new
British threat to its hegemony in the hills. Damant and thirty-six
members of his escort were killed while visiting Khonoma on October 13, 1879, and Kohima was then subjected to a siege that lasted
twelve days. The British garrison of some 180 men, women, and
children was surrounded by 6,000 Naga warriors who wanted to
sweep the British from their hills so that they could continue their
traditional practices unimpeded by the white man's law.

These sieges were a common characteristic of Britain's imperial
experience along the fringes of its empire. The siege of Kohima was
lifted only after the arrival from Manipur of a small army of 2,000
Manipuris and 40 sepoys of the Thirty-Fourth Native Infantry, led by
Lieutenant Colonel James Johnstone, the Manipuri political agent
based in Imphal, 120 miles to the southeast. The raja of Manipur
had long wanted to subdue these unruly hills, and supporting Johnstone's relief of Kohima helped him toward achieving this ambition. Sporadic skirmishes and bloodletting followed, with Khonoma
bowing its knee, finally, in March 1880. Shakespear concluded that
it was only by means of a strong hand that this troublesome tribe
was subdued: "It is also conceivable that the drastic punishment
meted out by Colonel Johnstone on Phesema village who attacked
his convoys during the winter may have somewhat taken the heart
out of the Angamis, who were in the end well punished by fines in
cash and grain, unpaid labor, the surrender of firearms, and demo-
lition of defenses; while Khonoma in addition had all its cultivated
lands confiscated, and its inhabitants dispersed among other clans.
Since then this powerful tribe have remained quiet."

In the hills to the east of Sibsagar, a tea-growing center in the
Brahmaputra Valley thirty miles northeast of Jorhat, trade had existed for centuries between the Nagas of the northwest hill area (the
Ao tribe) and their plain-dwelling neighbors. The British first came
into contact with the Ao people by virtue of a journey through the
hills by Captain T. Brodie of the Second European Regiment of
the East India Company in 1844. Their incorporation into a British

sphere of influence came about at the Nagas' own instigation; they even agreed without murmur to the annual tax of two rupees per household that the British political agent insisted was the price of British administration and security. From the outset gross violations of the king's peace were ruthlessly exterminated by the application of the law. The district officers served as magistrates and, when not sitting at Kohima, undertook regular—usually annual—tours into the remote villages to hear cases and apply the law. Significant infractions, such as murder or head-hunting, resulted in military expeditions setting out from Kohima to end the fighting, by force if necessary, and to capture and punish the perpetrators. But British government was for the most part benign, fitting comfortably alongside that of the village chiefs. Local customs and laws were largely left alone so long as villages behaved peaceably. In fact, through the *gaonbura* system the British were able to reinforce their power by passing down authority to the local headman, whose own authority was worn literally in red in the form of a blanket or waistcoat provided by the British. As the Naga historian Khrienuo Ltu explained, British "rule therefore didn't seriously affect the basic structure of the Naga society."

It remained traditional in character and content. Moreover, the system of administration which the British followed in the Naga Hills ensured social continuity and at the same time made it easier for the people to accept the British rule. The British intervened in the village administration only in disputes which could not be settled by the village courts. The main intention of the British Government in recognizing the village chiefs as undisputed leaders of the village was to make them loyal agents of the colonial administration. Thus, while continuing as leaders of their people they became an important link between the British Government and the tribal masses.

As British influence moved north from Kohima and east from Sibsagar, it became apparent that another administrative site was required in Ao territory. Mokokchung, eighty-seven miles north of Kohima, was duly chosen and became the location, beginning in 1890, of a British political officer responsible for the administration and security of a vast area of the northwest containing people of the Ao, Sema, Lotha, Konyak, Chang, and Sangtam tribes. But in what the Australian academic Geoffrey Blainey in another context described as the "tyranny of distance," the further reaches of the Naga Hills were too far distant even for the imperial power to apply its civilizing influence, and anything outside a directly administered area was, frankly, left to its own devices, even if it did (as was often the case) experience regular outbreaks of murder and mayhem. Until, that is, any lawlessness spilled over into the British Administered Area and upset the tranquillity of the order imposed by the deputy commissioner in the hilltop village of Kohima and his assistant, the subcommissioner in Mokokchung, farther north.

The process of administration quickly overtook that of militarization in terms of how imperial rule was applied to subject peoples in these parts. The period in the southern and western Naga Hills after 1881 was therefore marked by the development of political and civil administration, with the enforced acquiescence of the villages within British-administered territory if they stepped out of line. A regular question that arose during the tours of the early administrators was the extent to which they should control the activities of "British" villages mounting incursions into nonadministered territory, and vice versa. Considerable debate took place between those advocating a "forward" (interventionist) policy along the Naga frontier with nonadministered territory and those who argued for a more laissez-faire approach. Sir Robert Neil Reid, governor of Assam from 1937 to 1942, for instance, supported the former approach, dismissing the occasional "promenades," or punitive expeditions into nonadministered territory, as having no real impact on the incidence of feuding among the Naga villages outside the British Administered Area. The only solution to repeated and destabilizing lawlessness was for recalcitrant areas to be brought formally under British control. It was the latter view that prevailed and largely survived through the end of the Raj in 1947, with only a gradual, even reluctant, encroachment of British hegemony into previously unadministered areas. For much of the final four decades of British presence in these hills, attacks on British subjects inside and over the border would be punished, but feuding outside British territory was of no concern to the authorities in Kohima or Mokokchung. This policy didn't prevent the gradual expansion of British territory by 1910 to encompass the entirety of the northwestern hills and a zone of influence that extended well into the territories that bordered these.

There was another problem. The relinquishment of headhunting and blood feuds among villages in the Administered Area suddenly made those communities vulnerable to raids from the nonprotected areas. Because the newly law-abiding villages no longer responded in kind, they were suddenly soft targets. The British promise of security had now to be made real, or these villages would regret the decision they had made to pay tribute to a power that proved unable to protect them.

Occasionally, therefore, armed expeditions set out to punish villages for repeated infractions of the king's peace. The Pangti expedition of 1875, the Chang expedition of 1889, and the Yachummi expedition of 1910 were three such. A fourth, which remained in the collective memory of the region for another generation, was to the Konyak village of Chinglong, which lies northeast of Mokokchung toward the village of Mon. This expedition demonstrated that such ventures were not to be entered into lightly. In 1910 raids were reported from Chinglong against Chingtong, a village within British-administered territory. The subdivisional officer at Mokokchung, on investigating the situation, overreached his orders. He marched into nonadministered territory with Captain Hamilton and eighty men of the Naga Hills Military Police (later the Assam Rifles) and burned part of Chinglong. The subdivisional officer lost his job for this indiscretion of mounting an attack against a village that was outside his jurisdiction. Chinglong knew nothing of these imperial niceties and continued to be a thorn in the side of its neighbors and of the British inside their administered territory. In July 1912 the young men of this lawless village compounded a spate of recent raiding delinquencies by an act of treachery that outraged the sensibilities of colonial administrators. They were normally content to allow the occasional head to be removed from unsuspecting shoulders, but they could not turn a blind eye to a massacre. Chinglong deliberately lured a group of men from a neighboring village into its territory with the promise of a harvest of much-prized betel leaf and then attacked them en masse for their heads. Three were killed. The commissioner for Assam determined that enough was enough and ordered that a punitive expedition be dispatched at the end of the monsoon. The events that followed demonstrated, however, that there was a gap between the theory of an expedition and its successful execution.

Although a decision was reached in November 1912 to launch the expedition, a lack of suitable troops held up its departure from Mokokchung until January 1913. Repeated demands sent to Chinglong to hand over the murderers received hostile and scornful responses, and, emboldened by Chinglong's refusal to bow to British intimidation, the general attitude of other villages across the frontier became hostile. It was therefore considered prudent to reinforce the expedition with an additional 150 men of the Dacca Military Police. A military post that had been established at Chingpoi (thirty miles northeast of Mokokchung as the crow flies) reported that the men of Chinglong had a habit of advancing to the river separating the territory of both villages, waving their *dao*s, and chanting taunts at the British to come and die at their hands. By February 2 the men of the Dacca Military Police had arrived at Chingpoi, where they met up with seventy-five men of the Naga Hills Military Police. Leaving some of the men at Chingpoi, a mixed force of 196 soldiers and porters marched toward Chinglong on February 5. This was typical Naga hill country. Impossibly steep hillsides were bisected in the valley bottoms by rivers tumbling over rocky beds on their journey either to the Brahmaputra (to the west) or the Chindwin (to the east). Thick vegetation grew down to the water's edge and bloomed in intense green explosions that off the beaten tracks was impossible to cut through without considerable physical effort and a sharp *dao*. Even the paths were few in number and unless well tended fell into the habit of quickly overgrowing, a particular problem during the monsoon, when relentless rain allowed the exuberance of growth to know no bounds. In this terrain the advantage lay with those who knew it intimately, who could dart in and out of cover as required, using the jungle to move and to hide. It was ideal for the Nagas' favorite tactic: the ambush.

The British force departed Mokokchung happily enough. The rifle-armed troops were well drilled and in fine fettle, although few had fought in this rugged terrain and none knew the territory. They knew that the men of Chinglong had some weapons—probably ancient muskets, some homemade, or more modern single-shot Martini-Henry rifles—but these guns were no match for the disciplined firepower of the Lee-Enfield. Their camp equipment was carried for them by a cluster of locally recruited Naga porters, and this long, winding procession offered itself to the eager warriors of Chinglong as an ideal target. An advance guard of sepoys managed to push its way through a number of barriers set in its way, such as groups of *panji* traps (poisoned shafts of hardened bamboo driven into the ground and designed to penetrate the foot of a careless enemy) and trenches across paths that were overlooked by stone walls designed to offer cover to men firing the Naga's deadly crossbow. But it wasn't the armed troops whom the men of Chinglong targeted. A sudden and savage rush through the single extended line of porters caused shocking devastation. Frightened porters reported "hundreds" of Chinglong warriors appearing at speed through the long grass and cutting a swath of heads as they swept by. The onslaught was so swift and silent that men were killed as they stood without any chance to escape. As quickly as the swinging *dao*s appeared, they disappeared again into the towering vegetation that closed in against the winding hillside track.

Despite the sudden horror of the attack, the now empty village was occupied and much of it burned to the ground. This, after all, was the meaning of *punitive*. The bulk of the force rested there that night. The following day the remainder of the village and its surrounding fields were put to the torch, and the expedition withdrew to the relative safety of Chingpoi to lick its wounds. It was not strong enough to remain in Chinglong and to defend itself from counterattack, and in isolated and vulnerable position created a risk of having the withdrawal route cut off. Eleven men had been killed and thirty wounded already, most by swinging *dao*s in the close quarters of the jungle track where the porters had been ambushed. It was a serious loss, a casualty rate to the entire column of 22 percent. Unfortunately, three rifles had fallen into the hands of Chinglong, which didn't augur well for future peace in the region. Chinglong had been hurt but not subdued, and it took the arrival of Gurkha reinforcements the following month to finally bring its resistance to an end. It had been a long and painful experience for the British, and something of a humiliation. There were strong humanitarian and even legal imperatives to exert force across the frontier simply because it seemed the right thing to do, but such actions were fraught with danger, unintended consequences, and no guarantee of early or easy victory.

These lessons were to live with the colonial authorities for a generation. Far to the east, in the blue-shrouded hills of the Patkois, lay dozens of other villages that, like Chinglong, would no doubt resent any attempt to force the Raj and its rules on their way of life. One such was the mighty village of Pangsha, nestled at the western edge of the mountains that separated India from Burma, known of and feared by the entire region but entirely unreached by any white people. The Naga Hills were not to be easily tamed.

| | |

The generation of Britons who followed the soldiers into the Naga Hills as members of the Indian Civil Service (ICS) were a remarkable hybrid of colonial administrator and anthropologist. The first was J. H. Hutton, who led the way for Philip ("J. P.") Mills and Charles Pawsey, followed by Philip Adams and Bill Archer. The Viennese-born aristocrat and anthropologist Christoph von Fürer-Haimendorf, inspired by Hutton, joined Mills in the Naga Hills in the mid-1930s, and together they fashioned a golden age for the study of the varied tribes of the Naga people. Hutton arrived in 1912 at the age of twenty-seven. Despite the fact that he came as a member of the ICS in the role of colonial administrator, he felt an immediate attraction to the task of recording details of the cultures he encountered. The ICS had taken on the role of administering the Raj once Britain had taken on responsibility for India after the mutiny and the demise of the East India Company. A tiny, elite band of administrators—never more than 1,200 carefully selected Britons and, as time went on, an increasing smattering of Indians—ruled a population of some 300 million at the outset of World War II. Their jobs were hard, and the more successful were arguably those—such as this remarkable succession of ethnologically minded men in the Naga Hills—who were interested in their subject peoples and worked from a genuine desire to bring good to their lives. It was certainly not a glamorous life. It entailed living far from the bright lights, walking vast distances through difficult terrain, living a mainly camping lifestyle, and achieving very little material reward. It must have appeared a thankless task for the most part, their efforts seemingly a drop in the vast ocean of imperial endeavor. It seems clear, nevertheless, that a passion for the people they administered was the principal driving force of these men. What was primarily important for them was not merely the virility of the empire they represented, nor indeed the power and prestige of their positions, but the people among whom they lived. In this respect those in the Naga Hills were unusual members of the ICS. In 1909 the Hobhouse Commission concluded that across the ICS as a whole, few officers could speak the native vernacular of their district or knew anything about the customs, way of life, or habits of their subject peoples. This was not a charge that could ever have stuck to the administrators of the Naga Hills district of Assam.

Hutton desired more than anything else to understand the people whom he administered. It is fair to say that he became driven by the need to record the lives of this hill-dwelling civilization before it was washed away without trace by the surging tide of Westernization even then lapping against the Naga foothills. A measure of his success is the fact that his work as a civil servant has long been eclipsed by his anthropological work, which resulted in scholarly evaluations of Naga cultures, especially the Angami and Sema (Sumi) Nagas, both published in 1921, and his foreword to Philip Mills's *The Ao Nagas* in 1926. Hutton's great success lay not merely in *observing* his people but in living with them as intimately as a stranger was allowed and becoming their friend. He was especially well liked because his impish character fit in well with the characteristic playfulness of the Nagas. The historians Peter van Ham and Jamie Saul told the story of a Chang Naga once saying to Bill Archer, "You and Hutton Sahib come from the same village. Hutton Sahib was a thorough Naga. He was always fooling about."

Several Europeans—mainly tea planters and soldiers—had written of these people in the casual way common to travel writers and passing journalists over the previous seventy years, but none before had made the effort to become one of them; to see life—as much as one could—from their perspective and to understand their lives from the viewpoint of their culture. In the introduction to his monograph on the Sumi tribe, Hutton laid out, as if to head off any possible criticism, the reasons why he felt able to present this analysis to the world despite having no academic anthropological credentials (he had gained a third-class degree in modern history from Oxford in 1907):

The account of the Semas given in this book has been compiled at Mokokchung and at Kohima in the Naga Hills, during an eight years' acquaintance with them, during which I have learnt to speak the language fairly fluently and have been brought into contact with the life of the individual, the family, and the community more or less continuously and from many angles. For there is hardly any point of tribal custom which is not sooner or later somehow drawn into one of the innumerable disputes which the local officer in the Naga Hills is called upon to settle, and it is my experiences in this way which constitute my credentials in writing this volume.

He need not have feared. The University of Oxford conferred on him a doctorate of social science, formal recognition to accompany the honorary title he had been awarded in 1921 as the director of ethnography in Assam. Resigning from the ICS in 1935, he returned to Britain to join the academic fraternity to which he had long contributed while in the field, becoming the William Wyse Chair of Social Anthropology at Cambridge University, a position he held until his retirement in 1950 at the age of sixty-five.

Perhaps Hutton's greatest legacy was to inspire others to follow in his footsteps, two of whom were to play leading roles in the events of 1936. The first was Philip Mills. A product of both Winchester College and Corpus Christi College, Cambridge, he, like Hutton before him, became a member of that tiny, elite band of men in the ICS who ran India for the Raj. In 1916, at the age of twenty-six, he found himself the subdivisional officer at Mokokchung, where he remained until he became the deputy commissioner, based at Kohima, in 1933. His daughter Geraldine later described Mills as a man who came to believe "that anthropology often provided the key to a problem, by working with 'tribal' custom, rather than imposing alien western values" on native communities. He was "definitely not the 'white overlord' type," she recalled. Taking a lead from Hutton, Mills considered that cultural anthropology—the deep study of the indigenous people—would enable him to be a better administrator, the job that he was paid to do. He sought not to impose his own views on the people he administered—aside from the bare bones of the application of the law—but rather to interpret and apply the law in a culturally sensitive manner, striving to be fully cognizant of centuries-old customs and beliefs that were part of what it meant to be Naga. Mills modeled his approach on his mentor, Hutton, working hard to base his approach on friendship and mutual respect. "No one could despair who, like me, numbers chiefs among his real friends," he noted, "[and they] have time and again proved literally indispensable." His friend Christoph von Fürer-Haimendorf described Mills's "sympathetic and unbureaucratic approach to the Nagas and their problems," concluding that it was this that ideally "suited the administration of a loosely controlled frontier region." Ursula Graham Bower, the "Naga Queen," became very friendly with the Millses in Assam. She observed:

> The administration of hill districts was a very personal matter, depending almost entirely upon the individual officer and his influence. It called for men of integrity, tact, infinite patience and real devotion to their often obstreperous charges. Speaking as one who has seen the process of government from a worm's eye view and not from a coign of vantage in official circles, I should like to pay tribute to the remarkably high standard attained. The district of Naga Hills in particular was fortunate in its officers, and under men such as Hutton, Mills and Pawsey it enjoyed a long period of just and sympathetic control to which Naga loyalty and co-operation in two wars are a tribute.

In his 1953 presidential address to the Royal Anthropological Institute titled "Anthropology as a Hobby," Mills explained that friendship lay at the base of his approach:

> In my view, friendship, and by that I mean real friendship, is the master key to the amateur's work in the field. The hobby brings you friends, and without friends it cannot be properly pursued. Real mutual trust and confidence must be established, and if you show your interest in and appreciation of their institutions, your friends will in turn reveal to you their pride in them and tell you things you might not otherwise learn. Your friends will include priests, medicine men, warriors and so forth, and as friends you often see them in mufti as ordinary family men.

In September 1945 he prepared a secret paper for the then-governor of Assam, Sir Andrew Clow, arguing for the separation of the hill tribes in northeastern India in the event of Indian independence. He made no pretense of objectivity: "For nearly 30 years my service has been spent almost entirely on work to do with the hill tribes. I have not, alas, been able to see them all, but I have attempted to study those I have seen and to read everything available on those I have not. I am therefore writing about my friends, whose welfare I seek before all else, and to that extent I can fairly be called biased."

Like Hutton before him, Mills was appointed to the honorary post of director of ethnography in Assam, and, also like Hutton, he produced monographs on Naga tribes, concentrating on those tribes that Hutton had not, namely, *The Lhota Nagas* (1922), *The Ao Nagas* (1926), and *The Rengma Nagas* (1937). In his 1945 paper for Clow he described what the Naga were like and what they wanted:

(1) What is he like? He lives in a village, which may be very small or may contain 500 houses or more, according to the tribe. He and his fellow clansmen and villagers form a mutual co-operative society, helping each other to build their houses and cultivate their fields, and supporting each other in old age and times of sickness and need. He lives by agriculture, which usually yields a small surplus, and in a bad year he can always borrow grain, which he will repay in kind or in better times. . . .

Villages within fairly easy distance of the plains grow a considerable quantity of cash crops, such as cotton or *pan*, but in those further in the hills there is normally little or no money in circulation, since they are practically self-supporting except for salt and iron, and most transactions are by barter. Self-sufficiency has produced a strong artistic sense, which is virtually dead in the plains. . . .

Great pride and self-reliance are combined with a sense of humor so like our own that it forms one of the main ties between Europeans and hill men. The great majority of hill men are

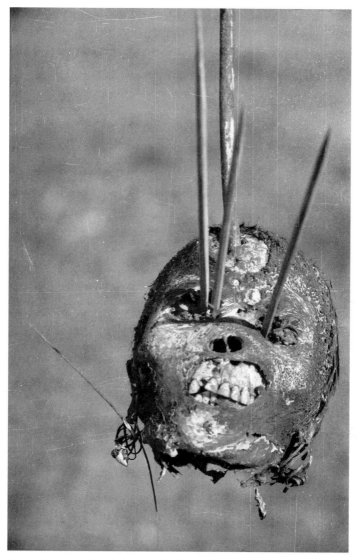

A recently severed head of a Saochu villager found at Yimpang Village by the punitive expedition on November 23, 1936. Head-hunting was the scourge of the region and the reason for the punitive expedition against the primary troublemaker, the village of Pangsha. *Fürer-Haimendorf*

Major Bill Williams and troops of the Assam Rifles on a track close to their target, Pangsha, on November 25, 1936. *Fürer-Haimendorf*

Under the watchful eyes of their Pangsha enemies, members of the expedition build a protective stockade on the bed of the Langnyu River to spend the night before battle, November 25, 1936. The Nagas, who never fought at night, failed to make use of the darkness to discomfit their enemy. *Fürer-Haimendorf*

The Pangsha leader and warrior Mongsen, seen here meeting the punitive expedition with a gift of goat, November 25, 1936, in the vain hope that it would persuade Mills to turn back. *Fürer-Haimendorf*

After spending the night in their stockade, the Assam Rifles moved up the Langnyu River to attack the Wenshoyl *khel*, a "suburb" of the large village of Pangsha, November 26, 1936. The men had their bayonets fixed, ready for action. Pangsha warriors tracked their progress from the high ground above. *Fürer-Haimendorf*

Sepoys of the Assam Rifles storming into Wenshoyl *khel*, November 27, 1936. It was undefended; the Pangsherites had withdrawn from the village, taking what valuables they could with them. *Fürer-Haimendorf*

Philip ("J. P") Mills, Major Bill Williams, and G. W. J. Smith resting on November 28, 1936, a day after the skirmish at Wenshoyl *khel*. *Fürer-Haimendorf*

Wenshoyl *khel* burns, November 27, 1936. The village was so large that only a small part was put to the torch. *Fürer-Haimendorf*

The march back from Pangsha to Chingmei, November 28, 1936. *Fürer-Haimendorf*

Porters and sepoys making their way to the safety of Chingmei, November 28, 1936.
Fürer-Haimendorf

The expedition stockade at Sangpurr, December 2, 1936. *Fürer-Haimendorf*

Victor: J. P Mills sitting with a young freed slave at Chentang, December 7, 1936. *Fürer-Haimendorf*

Chingmak, renowned chief of Chingmei and a great friend of J. P. Mills, December 1936. It was Chingmak and his two sons who protected the survivors of Flight 12420 in August 1943. *Fürer-Haimendorf*

One of the expedition Nagas—possibly Emlong of Mokokchung—showing off a captured head taken from Pangsha's extensive collection at ceremonies to welcome home the expedition and "share" the captured heads in January 1937. *Fürer-Haimendorf*

A collection of heads at Pangsha. *Fürer-Haimendorf*

The defeated Mongsen at Chingmei, November 30, 1936. Mongsen had come to parley and make terms with Mills, the victor of the battle of Wenshoyl. *Fürer-Haimendorf*

A Naga crossbow mounted as a trap. These were usually hidden overlooking a jungle path and were set off by a vine tripwire. *Fürer-Haimendorf*

Vindication for Mills: a party of slaves freed from Pangsha. Mills recalled that they looked miserable to start with but cheered up considerably as the days went by. *Fürer-Haimendorf*

Sworn enemies of Pangsha, the Chang warriors of Chingmei Village provided long-range intelligence to the British deputy commissioner in faraway Mokokchung, November 30, 1936. *Fürer-Haimendorf*

A Naga spear in flight. *Fürer-Haimendorf*

Konyak Nagas during the postexpedition victory celebrations, December 17, 1936. *Fürer-Haimendorf*

On December 14, 1936, Smith, Fürer-Haimendorf, Mills, and Williams gather somewhat shyly in the garden of the deputy commissioner's bungalow at Mokokchung at the conclusion of the punitive expedition against Pangsha. *Fürer-Haimendorf*

A Curtiss C-46 of the USAAF, similar to Number 41-12420, which crashed near Pangsha on August 2, 1943. *National Archives*

An aerial shot of the sprawling Chabua air base, Assam, in 1944. *National Archives*

Three survivors of Flight 12420 at the end of their ordeal, left to right: Jack Davies, William Stanton, and Eric Sevareid, September 28, 1943. *Corbis*

A photograph of Pangsha taken by Christoph von Fürer-Haimendorf the day before the Wenshoyl battle. *Fürer-Haimendorf*

A contemporary newspaper shot of some of the survivors back at Chabua following their return from Pangsha. *USAF*

A newspaper photograph of the three men—left to right, Richard Passey, Colonel Don Flickinger, and William McKenzie—who volunteered to parachute into Pangsha to look after the survivors. *Photo by Frank Cancellare, War Pool Photographer for Acme News Pictures, September 28, 1943*

Pangsha, March 2014. *Hugh Young*

Schoolchildren in Pangsha, March 2014. *Hugh Young*

honest and truthful, for not only would it be a matter of shame to be otherwise, but in a small and closely knit community dishonesty quickly meets its reward. In a country where all journeys have to be performed on foot visits to the outside world are necessarily difficult and infrequent, and this inevitably means a narrow outlook. . . .

Clan feeling is strong and governs daily life. All fellow members of a clan are not only invariably addressed as, but are actually regarded as "fathers", "sisters", "brothers", and so on. . . .

(2) What does the average hill man want? The answer might be summed up by saying that, like most people, he wants a Government which will leave him alone except when he requires help.

For his part, Dr. Christoph von Fürer-Haimendorf arrived in the Naga Hills in 1936 after securing a Rockefeller Foundation Fellowship, having received his doctorate from the University of Vienna in 1931 on the subject of the hill tribes of Assam and northwest Burma. He had met up with Mills in Britain and eagerly accepted the offer of friendship and support for his studies while in Assam. Taking up residence in the Konyak village of Wakching, he immersed himself in the study of his subjects for thirteen months, learning the language of his hosts and becoming the first Westerner to spend more than a few days in the midst of this ancient race. He described his experiences in *The Naked Nagas* (1946), and the fruit of his time among the Konyak villagers came to print as *The Konyak Nagas: An Indian Frontier Tribe* in 1969.

The men who followed Hutton and Mills also possessed deep ethnological instincts, even if they could not be called "collectors" or anthropologists in their own right. Deeply sympathetic to the people with whom they lived, men such as Philip Adams and Bill Archer all followed the same dictum: to administer the people for whom one had responsibility, the best, indeed the only way, was to live among them and become, as much as was possible, their friends.

| | |

For the East India Company and the Raj that followed it, the "Naga problem" began as one of security and transformed itself over time into one of cultural dissonance. How could the imperatives of Christian civilization—living peaceably under the rule of law, respecting other people's lives and property, and thus allowing the structures of mercantile commerce to benefit everybody—be in any way compatible with the indiscriminate lopping-off of heads, even if the imperatives that drove this behavior were deeply ingrained in the local culture? Thus it was that the great ethnological impulses motivating humanitarians such as Hutton, Mills, Pawsey, and Adams were trumped by their horror at the "cultural" practices enjoyed by the people they otherwise so much admired. This was the challenge for the colonial ethnological administrator: when to admire and record, when to punish and destroy? They were not missionaries. Although Mills was a practicing Anglican of the High Church variety, the others had no strong religious convictions. Indeed, they were all suspicious of most of the evangelical missionaries in the Naga Hills because the preaching of such people tended to change the way in which the native people lived their daily lives—for example, the Christians encouraged the near-naked Nagas to wear more rather than fewer clothes—and therefore impacted the culture. In actuality not one of the ethnologists who recorded the history and culture of these remote hill people in the early twentieth century gave the question much thought—life and freedom always outweighed culture, especially when that culture involved any one of the three great prohibitions: slavery, head-hunting, and the casual abuse of animals.

Native "culture," in the minds of these men, though important to capture and record and unarguably important to the lives, histories, and experiences of the Naga tribes as a whole, was not a perfect right in itself and did not trump the claims of other practices in other, competing cultures. In their view head-hunting and slavery were manifestly so abhorrent to right-thinking men and women that not an inch of the written word in the diaries, papers, and reports they left behind in any way condones or supports the practice. Could head-hunting be acceptable simply because it was part of an ancient culture? Was it, in other words, inviolable simply because it was an essential ingredient of that culture? The answer was no. To all of these men, to remove an innocent person's head simply because it was a cultural practice was indefensible. Mills argued in 1945 that the tribes must not be put into "human museums," as that "would be both impossible and wrong, for change is inevitable." If a head was removed in battle, then that might be a different matter, but if the battle was itself the consequence of indiscriminate lawlessness between villages flouting the prohibition against the use of armed force against each other, then it too was unacceptable. This is not to say that the attempts of these men to remove head-hunting from Naga culture was easy. They may actually have been self-defeating. The ethnologists Peter van Ham and Jamie Saul argued that the work to stamp out head-hunting as an occasional cultural practice in fact fed the flames of an illegal head-hunting culture:

> By imposing their "Inner Line System," the British changed the delicate balance of power between certain villages and their subordinates and, as a result, were confronted with a lot more headhunts than before, involving a much higher loss of lives than had previously been the case. For example, when villages were no longer allowed to wield power to keep others in check, the threat of possible raids increased. It is known that Naga at times undertook week-long marches to take a head from an enemy village because, although there were many villages in their vicinity, they were not hostile. The subordinate villages often lay in the unadministered zone and, consequently, villages that had been weak now formed alliances among themselves and set out, united in hatred, to fight a powerful village located within the administered zone. Then the long-established rage was often unleashed in bitter killing of sometimes hundreds of victims. Since,

however, it was British policy to guard its "citizens of the Empire," the colonial forces on their part were compelled to set out on a punitive expedition in order to avenge the raid against its citizens—expeditions that presumably could have been waived if the random border hadn't been drawn in the first place.

This assessment confuses two issues, however. The first concerns the exercise of head-hunting as a cultural rite and the second the exercise of power by local villages determined to use force to maintain that power. This point is sometimes missed in the scholarly discussion of head-hunting. Head-hunting as a cultural practice was one thing (and bad enough), but the head-hunting that took place because of an absence of a universal system of law across the hills was another, and it was the latter that drove the colonial administrators in their quest for order in their universe. In other words, their principal concern lay not in what was, as some argue, a relatively insignificant (in numerical terms) cultural activity but in the widespread lawlessness caused not because villages wanted heads, but because they wanted to exert their own power over others, which itself was a consequence of having no overarching system of effective government.

9

THE 1936 PUNITIVE EXPEDITION

By the mid-1930s the farthest east any previous expedition—punitive or otherwise—had reached into the Naga Hills was Tuensang. From here one could look out at the dark blue smudge on the horizon that denoted the Patkoi Range, on the other side of which lay Burma, but no white man had ever reached these distant hills, from the Indian side at least. There was no intelligence to suggest that any European had ever set foot in these hills from the Burmese side either. One Naga chief from the village of Chingmei, Chingmak, had nevertheless visited Mokokchung several times, beginning about 1920, and did so again in 1934 to complain that Tuensang was restricting his village's trade—and to swear his fealty to the British king-emperor, George V. This visit followed a tour of Chang territory in January that year by Philip Mills, the subdivisional officer in Mokokchung. Chingmak and Mills got on famously from the first time they met and remained firm friends thereafter. Chingmak had even gone so far as to send one of his sons, Sangbah, to Mokokchung to learn something of the ways of the British overseers of this green and pleasant land. Although the relationship was a distant one, geographically speaking, Chingmak nevertheless kept Mokokchung abreast of affairs in eastern Tuensang as regularly as was needed.

One day in early 1936 a man named Matche, a Kalyo Kengyu from the mixed village of Yimpang, rushed into Chingmei asking for sanctuary. He was lucky to be able to do so without losing his head—Christoph von Fürer-Haimendorf described traveling alone in the Naga Hills as akin to suicide—but Matche brought news that was of considerable use to Chingmak, as he was able to provide the chief with information directly from the seat of power of their greatest rival: the village of Pangsha. It is unclear why Matche fled to Chingmei in the first place, but he had upset the people of Pangsha for some reason and was now in fear of his life. The news he brought concerned the extent of the recent ravaging of local villages by Pangsha and its allies on the Burmese side of the Patkoi Hills. Chingmak duly fed this information to Philip Mills in Kohima, where Mills had moved following his promotion to the rank of deputy commissioner in 1935.

Pangsha's reign of terror was well known in these territories, of course. Survivors had managed to escape the pillaging to spread the alarm to other villages, which served to further propagate Pangsha's message. Under the leadership of its three principal *khel* headmen—Mongu, Mongsen, and Santing—it had recently attacked the neighboring villages of Saochu and Kejok, taking a substantial number of heads, and young slaves, in the process. Reports reaching Mokokchung on January 6, 1936, stated that Pangsha and Yimpang had exterminated Kejok on Christmas Day 1935 and that fifty-three heads had been taken. Pangsha had already taken nine heads from Panso and seven from Ngobe in recent weeks. Then, on April 16, 1936, the subdivisional officer reported to Kohima that Pangsha had raided Agching or Saochu and killed about fifty and that since the start of the year Pangsha had taken 140 heads from this village.

Mills estimated in a letter to Shillong on April 29, 1936, that 200 people had lost their lives as a result of this raiding. The future for those who survived as slaves was a terrifying one: they could look forward only to being put to death at some later date as part of a human sacrifice, their heads to adorn the village head tree and other body parts—limbs, hands, and so on—to decorate various parts of the village. Both villages were close to the Control Area—the boundary of which ran through Tuensang—and instability caused by Pangsha, in addition to its rank lawlessness, could have a destabilizing effect on the whole of the Naga Hills. It was also a direct challenge to the authority and prestige of the Raj. Could it not enforce its law even in these remote places? Pangsha didn't think so and was content to thumb its nose at the king-emperor as a result. Pangsha's aim was to sow terror among its neighbors; by so doing, it could dominate the region and guarantee its own security from attack. It was the only village in the Naga Hills that had no defenses. As has been seen, intermittent head-hunting was tacitly accepted by the British as part of the Naga way of life; widespread and systematic terror could not, however, be condoned.

For Philip Mills, the reports of Pangsha's depredations were deeply worrisome. His primary worry was that, if left unchecked, such lawlessness would lap up against the administered territories, for whose security he was directly responsible. He was also concerned for the security of those Naga villages in the Control Area—such as Chingmei—that had demonstrated loyalty, albeit in a distant sense, to the Raj. In these circumstances the question "Who is my neighbor?" was not a difficult one to answer. His friends were in trouble, the peace of the realm was being threatened, and Mills's conception of his role as the upholder of the king's peace demanded action. The government of Assam in Shillong and the government of India in Delhi agreed, and Mills was authorized to proceed with a military expedition to punish Pangsha and by so doing to persuade it to desist from its violent practices. The role of the mission was to proceed into the Control Area not to threaten Pangsha but expressly to punish it. If Pangsha, under the threat of British action, appeared to back down during the operation, it was not to be forgiven for its recent activities without formal retribution.

From the outset, the sacking of Pangsha was to be the principal purpose of the raid. New Delhi's permission was carefully couched in terms that Mills had first advised, namely, the abolition of slavery as an adjunct to both head-hunting and human sacrifice.

India is a party to the Slavery Convention, 1926, and has undertaken to bring about progressively and as soon as possible the complete abolition of slavery in all its forms. It was, however, found necessary to make a reservation in respect of certain outlying and inaccessible areas bordering on Assam and Burma where, it was thought, it would be difficult to implement our undertaking effectively. Recently the Government of India have agreed to the reservation being withdrawn in respect of certain cases including the Naga Hills area in Assam. As a first step towards the fulfilment of the requirement under the Slave Convention to bring about the abolition of slavery in this area, the Government of India, at the request of the Government of Assam, agreed to an expedition, headed by the Deputy Commissioner, Naga Hills, and composed of a column of Assam Rifles. The object of the expedition was to acquaint the headmen of the villages with the determination of Government to suppress the practice of slavery and, if they persisted in an attitude of defiance, to punish them. This action was rendered imperative by the conduct of one of the villages in that area, namely, Pangsha, which, with the assistance of certain other villages, had been raiding and destroying the weaker villages in their neighborhood and holding their captives as slaves in defiance of warning from Government.

It wasn't the prospect of punishing Pangsha, however, that excited the anthropologist, as well as the administrator, in Mills but rather the prospect of traveling as far as the Patkoi Range, to which no white man had ever journeyed. The entire area beyond Tuensang was unsurveyed, and there was much to discover about the tribespeople living in areas never before exposed to the gaze of Europeans. He knew of the villages that lay beyond—he had met Chingmak, of course—but he had never, nor had any of his predecessors, set foot in these territories. The prospect was an exciting one. He half suspected that it would be his last professional opportunity to undertake a journey of this kind.

Shillong had agreed to Mills's request that an invitation be extended to Christoph von Fürer-Haimendorf to accompany the expedition, and it was an eager Austrian at Wakching who received instructions from Mills to proceed to Mokokchung to prepare for the start of the expedition on November 10, 1936. He traveled— delayed for five days by a bout of malaria that he worried might cause him to miss the expedition altogether—accompanied by his Konyak friend Nlamo and some porters carrying the camping equipment Europeans regarded as indispensable in this terrain: a canvas tent, bedroll, mosquito net, and camp bed.

The normally tiny settlement of Mokokchung was a hive of noisy activity. The home of the local subdivisional officer, G. W. J. Smith, who occupied a European-style bungalow in the town, was now swarming with hundreds of Nagas from neighboring villages—Aos, Lhotas, Rengmas, and Sangtams in particular—who wanted to be hired as porters. They were unable to bear arms against the brutal Pangsherites, who were legend in these parts, so traveling with the expedition as porters was the next best thing to being warriors on a war party. Mills had determined that to sustain the 150 men of the Assam Rifles and the command party, they would need 360 porters to carry their food and camp equipment so far into unknown territory. It was Smith's responsibility to hire the porters and allocate their loads.

One of the distinctive features of Nagadom was and remains the complete linguistic separation of each tribe. This separation is not so much a difference in dialects as it is entirely different languages. Accordingly, British-appointed interpreters wearing the distinctive red sashes, *dobashi*s, denoting their appointment bustled about, attempting to create seamless communication between the British overseer and the men of many different Naga tribes—few of whom could communicate with each other in their own tongue—who were queuing up for the chance of being a warrior once more. The local doctor, Dr. Vierya, who accompanied the expedition, insisted on inoculating those selected, much to the annoyance of Philip Mills, who regarded the eager medic as something of a fusspot and meddler.

They would be able to count on very little provisioning from the villages through which they passed, even those that were friendly. As subsistence farmers, Nagas rarely had spare food available, barely extracting a living for themselves from the thin soil of their hilltop homes. The expedition would need to carry all its provisions on its back. It would receive gifts from friendly villages along the way, but not enough to support the requirements of 500 hungry mouths. Of course it wasn't portering that these Nagas in Mokokchung wanted but *battle*. The prospect of joining a punitive expedition whose task was to fight the rebels at Pangsha was an exciting one for young Naga men whose warrior culture had been emasculated by British laws prohibiting head-hunting and yet for whom taking a head was an important part of their tribal and masculine identities. The irony that they were joining a British military expedition designed to stamp out head-hunting in territories far beyond their own so that they could have the opportunity to take heads probably passed them by. In any case this moral confusion—if it was ever seriously contemplated—was quietly ignored in the face of the eagerly awaited prospect of a fight. The presence among them of the uniformed platoons of the Assam Rifles, smart in their light blue uniforms, canvas webbing, and British Service Lee-Enfield .303 rifles, together with the long sword-bayonet that, when fixed to the end of the rifle, looked very much like a Naga spear, only served to generate more martial excitement.

For their part, Mills and Major W. R. B. ("Bill") Williams, the commandant of the Third Battalion, Assam Rifles, were considerably less enthusiastic about the prospect of violence. Their task was to execute the law, not conduct a war, and if the expedition could be undertaken without bloodshed, so much the better. The prospects of a nonviolent resolution were slim, however, they mused over supper that night with Fürer-Haimendorf and Smith. The Nagas' favorite military tactic was the ambush, in which they were very proficient, and the deep ravines and thick vegetation of the hill country made attacks of this kind very successful against long, strung-out columns. They thought of the previous infamous punitive expedition against the Konyak village of Chinglong on February 5, 1913, when so many men had been killed. It had taken four months to subdue the Nagas on that occasion. Would this be any different? Whatever happened, they all believed—unlike the excited porters who were already considering the prospects of victory—that the subjugation of Pangsha would not be a walkover.

Two days of organization were required before, at 8 a.m. on Friday, November 13, the long files of men left Mokokchung for their distant adventure. Bamboo cups of *zu*, a traditional farewell gift to departing war parties, were offered by the *gaonbura* to the command party (Mills, Williams, and Fürer-Haimendorf) as the mile-long column began to wind its way down into the valley leading east, most of the village watching the events with a solemnity that contrasted starkly with the excitement and noise of previous days. After leaving Mokokchung the route wound down around the cultivated hillsides deep into the Dikhu Valley and crossed the river, which flowed lightly in this postmonsoon period, before climbing stiffly into the hills once more, with the first day's camp located at Chare. An advance guard of twelve sepoys led the way, followed by the command party leading the main party of Assam Rifles. The porters followed, led by Smith and guarded by small groups of sepoys, a group of whom also brought up the rear.

The track down to the Dikhu River was poor, and the ramshackle bridge across it was too slight to accept more than a few men at a time. Most men waded across. It was a hard first day's march. The weather was warm, and Mills described himself as "fairly cooked" but was somewhat dismissive of the fitness and attitude of Smith, who appeared to struggle with the terrain. It would get worse, Mills considered. He was right. That day's march was a foretaste of what was to come, as the route east ran against the grain of the country, in which the mountain ranges ran roughly north-south. Steep climbs into the hills were followed by equally steep descents into thick, warm valley bottoms before heading, it seemed, directly up into the skies again.

When they reached their destination toward the end of the afternoon, they were met by a delegation of village elders offering gifts of fish taken from the Dikhu. Later these gifts were added to

by five enormous pigs, four goats, "and chickens without number."
"Of course," Mills noted, "we shan't do as well as that everywhere."
The first task on arriving outside Chare was the organization of the
campsite for 500 men. The village had prepared the site and built a
number of rudimentary shelters, which the porters and sepoys immediately got to work improving. There were tents for Williams's
sepoys and the command element, but most of the porters slept
under the stars. Chare was friendly territory, and defenses were
not required. Before long fires were lit across the hillside, soon followed by the smell of roast goat, pig, and chicken that would satisfy
the hungriest of appetites.

The following day—Saturday, November 14—dawned wet and
cold. A heavy mist had draped itself over the mountains. It failed,
however, to dampen the enthusiasm of the expectant warriors.
What did this more effectively than anything else was the extreme
difficulty of the march. As the crow flies, the distance between
Chare and Phire-ahire, their destination that night, was a mere ten
miles. But in miles walked it seemed three or four times as long.
Mills admitted to his wife, Pamela, in his daily letter that he had
had a "bellyful of hills today." On leaving Chare the path dropped
steeply 2,000 feet into the valley (a descent undertaken in heavy
rain), climbed 1,500 feet to the village of Thurigare before dropping into another valley, through which flowed the Chimei River,
and then rose yet again some 3,000 feet to their camp.

The welcome they received from the villagers of Phire-ahire
made up for the agony of the march. Mills and Fürer-Haimendorf
(to whom Mills referred affectionately in his letters as "the Baron")
were well received by the villagers and were given a demonstration
of the crossbow, a weapon in common use in the Sangtam territory into which they had moved, and the usual gifts of food—"three
enormous pigs, a cow, three goats, ten chickens, some excellent
fish." Mills was quick to identify deficiencies in Smith, who was
responsible for the logistics of the expedition and for managing
the porters, who by some oversight (one of many, it seemed) had
neglected to provide sufficient vegetables among the foodstuffs to

feed the column. They enjoyed a pleasant meal of soup, fish, bark-
ing deer, dried fruit, and, because of Smith's carelessness, tinned
baked beans rather than fresh vegetables. For his part, Fürer-
Haimendorf was less concerned with the lack of vegetables than
with the demonstration by Phire-ahire's *gaonbura* of the crossbow.
It was a wicked-looking weapon firing foot-long poisoned bamboo arrows tipped with iron-barbed heads.* The *gaonbura* boasted
that a wild boar struck by such an arrow would not run more than
thirty yards: "The poison is applied in thick layers just behind the
head, and the shaft nicked so that it breaks off easily, leaving the
poisoned head in the wound. Sometime ago Mills had obtained
a small quantity of this substance and sent it to Calcutta to be analyzed. It had not been identified, but experiments proved that it
was a powerful poison, causing death by paralyzing the respiratory
organs. The victim, the report continued, could be saved by the
administration of oxygen through artificial respiration. Not exactly
a comforting thought many days' march from medical aid."

A calm and much more pleasant day followed as the column
wound its way through Sangtam territory to the village of Chongtore, where the men were to spend two nights. They left Phire-ahire
at 7:30 a.m. The first steep descent of some 2,500 feet was followed
by a long climb to 6,500 feet. Mills and Fürer-Haimendorf left the
column to find its own way to Chongtore while they indulged their
anthropological instincts by visiting a string of Sangtam villages
never before visited by Europeans—Holongba, Sangsomo, and
Anangba—but whose inhabitants knew Mills through their own regular visits to Mokokchung. Many of these villagers had volunteered
to serve in the 2,000-strong Naga Labour Corps, which had been
recruited by the British to serve in France during World War I. Most
had thought they were signing up for the head-hunting expedition
of a lifetime and had been disappointed to find that they were not
even allowed to fight against the enemies of the empire, instead
expending their martial energies in road building in France. One

---

*See the drawing in Appendix A.

of these veterans whom Mills wanted to visit at Anangba was Chirongchi. It was with some amusement that he discovered that this
incorrigible old rogue—a "magnificent specimen" who had plenty
of enemies—had secreted a Lee-Enfield rifle down his trouser leg
when he was discharged and brought the weapon, together with
ninety rounds of ammunition, back to his *khel.* How many bullets
had he discharged over the years? Rather reluctantly, Mills was
forced to confiscate the gun. "I simply couldn't let him go round
slugging his enemies with it," he told Pamela. The expedition left
Anangba after Fürer-Haimendorf had taken a photograph of Chirongchi with the skull of Pukovi, a notorious Sema scoundrel whom
he had killed, presumably to local approbation. With his military rifle? Possibly. Mills looked at the Viennese anthropologist's camera
with envy. Such things had not been invented, he observed, when
he had begun his work twenty years before.*

They stayed comfortably at Chongtore, the last place in the hills
where they didn't need to consider security and therefore have to
build a palisade around the camp. When they traveled farther east
into Yimsungr and Chang territory, their safety would become increasingly less sure. The gifts of food from Chongtore that night
were listed by Mills as "one cow, five pigs, four goats and a mass
of chickens and eggs." That evening they received visits from the
gaonburas of the neighboring villages, all coming to pay their respects to the deputy commissioner for the Naga Hills—"a pretty
hard bitten lot," Mills noted as they drank their proffered *zu.* As the
campfires blazed across the hillside that night, the column enjoyed
its last night of peace.

Although the next day was spent in Chongtore and was designed
to be a rest day for the porters, who were bearing the brunt of
the expedition's physical challenge, the day was wet, bitingly cold,
and miserable. The expedition was being conducted outside the

---

*Fürer-Haimendorf took some 1,157 photographs during 1936 and 1937 and ap-
proximately 291 during the punitive expedition to Pangsha. All can be seen online
at http://himalaya.socanth.cam.ac.uk.

monsoon period, which runs from April until October, as travel in the hills was much more difficult during the rainy season. Yet here was weather that was unusually unseasonable. Mills and Fürer-Haimendorf managed to visit both Chongtore and a neighboring village, Liresu, but concluded that these communities were rather poor and miserable. That night a storm blew wildly through the hills, blowing the flimsy roofs off the porter's shelters and soaking them before the day's march to Helipong, which Mills knew from experience would be a hard one. Yet it would also be a high point of the journey, as Helipong sat majestically at the highest point between Mokokchung and the Patkois. From its peak one could see all the way back to the Brahmaputra, glistening in the far distance to the west, and the long blue stain in the lower sky of the Patkoi Hills to the east.

On Tuesday, November 17, the entire caravan packed itself up and, in good heart despite the rain, begin the inevitable descent far into the valley below. The river crossings in this valley—four in a row—were made over logs, which Mills hated because he had very poor balance. Then began the steep ascent to Helipong, some 7,280 feet above sea level. The forest ran out at about 7,000 feet, and the men climbed slowly upward into the cold clouds. As they reached the summit of Mount Helipong, they emerged from the mist into bright sunshine and the welcome of the tiny Chang village of some twenty houses, an outpost of the Yimsungr tribe. The view in every direction was magnificent, making up for the poverty of the hamlet. Mills was always astonished at the view from Helipong: "You can see from the Burma boundary to the Plains. . . . I loved every minute of the view, for I saw for the first time villages I had heard of for years. I could see from the Konyak country I visited in the north, to the Sangtams I have been to in the south." Fürer-Haimendorf was equally astonished at the view:

We overlooked the land of the Lhotas and Aos and beyond the distant hills of the Konyaks. The country of the Changs and Sangtams lay at our feet and in the east the unexplored mountains of

the Kalyo Kengyus and the Patkoi Range, with the 12,622 feet
peak of Mount Saramati, were clearly visible. Here in Helipong
we were on the watershed between the Brahmaputra and the Irrawaddy. The rivers to the east belong to the basin of the Chindwin; following them, if you were lucky enough not to lose your
head en route, you would arrive in Burma. All these high ridges,
running almost at right angles to our proposed route, were not a
very encouraging sight, and yet the glimpse we had caught of the
distant Patkoi Range only sharpened the wish to set foot in that
distant, unknown land.

This was a location from which the sun allowed the Assam Rifles'
heliograph to send messages in Morse code back to the rear party
at Mokokchung, confirming the status of the column. The next
time they would be able to communicate with Mokokchung would
be on the return journey—if they got back, and if the sun allowed
the heliograph apparatus to function.

Camp was set up, and for the first time security drills were practiced by both the sepoys and porters. Local *gaonbura*s were entertained in traditional fashion as they came to discuss the affairs of
their villages with Mills while Williams busied himself with ensuring that his sepoys and Smith's eager porters were prepared for
any alarm now that they were entering territory that harbored
uncertain sensibilities. As quietness fell over the camp that night,
the rain began to drum against the canvas of the Europeans' tents,
thudding heavily against the flimsy banana-leaf roofs of the shelters and saturating the blankets of those unfortunate enough to be
huddled around the dying embers of the fires. No threat emerged
during the night, as indeed none was expected, but it was best to
be prepared.

As the dawn struggled to appear the following morning—
Wednesday, November 18—the camp emerged quickly from its
sodden slumbers and the column made haste to climb down from
Helipong's heights. The objective that day was to move from the
territory of the Chang to that of the Yimsungr, resting at the end

of the day at the village of Kuthurr. There the column found that although outward appearances were civil, an underlying hostility sat like a heavy blanket over the village. Despite the customary gift of pigs and chickens, considered Fürer-Haimendorf, had "we arrived singly, or even in a small number, there can be no doubt that their joy at such unusual guests would have taken other forms, and our chances of ever leaving Kuthurr would have been slight, for our skulls would have certainly occupied places of honor in the men's house." That night, for the first time, Williams supervised the construction of a strong bamboo palisade and practiced the call to arms several times before he was satisfied that his men, and the porters, who formed a second line of defense inside the perimeter, were satisfactorily prepared for the possibility of an attack. None came, however. Indeed, Nagas tended not to attack at night, which was a boon for the exhausted column, giving it a chance to recover each night from its daily exertions up hill and down dale. But the palisade was an insurance policy, and an attitude of alertness generated by the practice alarms and nightly picket duty ensured that all the men knew the expedition was a military and not an anthropological one, with the ever-present prospect of danger.

Kuthurr's reluctant duty was followed the next day by a march to the village of Chentang. Although some villages beyond—most notably Chingmei—would be overwhelmingly friendly, the affections of the rest of the region were uncertain. This was a traditionally troubled area, the ethnic nexus of three often-warring tribes: Changs, Yimsungrs, and Kalyo Kengyus. While the expedition was encamped outside Chentang on November 19, the last message came by runner from Pangsha, laughing at Mills's diplomatic overtures and suggesting that the villagers would not give up their legitimately acquired slaves and that the members of the expedition "were probably all women, and the sooner they came to attack them the better."

News of the progress of the 500 or so imperial troops, the bayonets of the 150 sepoys fixed to the ends of their rifles so that the sun—when it shone in these unusually cold and overcast days—could glint off the highly polished steel and resemble the long Naga spears of their enemies, was being reported nervously through the hills. Mills's hope was that this threat of force would persuade the Pangsha leaders to parley rather than commit their menfolk to what must inevitably be a one-sided battle given the difference in armaments. Early indications, however, were that Pangsha refused to be intimidated. Would Pangsha fight? If so, it represented a fearsome proposition: over a thousand warriors desperate both to demonstrate resistance to the demands of the distant Raj and to protect their village, massive by Naga standards and the center of all power in the mid–Patkoi Range. It would be a mistake for anyone, even armed with the dead-accurate Lee-Enfield rifle, to take this threat lightly. A wrong move in unknown terrain or an ambush by Nagas, for whom this country was their well-known backyard, could quickly upset the balance between the two sides that in terms of firepower clearly favored the Assam Rifles but in terms of local knowledge vastly favored Pangsha. Not only were the Nagas adept at close-quarters fighting in this terrain but they were armed with weapons that favored fighting in the close scrub, high grass, and thick vegetation of the hillsides and valleys. The traditional Naga spear—deadly at twenty paces in the hands of a trained warrior—was accompanied by poisoned arrows (with fearsome iron-barbed heads) fired from crossbows of the sort they had seen at Chare, with an effective range of seventy-five yards. In addition, the many paths and tracks leading into the village would be thickly covered with *panji*.

Nagas rarely attacked at night, preferring ambush. Because Naga villages were perched precariously on the tops of mountains and were well protected, pitched battles were unusual. Heads tended to be taken in one-to-one combat or when lone individuals or groups of unprotected villagers—such as women and children fetching water—were caught by their enemies and slaughtered. Ambush was perfected. *Panji* were one threat, but there were others. Pits dug deep into the ground on paths, in which sharp spikes were hammered into the bottom to impale their victim, were another, as were rope tripwires stretched across jungle paths to release a poisoned bolt from a hidden crossbow into the chest of the unwary victim. But at no stage were Mills and Williams concerned that they might come off worse in an encounter with the rebel Nagas, even though the possibility that they might receive a bloody nose was a very real one. On November 22 Philip Mills wrote to Pamela in far-distant Kohima with instructions should he not return, noting, presumably for her comfort, that if he were to die, the "effect of the local poison is pleasingly instantaneous."

In all other respects the two men were confident of success. They had enough friendly Nagas around them in the region from villages that had long borne the brunt of Pangsha's slaving and head-hunting aggression; their force of 150 Lee-Enfields was strong; most of the sepoys, although now members of Assam's paramilitary police regiment—the five-battalion-strong Assam Rifles—were former long-service regular Gurkha soldiers who would be staunch in a fight, and they were commanded by a professional Gurkha officer, Major Williams. Mills and Williams also knew from personal experience the truth of Hilaire Belloc's dictum in this kind of imperial encounter, expressed powerfully only a few short decades before in the ditty "Whatever happens, we have got / The Maxim gun, and they have not."* It wasn't Maxim guns with which the force was armed but drum-fed Lewis guns and bolt-action .303-inch Lee-Enfields that, well deployed by disciplined troops, would be more than a match for even the fiercest Kalyo Kengyu army. The expedition was now deep in hostile territory, and Mills and Williams went to some lengths to drill their baggage train—the 360 Naga porters ("coolies," as Mills described them) carrying the expedition's supplies—in erecting, patrolling, and defending the bamboo stockades they now had to build around their encampment at the end of each day's march.

Mills observed that the village of Chentang was overlooked by the huge enemy village of Sangpurr, which belonged to the Yimsungr

*Belloc, *The Modern Traveller.*

tribe, and was shown the location outside the village where recently a Sangpurr raiding party had caught a Chentang villager unawares, first spearing him and then lopping off his head. Chentang was a miserable, muddy assortment of ill-made houses, the dilapidation the result of repeated Sangpurr attacks that placed its unfortunate villagers in a perpetual state of insecurity and anxiety, not to mention homelessness. There was in effect a continuous, if somewhat spluttering, state of war between these villages, and it is no surprise that the hard-put-upon people of Chentang were delighted to see Mills arrive in such force, the neatly accoutered sepoys impressive in their uniforms and canvas webbing. Allegiance to the Raj would deliver substantial security benefits for those villages on the side of the (British) law from far-distant Mokokchung, but it took a brave *gaonbura* to ally his village wholeheartedly with a far-distant power when this was its first armed foray into territory not in either the Administered or Control Areas, and there was no guarantee of return visits anytime soon. But the "stout hearts" of Chentang, as Mills described the villagers, seemed to be doing well enough on their own account.

One of Mills's ambitions was to persuade, by his version of armed diplomacy, any villages in the region that might otherwise side with Pangsha. His intent quite simply was to divide and rule, and while at Chentang he invited emissaries from the local villages to parley. He succeeded in persuading elders from Sangpurr to meet him, and they were offered gifts of food and clothes, all the while eyeing the impressive parade of heavily armed sepoys. Likewise, too, the village of Panso, which Mills described as "big and truculent," sent representatives. They received gifts of rum and red cloth (prized by Nagas because the color red denoted high social status: *gaonbura*s in the Administered Area received red blankets from the British as a sign of their exalted status as village leaders) but accepted them with impassive faces, undoubtedly nevertheless drinking in with their eyes, as Mills intended them to, the large size, purposeful demeanor, and disciplined authority of his small army. He had every intention of ensuring that the authority of the Raj and of the king-emperor, Edward VIII, was respected throughout these fractured lands. And he was pleased with the effects of his overtures at Chentang. "I could not help admiring the pluck of the Sangpurr and Panso headmen," he recalled. "There they were, in our camp, disarmed and surrounded by Sepoys, yet they showed no emotion. I told Panso I would visit their village and that if they did us no harm we would do them none."

The following day the expedition said its farewells to Chentang and marched to Chingmei, which would be the advanced base for the final move to Pangsha. The village and the nearby camp were at 6,000 feet, although the men had to climb a saddle at over 7,000 feet to reach their destination. Chingmei, forewarned, send an advance party to guide the long single file (it stretched for over a mile) to safety, as the region was notorious for ambushes and the sepoys, who marched together, could not protect every one of the porters when they were strung out on the march. In his report Mills recorded, "On November 20th we reached our advanced base at Chingmei where the loyalty of my old friend Chingmak was of inestimable value. There we found that Pangsha had handed over to him all their slaves but one; they still defied us to visit them, and I found they had terrorised the whole neighbourhood, threatening to destroy any village which helped us." Chingmak had already prepared eleven large bamboo huts in the midst of the camp area. Chingmei lived in a perpetual state of war with its neighbors, and Chingmak proudly displayed the head of a notorious Panso rogue who himself had had fifty heads to his credit. Chingmei gained some consolation from the sight of this withered specimen being stuck ignominiously on the "head tree" at the outskirts of the village, where it would be seen with a shiver (hopefully) of fear and concern by any Panso native approaching the village with nefarious intent. The biggest surprise was the news that Pangsha had voluntarily given up three of the four slaves it had taken and had left them with Chingmei as a sign of its good intentions. The fourth slave had already been sold into Burma and was, by all accounts, unrecoverable. By now five surrendered slaves had been collected. Mills looked at them with interest: "A girl about 17 or 18, a boy about 12, two little boys and a little girl. All except the little boy are in a pretty bad way, and seem stupid with all they have been through. . . . A very pathetic sight. I am having them fed on the best in the land and they are being treated with every kindness. Language is a real difficulty, as four of them are from up north and can't understand more than a word or two of Chang."

It was imperative that the stockade be secure and the discipline of the porters exemplary if they were not to be picked off individually by Pangsha raiders, or if by their inattention they inadvertently made the entire camp vulnerable to attack. And yet Mills fumed at the ineptitude of the men. It had been many years since the last punitive expedition, and the skills and drills of setting up such a large camp in the midst of enemy territory had clearly been lost. The retreat was sounded repeatedly by the bugles of the Assam Rifles as a practice to rehearse the camp for any attack, the bamboo gates of the stockade being closed and barred at each time. Slowly the performance of the porters improved, and Williams, Mills, and Smith were gradually satisfied that a disciplined routine was being adopted and that the Naga porters understood what to do in an emergency. Despite the drills, as darkness fell a foolish sentry opened the gate to allow a number of men to wander out and collect water, strictly against orders. They managed to return, however, with their heads still attached to their bodies in time for a severe admonishment from an angry Williams.

Mills continued his policy of armed diplomacy in the area of Chingmei, although the following day, November 21, was unseasonably wet, with heavy rain all day. But on November 22 he set out to visit the village of Yimpang. It was a slave-raiding village, and although Mills expected it to be relatively friendly, he took with him fifty sepoys and a piper. It was to be a day of firsts for the people of Yimpang. None had ever before seen a white man, and none had ever enjoyed the pleasure until then of hearing the skirl of the great Highland bagpipe.

To say we got a hearty welcome would be an exaggeration. The people were pretty frightened for no white man has ever been there before. It is over 7,000 feet up, and the first thing we did was to look at the view. It was rather thrilling, looking down on to unsurveyed country, and we were busy for some time taking bearings and putting on the map villages which were mere names before. . . .

The sight of the Sepoys with rifles and fixed bayonets must have been rather shaking to Yimpang's nerves, but we had a piper with us and after [a Scottish air] the people began to look more cheerful.

One needed to look no further than the prominent head tree in the village to see the grisly fruits of the villagers' recent labors. Five heads from the village of Saochu were impaled on it. The villagers' pride in taking these heads, Mills determined, needed to be tempered, and he decided to insist on their confiscation. But he would not do so while inside Yimpang, where he and his men were at a disadvantage. He bided his time until safely outside the village's fortifications and was able to observe carefully that these comprised a "double fence with a ditch in the middle [that] was simply bristling with poisoned bamboo spikes." Once outside, he successfully demanded the heads, which he told his wife he would send to his friend Henry Balfour at the Pitt Rivers Museum in Oxford. Yimpang at least was trying to be friendly and was determined to make peace, which Mills hoped would also have a positive effect on Pangsha.

The next and last village that the expedition would reach before Pangsha was Noklak. Mills likewise wanted peace there, but so far no emissaries had been received from the village, which was an ominous sign. After the twelve-mile march to Yimpang was concluded, however, Mills was told that a Noklak war party had been keeping track of his progress on a parallel ridge. Would Noklak fight? Mills could not be sure, although as each day passed the certainty of a fight with Pangsha became surer.

On November 23, 1936, tumultuous news arrived in the camp with the mail, which was followed by a runner from Mokokchung. The newspapers were full of rumors that the king-emperor, the man who underwrote Mills's very authority, was threatening to marry the divorced American Mrs. Wallace Simpson. It was simply not possible, Mills remarked indignantly to his wife—because the people would not support it—for Mrs. Simpson to be crowned queen of England. Something would have to give. The loss of prestige for the monarchy suddenly loomed large in both Mills's and Williams's consciousness, and they determined to deploy a stiff upper lip and not to say anything of it in the camp so as not to depress the men.

10

THE BATTLE OF PANGSHA

Tuesday, November 24, began with reveille at 4 a.m. Mills wrote in his daily letter to Pamela that the immediate tragedy was that the bitters for the gin had somehow been left behind, but to all other intents and purposes, progress was good. The 150 sepoys and 120 porters (240 porters remained at the forward camp at Chingmei) of the "forward" expedition were under way by 6 a.m., dropping down a steep hill to a stream running through the valley below. It was now that they heard from Noklak. The villagers would not clear the path to their village, they said, and although they would not impede the expedition, neither would they help it. The message demonstrated neither hostility nor friendship, merely fear. The people of Noklak were unsure who would be successful in the coming fight with Pangsha and clearly wished to hedge their bets, even if it meant incurring Mills's wrath. Chingmak, however, was eager to lend a hand and provided Mills and Williams with six men to show them the way and to scout out the land as the expedition wove its slow way through the hills. The immediate problem was that the boundaries between Chingmei and Noklak were liberally spiked with *panji*, since the two villages of course were at war. Clearing the path was tedious and painful. The last two hours proved very slow going, with thick vegetation having to be removed slowly by *dao* along an overgrown path that boasted a steep precipice down its right-hand side. And the *panji* began to take their toll: "One Chingmei man got a panji clean through his foot, and one was badly cut up by a panji on the shin, and one Sepoy was badly cut in the calf. Also one Sepoy was terribly stung in a mysterious way and had enormous swellings on his throat, arms and thighs." When Noklak finally appeared before them the village seemed entirely devoid of life. Then a large body of armed men appeared on a path farther down the hill. Williams ordered his sepoys to advance purposefully on the Noklak warriors with their bayonets fixed, and the confidence and discipline of the troops made an immediate impact on the Nagas, who offered if not obeisance then certainly nervous subservience. More practically, they made a peace offering of ten pigs, ten fowls, and an enormous smelly goat. Two men who came forward, clearly leaders, greeted Chingmak like an old friend, to Mills's amusement, given the two tribes' historic animosity. The Noklak men showed Mills and Williams an area of grass that provided cramped but adequate space for the tented camp but did nothing to help in the construction of the final camp and stockade. As a result of their noncooperation, the village's precious stocks of bamboo were pillaged freely by the expedition to build the palisade. The work took all afternoon. All the while, as Mills admitted, they nervously waited for the flights of arrows that might come from the thickets of vegetation. But they were unmolested by the people of Noklak, or anyone else, for that matter, and the expedition settled into its last night before battle.

The morning of the final march on Pangsha—Wednesday, November 25—began early, with the camp stirring at 3 a.m. At 6 a.m. the sepoys and Naga porters began moving out in a long line toward their destination, the Langnyu River just below Pangsha, where they aimed to arrive, notwithstanding any impediments (such as ambuscade and *panji*) they might encounter on the way, by early afternoon. The plan was to build yet another stockade in which to demonstrate the military strength of the expedition and to conduct what Mills intended to be one-way discussions with the headmen of the village about the problem of persistent slaving, after which a major part of the village was to be burned in punishment for Pangsha's historical rejection of the imperial antislavery injunctions. During the day little was seen of anyone from Pangsha, although the expedition moved warily, anticipating an ambush at any moment. It was during the advance that the expedition was at its most vulnerable, yet the Pangsha warriors failed to exploit the opportunity. On one occasion the voice of a Pangsha scout was heard calling, "They're coming," and to reinforce the point Mills had an entire hillside of ripening millet burned to the ground. He meant business, and it was important that Pangsha realized it.

At midday a party of Pangsha natives was encountered on a track, and after much long-distance shouting four men were persuaded to come and talk. They came with a peace offering of a goat and a chicken, perhaps in the hope that this would be sufficient to persuade the British to withdraw. Mills spoke to them, reinforcing the message that the village was to be burned for its wanton disregard of the law and to demonstrate that the arm of the Raj extended into the Patkoi Hills even if representatives of the king-emperor were not seen in these remote parts every day. Unknown to Mills, one of the Pangsha party was Mongsen, one of the village's headmen and a famous fighter. They would have cause to meet again very soon. After keeping the four men as hostages as the expedition moved through a particularly dangerous stretch of jungle, Mills had them released in the hope that the message would get to the village so that precautions such as the evacuation of women and children to a place of safety could take place. It was already accepted that the element of surprise had been lost and that Pangsha would be well defended, but Mills's hope was that fear would do the rest and that a pitched battle—with inevitable loss of life on both sides—could be avoided. In his official report Mills wrote of this encounter:

Soon after passing the Noklak-Pangsha boundary we saw a small unarmed party of Pangsha men in the distance. Four were induced to come and speak to us, and brought with them a goat and a chicken. They asked whether we would make peace. There was not the slightest doubt as to the only possible answer. To have made peace, turned back and abandoned the remaining slave at the price of a goat, a fowl and some smooth words would inevitably have been interpreted as a sign of weakness. Friends who'd helped us would have been massacred and raids would have continued. I therefore told the envoys, that I did not believe their statement that they could not produce the slave girl, and that I was going to punish them for their conduct and insults to the Government.

For the next two hours the expedition moved along the western edge of the Langnyu River Valley and saw large bodies of armed men in front crossing the river with what Mills and Williams assumed to be a plan to block their further advance. Instead of engaging with this group, Williams turned the column right, down to the river bottom, in order to build a stockade for the night. He wanted to avoid a direct confrontation that might lead to battle, as his purpose was to burn the village, not fight its populace. If the latter wanted to attack, then so be it, but he didn't wish to provoke it. The march had taken longer than expected, and instead of challenging Pangsha that day, they decided to rest after an exhausting approach march and deal with Pangsha, on the east bank, the following day. A grassy island in the middle of the river valley was chosen for the defensive position, and the men immediately started building the palisade. Thirty porters were sent across the river to cut bamboo, protected by a section of sepoys. Williams mounted watch within the stockade with a Lewis gun. Before long three armed Pangsha men could be seen 300 yards away, edging their way down the eastern slope toward the working party, clearly with the intention of taking a coolie's head. Without much ado the Lewis gun promptly opened fire and knocked over two of the three. Mills, watching, was annoyed that both men were able to pick themselves up and limp away, but he noted that it was good shooting at long range.

Would Pangsha fight on the morrow? Mills couldn't believe that in the face of such force the villagers would take the risk, but there was no guarantee that the Pangsha headmen—Mongu and Mongsen—would consider that numbers were not in their favor. Was the prospect of attacking the interlopers riskier than giving in to this egregious threat of British force? A possibility, Mills considered, was that the stockade would be attacked that night. They were well within crossbow range of the eastern slopes, where dense vegetation provided cover for attackers down to the water's edge. The following day, he thought, the culminating point of the expedition, would be a very hard one for all. His plan was to leave a guard on the river stockade before marching on the main Pangsha village and burning it, or a major part of it, to the ground. They would then return, pack up the stockade, continue down the river valley for three miles, and repeat the procedure on the Pangsha *khel* of Wenshoyl. Afterward, as dusk drew near, they would pretend to make another camp in the Langnyu Valley but would slip away at moonrise to the comparative safety of the stockade at Noklak. Remaining in the Langnyu River for a second night, especially after the burning of the two Pangsha villages, would be too much like tempting fate.

The stockade was unmolested again that night, and Mills got his sleep without any of the arrows he half expected to be fired at his prominent white canvas tent. Once again the Pangsha strategists had failed to take advantage of the night. This, of course, was understandable. They had never battled Europeans before, and Mills's expedition had arrived in considerable numbers. The British also possessed discipline and a disturbing purpose, and the Pangsherites must have been nervous that they no longer held the military advantage, even on their own ground.

The night was bitterly cold. The arrival of dawn did little to bring any much-needed warmth. During the night only the Europeans enjoyed the benefit of a canvas tent; each of the Naga porters and sepoys stretched out on the grass protected from the cold by a single blanket. With dawn fully upon them, the troops marched out at 6:30 a.m. after a brief, cold breakfast. Even before the stockade gate was opened, the Pangsha scouts were able to observe what was going on below them, and when the gate finally opened to release the sepoys they began to shout, "Come along, come along!" as if urging them on to their destruction. It was bravado, of course; the men of Pangsha clearly worried about the disciplined determination of all those sepoys advancing toward their village with their Lee-Enfield rifles fixed with long, shiny bayonets pointing menacingly in their direction.

From the outset of the march on Pangsha that morning a running fire was maintained with any Naga warriors who were impertinent enough to try to come close to the sepoys. Williams sent an advance guard to the front, in sight of the main party, and flank guards with Lewis guns protected the extremities. Most of the firing, Mills observed, was at long range except for an occasion when one of the Assam Rifles officers, Subedar Balbahadur, fired at a group of men at about 300 yards and bowled over six. Much to Mills's chagrin, the men seemed only lightly wounded and all got away. "These modern bullets go right through without doing much harm," he observed crossly to Pamela in his daily letter. "They are meant to be humane and to wound a man without killing him. The porters' feelings can be imagined at seeing no one killed. I am very sorry, too. Pangsha will be able to boast that they lost no lives."

Mills's irritation at the sight of six wounded Nagas picking themselves up off the ground and making their escape was compounded by his failure that day to inflict the sort of damage on Pangsha that he would have liked. The village was extensive—far larger than he had expected—and divided into many separate *khel*s, some with deep ravines between them. It would have taken many more men, and more time than they had available, to destroy everything they saw. The inhabitants had had time to remove their most precious possessions and livestock into the hinterland, and there was little left to do but to destroy as many of the houses as possible by burning. One *dobashi* later admitted shooting thirteen *mithan* cows; certainly any livestock found alive was unceremoniously slaughtered. Mills's aim was not to destroy everything, however. That would end up hurting many of those—such as the women and children—who were the unwanted victims of the political policies pursued by the village's elders.

The sheer size of the place almost got four of the Lhota porters into trouble. They had wandered away from the main party into a different *khel* in search of material wanted by Fürer-Haimendorf and didn't hear the bugle calls giving the order to withdraw. The bulk of the expedition had returned to the Langnyu River stockade by 11:45 a.m. when they realized that the four men were missing. They could hear Pangsha men shouting, "Cut them off, cut them off!" Mills wrote, "We thought they were certainly dead and a party was just going out as a forlorn hope when they appeared, breathless and sweating. The idiots had gone the wrong way and met Pangsha men at short range. I can't imagine which side was most surprised. Nlamo [Fürer-Haimendorf's Konyak friend] peppered a man with buckshot and they got away. It was a near squeak."

Mills finally had his battle on Friday, November 27, a day after the burning of the main part of Pangsha and by his own reckoning "by far the most serious there has been in these trans-border shows here." All of the Naga porters and the bulk of the sepoys were sent back to Noklak after the firing of the main village, and Mills, Smith, and Fürer-Haimendorf accompanied Williams and a reinforced platoon of fifty men to march along the Langnyu River Valley to the Pangsha *khel* of Wenshoyl, about three miles from the main village. As on the previous day, the plan was to burn the *khel* to the ground. But Wenshoyl proved difficult to reach, and after struggling for most of that afternoon they were forced to camp out in the open because it was too late to attempt an attack and achieve a successful withdrawal that evening. The following morning the small party climbed into the hills and found the *khel*. Fortunately, it was undefended, for it sat on a prominent spur and could have easily been protected, even against troops armed with rifles and Lewis guns. But it was during their withdrawal that the Pangsha attack finally came. "We had to go about 3,000 feet down a long spur," recalled Mills, when they were suddenly attacked by a huge number of screaming warriors. He counted as many as 500: "Very soon down on our right we saw hundreds of men from the main village streaming along a path to cut us off. We knew the supreme moment had come, and that Pangsha were going to try and overwhelm us and annihilate us by sheer weight of numbers.

They disappeared into dead ground, and then came at us over a ridge with a roar." The Pangsha attack came at the small group of sepoys through fields of millet standing some ten feet high, so the first running warriors were not seen until they were through and into the open, a matter of yards in front of the troops. The intention was to wipe out the British in one overwhelming and terrifying attack. Williams, however, had positioned a section of his platoon on high ground to provide covering fire if it were needed. It was. They were able to fire over the heads of their fellows when the first wave of warriors broke from the millet field and swarmed against the British position. "It was an experience I shall never forget," recalled Mills. "I should think the nearest man rolled over like a rabbit with a bullet in the chest not more than 50 feet away. They were just drawing back their arms for a shower of spears. Of course they outnumbered us by ten to one. We beat them off. The men were splendid, firing calmly and carefully. At one point, Williams, two yards from me, snatched a rifle from a Sepoy's hand and fired himself." Once the initial enemy charge had been so decisively halted, Williams organized a textbook "withdrawal in contact," which Mills admired for its slick professionalism. While one line of sepoys engaged the enemy in deliberate aimed fire in ragged volleys, the remainder withdrew down the slope at a run. The Lewis gun pumped automatic fire in short bursts into the mass of rushing Nagas, leaving them to fall in crumpled heaps amid the millet. After every fifty yards the sepoys stopped, turned, and fired their rifles to give cover for the first section to retire. So it was that the entire platoon of sepoys leapfrogged down the spur to the riverbed, all the while ensuring that the Pangsha warriors were unable to interfere with the withdrawal in any meaningful way. Again, Pangsha failed to exploit all its advantages that morning and didn't ambush the retreating British force when it reached the river. Perhaps the Pangsherites had considered that an all-out frontal assault at the top of the spur, through the high millet, would be sufficient to overwhelm Williams's men, but they had not, to their ultimate discomfort, properly considered the true potential effect on their own ranks of volleys of Lee-Enfield fire. In his daily letter to Pamela, Mills wrote, "We got down and across all right without a single casualty. We had to keep them off, we couldn't afford to have even a few wounded. In civilized warfare you can leave wounded knowing they will be looked after, but in Naga warfare every man has to be brought along, even in a retreat, and that hangs up things frightfully."

The truth was that the withdrawal to Noklak was something of an exhausting scramble for the men of the Wenshoyl force. They rushed back to the protection of the remainder of the column somewhat in fear of the possibility of aggressive follow-up by a swarm of angry Pangsha warriors, stung to anger by the Lee-Enfields of the Assam Rifles. The sepoys had largely exhausted their ammunition in the frantic volleys fired to staunch the Pangsherite counterattack. The sun blazed down as the eight miles were rapidly covered, four heads that had been confiscated from Pangsha banging uncomfortably on Fürer-Haimendorf's back. The discomfort, however, was not enough to persuade him to relinquish these prizes. No sign of follow-up appeared, and the welcoming sight of Noklak soon emerged on the high ground in front of them, rising above the tall grasslands of the valley. It was a hard and hot climb into the hills, and when they reached the stockade and the remainder of the forward expedition at Noklak, they were all completely exhausted. Two sepoys were close to collapse, and Smith took himself straight to bed. "The worst part was a frightful thirst," noted Mills to Pamela. "We were running hard in boiling sun, and my running days are really over."

So ended what Mills was to describe as "one of the most exciting battles there has ever been in the Naga hills." He wrote in his report, "It was only the skill and coolness of Major Williams and his force that enabled us to make a safe withdrawal to Noklak without losing a man and after inflicting losses on the enemy, whom ground and cover enabled to charge to within 50 yards before they were stopped." The Pangsha Nagas admitted to losing five killed in the battle. No attempt appears to have been made to evaluate this number: by the accounts of those who were there, the Pangsha estimate appears remarkably low and almost certainly a fabrication. It may have been concocted to minimize the extent of its military humiliation, a devastating blow for a once proud and seemingly invulnerable village chastened under the disciplined Lee-Enfield and Lewis fire of well-drilled sepoys. Hilaire Belloc had been right.

Once safely behind the village's formidable defenses the men were able to relax for the first time since setting out for Pangsha the morning before. Noklak men had greeted the returning force with the traditional cups of *zu* to celebrate the homecoming of warriors from battle. Perhaps, mused the Viennese anthropologist, they were quietly happy that their traditional rivals had been humbled so decisively. Smoke still straggled skyward from Pangsha, easily visible from Noklak on the far side of the valley. Mills was careful to observe that the women and children remained out of sight, a sure sign that Noklak didn't fully trust its visitors. The locals were concerned, no doubt, that what had happened to Pangsha might well happen to them if they stepped out of line.

With the adrenaline of the withdrawal rapidly subsiding, Fürer-Haimendorf and Mills took the opportunity to examine Noklak. It was, and remains, one of the largest villages in the eastern Naga Hills, a long, thin aggregation of houses sitting astride the entire ridge that forms the western valley through which runs the Langnyu River. It was densely packed, as though each stilted house were trying to force its way ahead of its fellows for the right to sit at the highest point of the ridge. It was the architectural expression of fear, the people wanting to be as far from the dangerous lowlands as they possibly could get, each straining for the protection of the high ground. What constituted the main street ran along the top of the hill. Unusually, the roofs were constructed mainly of slate rather than the more common woven banana leaf, although the *morung* in the center of the village, outside which was a large stone circle where the menfolk would gather to talk, was built of traditional woven material. The defenses—entirely unlike those of Pangsha—were formidable, with a double layer of outer wall built from thorny palm, in the middle of which was packed impenetrable brush. Fürer-Haimendorf observed that the thickest defenses were reserved for the area facing off against Panso. A narrow path wound its way between the two walls to allow access to the village, which at the point of entrance, opposite the *morung*, was guarded by a thick wooden gate common to most Naga villages.

Sightseeing over, the men were guided to the temporary encampment prepared for the column, where the remainder of the expedition had been safely ensconced since the previous evening, awaiting the raiders' return. Exhaustion set in as the adrenaline of the fight and the physical exertion entailed in running uphill for eight miles to reach the relative safety of Noklak hit home. Fürer-Haimendorf was so tired that he struggled to put one foot ahead of the other. They all took to their camp beds for a rest, out of the beating sun, with considerable gratitude.

Late in the afternoon a flurry of activity was observed outside the stockade, and the guards brought some surprising news. At the gate were some men of Ponyo who wanted to parley. Ponyo was a village known to exist on the eastern slopes of the Patkoi Range, in Burma, but no white man had ever visited it.* It was known to be in cahoots with Pangsha and ruled the entire territory between the Patkois and the Chindwin. There were slight differences in dress and in appearance from those of the villagers living on the western side of the hills, which excited Fürer-Haimendorf's anthropological instincts; for example, the men of Ponyo wore their hair tied at the back in a ponytail. It was not immediately clear why they had made their way to Noklak, but Mills invited them in to talk, welcoming them with *zu*. Perhaps they wanted to act as brokers between the government column and Pangsha?

As the *zu* was drained and the men relaxed, it became apparent that they had been in Pangsha that day after the fighting and reported that five Pangsha men had been killed and many more had been wounded. They had instructions from Pangsha to parley and appeared to have traveled to Noklak to get a closer view of

---

*Ponyo's location is N 26°21'4", E 95°16'30".

these people who had humbled the mightiest village in the area. Mills decided to use the visit to his advantage and asked the Ponyo emissaries to go back to Pangsha and invite its leaders to Chingmei on the day after the next for talks. He instructed them to say that he wanted peace but that a precondition was the release of the last remaining slave girl, whom they were to bring with them. If they were unwilling to acquiesce, he would be forced to consider further action. The Pangsha delegates would be provided with a safe passage to Chingmei if they came with peaceful intent and were determined to hand over the slave girl as instructed.

Sunday, November 29, saw the expedition bid farewell to Noklak—despite the government's victory, the citizens were relieved to be rid of their uninvited guests but careful nevertheless to show wary politeness at all times—and begin to wind its way to the more certain welcome of Chingmei. "It was a long and rather beastly march to get here, the path like the side of a house," Mills wrote to Pamela. They were all now "sick of climbing up and down hills," but the welcome they received in Chingmei more than made up for the exhaustion of the trail. Chingmak and his sons, Sangbah and Tangbang, as well as the portion of the column that had stayed at the Chingmei stockade to serve as the base camp, greeted them as returning conquerors. Chingmak would have been relieved that his British ally had been triumphant and had avoided humiliation at the hands of the Pangsherites. His loyalty to the Raj had been vindicated and his position in the region reinforced. Noklak's leaders accompanied the column, eager to make peace with Chingmei and bringing with them, on the hoof, payment for the fine levied by Philip Mills for placing those deadly *panji* sticks on the path into the village, and portions of a *mithan* cow were soon roasting flavorfully on spits across the camp. Mills and Fürer-Haimendorf dined that evening on one of Mills's favorite dishes, boiled *mithan* tail. "The succulent meat on the tail vertebrae of one of these huge animals is surprisingly tender," the Viennese man noted, "and much more tasty than any ox-tail."

Mills's plan was to rest and recover at Chingmei for two days while using the combined threat of force, with diplomacy, to ensure that other villages in the region also firmly received the antislaving message, gave up their captives, and agreed to desist from these practices in the future. It was also an opportunity to read the mail that had arrived in Chingmei by runner from Mokokchung. The letters brought news from home, some of which was deeply disturbing to these servants of the empire. Mills and Williams were horrified by the news from London about the scandal overwhelming the king-emperor, which in their view was every bit as damaging to imperial prestige as the refusal of recalcitrant places such as Pangsha to bend to the imperial yoke. The bad behavior of the king and the gossip in the American newspapers of Mrs. Simpson's scandalous shenanigans placed the empire in a poor light, and a deeply embarrassed Mills and Williams agreed to keep the information from Fürer-Haimendorf. "One can't discuss the King of England's affairs with foreigners," Mills wrote to Pamela. "If he [King Edward VIII] were to go off the deep end it might break up the Empire!"

The following day dawned bright and clear, although it was bitterly cold and a thin frost lay on the ground at the start of the day. Would Pangsha come to Chingmei to secure terms? Mills was certain that the Pangsherites would do so despite their loss of life in the Wenshoyl skirmish. They could not afford to be weakened any further and thus fall prey to the potential depredations of their neighbors, who might now be keen to capitalize on the sudden weakness of their former overlords and seek to prevent a resurgence of their power. The sun climbed gradually into the sky, quickly dissolving the frost, and as the day warmed the entire column lazed on the grass, enjoying its first real respite from the rigors of the campaign. Sepoys of the Assam Rifles, bayonets fixed to their Lee-Enfields, kept watch at the gate and at sentry positions around the stockade. A sudden commotion at the gate after lunch brought news that they had visitors. A *dobashi* rushed into the hut occupied by Williams, Mills, Fürer-Haimendorf, and Smith as a temporary "officers' mess," blurting out excitedly, "Sahib, Pangsha men are at the gate!"

If they had come to submit, decorum was demanded. The four Europeans sat at their portable table while eight visitors were brought in, one by one. The *dobashi* relieved each of his fighting *dao* as he entered and was ushered to a seated position on the ground in front of the table. Nakhu—a distinguished Ao *gaonbura* and *dobashi* accompanying the punitive expedition—and a somewhat nervous Matche stood by the side of the table, serving as interpreters. Fürer-Haimendorf felt his pulse race as he looked into the faces of the men who only two days before had been intent on removing the head from his shoulders. Only three of the men, it transpired, were from Pangsha. The other five were from Ponyo and a further ally of Pangsha, Tsawlaw ("Shiwu," recorded Mills), on the Burmese side of the Patkois. The three Pangsha men looked glum, Fürer-Haimendorf thought, and seemed to have been brought along by pressure from their allies.

The leader of the Pangsha delegation was Mongsen, one of the men who had approached the column in the Langnyu Valley rather optimistically offering a goat as an inducement for the expedition to depart. Mills and Williams had already been told by Noklak that Mongsen was one of the most famous warriors in the area and that he had been responsible, with his fellow Pangsherite Santing, for the recent devastating raid against Saochu. Santing, however, had been one of the warriors to die at the hands of Williams's sepoys in the mad dash to escape from Wenshoyl, which left Mongsen as the preeminent *khel* leader. Fürer-Haimendorf captured the discussion in his diary. Mongsen was invited to speak first.

His speech is open and dignified. He attempts neither defense nor accusation. What has happened, has happened; we have burnt their village and killed some of their best men—they, too, have tried to kill us. But now they wish to make peace, and so they have come to Chingmei in answer to Mills' message. Mills replies that peace is also his wish. He bears them no grudge, but Pangsha must swear not to take revenge on any of the villages who have befriended us. It would be futile to exact from Pangsha a promise to desist for ever from all head hunting, and Mills demands only that in future they shall not raid "this" side, leaving it open what is to happen "that" side, i.e. in the unexplored area to the east. But above all they must return the slave-girl. All the other terms are agreed to, but in this last demand there lies a difficulty, for the Pangsha men assure us that the child has really been sold across the Patkoi through the mediation of Tsawlaw, but they know which village bought her. The transaction must have been carried through shortly before our coming, and in a great hurry, for Mongsen complains that the price is still owing. Well, so much the better; it should be easy to recover the child from a defaulter, and Mongsen promises to bring the slave-child as soon as possible.

Peace was thereby concluded. "The scene was really rather an amazing one," Mills wrote to Pamela. Mills gravely drank *zu* while touching Mongsen's hand as a sign of their agreement before passing the cup to Mongsen for him to do likewise. Solemnities over, the party, rather incongruously, Fürer-Haimendorf thought, began a relaxed conversation about the fight. It was a little like two opposing teams discussing a hard-fought game of sport after the event, when passions had cooled and the rivalries of the field had been replaced by friendly camaraderie over a glass of beer in the bar. Previous enmities seemed to have entirely dissipated, and they chatted matter-of-factly about the man-to-man fight they had "enjoyed" three days before. Mongsen told Mills that although four bullets had brushed his hair, he had survived because at their first meeting Mills had described him as a *lambu*—a sacrosanct ambassador—and therefore he could not be killed by the British bullets. Noticing that Mongsen had a burned foot, Mills arranged for Dr. Vierya to treat and bandage it. Rushing back into Pangsha after it had been fired, Mongsen had trodden in the embers of one of the fires. It had not stopped him from leading the counterattack at Wenshoyl, however, or from making the long journey to Chingmei. He was clearly a remarkable man. Now that they were formally friends, the eight visitors were to stay that night in the village as guests of Chingmak, together with the emissaries from Noklak—who had also made peace with Chingmei—and the *zu* flowed freely into the evening (the Europeans reverting to gin and bitters). As the tired interlocutors went to sleep that night, there was no thought but that they were all lifelong friends getting together for a happy reunion after spending time apart. Mills had every right to be pleased with this outcome, Fürer-Haimendorf concluded. He had brought Pangsha to heel and secured a peace that would prevent it behaving in such a high-handed way in the future. Importantly, the punishment should also have a dampening effect on the trade in slaves for human sacrifice. With any luck, he thought, this terrible practice would die its own natural death.

The following day—Tuesday, December 1—none the worse for their imbibing of the previous night, Mongsen and his two fellow leaders from Pangsha were ceremonially bestowed with the signs of their preeminent status in the eyes of the Raj: red waistcoats and blankets. More practically, and as a reward for their obeisance, they were provided with the most valuable gift that could be made in these hills: salt. It was entirely absent in the mountains and as a commodity was obtained from either the Brahmaputra or Chindwin Valley. "All three villages swore an oath of friendship," Mills wrote in his report. Peace concluded, and now the best of friends, the men of Noklak and Pangsha departed for home.

11

RETURN TO MOKOKCHUNG

Mills's plan was to delay the expedition's return to Mokokchung, making the most of the fact that he was deep inside territory that had never before been visited and in which a number of recalcitrant villages skulked. One of these was Panso, which, although only eight miles south as the crow flew, lay on the other side of the rugged Mount Yakko, a prominent obstacle rising to a height of 7,687 feet on top of which lay the village of Sangpurr. Another was Noklu, also deeply implicated in local slaving, although Mills wanted to find a way of securing the freedom of slaves there without having to visit the place. Accordingly, he sent armed warriors with messages to Noklu to ensure that it sent emissaries to meet him at Panso. Chingmak, Sangbah, and Tangbang were to accompany the column, which was now to take on the style of a diplomatic tour rather than a punitive expedition. The practicalities of dealing with issues of localized fear-based power were very evident in these parts. "Diplomacy is completely jammed at the moment" in the area, Mills reported. "In the area through which I want to get messages, no one dare visit anyone else's village." The route to Panso would be a difficult one, taking three days. The route was known to be dreadful and would pose a significant physical challenge for them all.

Soon after the Noklak and Pangsha farewells had been said, the column said good-bye to the hospitable people of Chingmei and began its own march toward Chentang, where foodstuffs were replenished and preparations made to travel over Mount Yakko the following day. "We plunge into it tomorrow," Mills wrote to Pamela. "It's going to be one of our worst marches. We go down into a valley, over a hellish range on the other side [Mount Yakko] and down into another valley." Before leaving Mills did his best to determine the future of the slaves who had previously been handed over to Chingmei. He wrote to Pamela:

"Girly" is a young widow. Her mother was killed when she was captured and her father died a few days ago. She wants to stay on at Chingmei with Mrs. Chingmak. Really, she is hardly fit to be moved, as her mind is still dulled with shock and fear. "Bert" is the youth. He has some relations left so I am taking him back to them. One of the children has a grandfather in Chingmei, so will stay with him: another deaf and dumb poor little rabbit is going back to his father, the last has no one left in the world, all killed in the raid, so he is being adopted by a dobashi and his wife, a nice childless couple who live in Mokokchung.

The journey from Chentang to Yukso on Wednesday, December 2, 1936, was every bit as difficult as Mills had anticipated. A streaming cold that had come on Major Williams at Noklak remained with him, and Mills recorded that "we are all sick of hills and battles and rather short rations." A drop of 1,000 feet that took them to a stream was followed by a direct climb to the top of Mount Yakko, where lay the village of Sangpurr. Fortunately, despite the blazing sun, most of the walking was achieved under the shade of the jungle canopy. At Sangpurr they met a small group of men from a Nokhu *khel*. Mills told them to return home and ensure that the ambassadors whom he had demanded from Noklu were ready to meet them at Panso in two days' time. Just in case they were not believed by their own people, Mills gave them each pages of the *Statesman* (an English-language newspaper published in Delhi), one for each *morung*. "They will never have seen paper before and will believe that the people who came in today really saw us!" he told Pamela. Not one of the Nokhu men had seen a white man before, he observed, and noted that their faces remained inscrutable while they received these instructions. They said they had returned all their slaves on hearing that the British were making a fuss about slavery. That night the column camped in thick jungle on the side of Mount Yakko.

On Wednesday, December 3, the expedition had something of an easy march for five miles before reaching a camp prepared for it by the village of Panso. A gentle uphill climb included traversing a large log on an incline, and Mills could not begin to understand how he would be able to climb down it on the return journey. "At the top of our climb was Yukso village, a place of about 50 houses in which no white face has ever been seen before. They were a little sore at having lost a head by treachery a few days ago, but were *most* friendly to us." For the excited Mills, with his eye on collecting artifacts for the Pitt Rivers Museum in Oxford, Panso was like entering an ethnological treasure trove:

> I collected one or two things I wanted, including a real "crash helmet," a huge thing of cane with rope coiled round it, and padded inside with a filthy rag! They use them in village fights when it is "genna" (against their own tribal laws) to use steel, but you may hit the other fellow on the head with a club, as hard as you like! Also a very fine drum in the village of the curious type one gets round here. I also collected a set of ladies' combs. One for the scalp has fine teeth, and the other one has a long handle and blunt bamboo teeth. This is used for twisting the back hair when it is being done in the morning.

Instructions had been sent ahead and a large encampment prepared for them by Panso, separated from the main village. "It was of vice-regal proportions," a surprised Mills observed. The views were spectacular. Across the broad valley looking northeast they could see the slope at Wenshoyl from which they had made their rapid withdrawal five days before. What surprised Fürer-Haimendorf, however, was the warmth of the welcome they received. On reflection, he considered, it had much to do with the humbling of Pangsha as, like Noklak, the village lived in an uneasy relationship with its aggressive neighbors. "They are all *very* pleased with us for burning Pangsha," Mills told Pamela. Christoph von Fürer-Haimendorf explained why:

They have seen the smoke of the burning Pangsha in the distance, and are beside themselves with joy at the defeat of their enemies. There is a certain maliciousness in their remarks on Pangsha's ruin when they meet us before the village; and we soon realize that it is not altogether without reason, for early this year a troop of Pangsha men, appearing before the gates of Panso and challenging them to fight, had taken without any losses to themselves no less than twelve heads. The Panso men were inside the strong fortifications of their village; why, then, we asked, had they ventured outside? But Panso prided themselves; they were famous warriors, they said, and could not allow such a challenge to go unanswered. Well, Pangsha had taken twelve heads, but the white men have burnt her to the ground, and she has paid for those last insulting remarks her warriors had thrown over their shoulder as they left: "We only wanted to show you what sort of men we are; you have nothing more to fear, only be careful! Don't follow us." Sadly the men of Panso tell us they had not had the courage to follow and take revenge. Now we have destroyed their enemies, and the people of Panso joyfully acclaim the victors.

It was yet more confirmation to the Europeans that fear was the driving ingredient in the exercise of power in the eastern Naga Hills. The celebrations of the victory over Pangsha were, as a consequence, fulsome and elaborate. Fürer-Haimendorf described the color and spectacle:

The great dance in honor of the victors is soon to begin, and a wonderfully colorful crowd gathers on the open space outside the village. The men stand in a long row, stretching from

our camp down the slope, and start the dance with slow, measured movements. They wear full ceremonial dress—you might
be tempted to describe it as full war-dress, but the Nagas never
risk their costly feathers and ornaments in a raid. They treasure
them for the glory of the dance. They have conical hats of red
and yellow plaited cane, tufted with flaming red goat's hair, and
surmounted with two white hornbill feathers striped with black.
Warriors who have themselves captured heads are permitted to
load their hats with shining mithan horns and hold their hats in
place with chin-straps set with tiger claws. Cowrie shells are em-
broidered on most of the dark blue cloths and the small aprons
reaching from the belt to the knee. The broad belt is set with
white seeds, and supports a wooden sheath at the back, which
takes the long dao when it is not in use. In fact, their ceremonial
dress is very like that of the Changs, except that, in addition, they
wear leggings of bearskin which not only protect the legs against
panji but complete the harmony of the costume.

Mills was less enthralled with the proceedings. "I have seen too
many Naga dances to be very interested," he told Pamela, and "he
was tone-deaf [although the] . . . Baron loved every moment of it,
and rushed about like a press photographer. He wants spectacular
pictures which he can sell." The day following—December 4—Mills,
Smith, and Fürer-Haimendorf had the opportunity of examining
Panso at close quarters while Major Williams attempted to throw
off his cold by lying in the sun at the encampment. Like Noklak, the
village was enormous. It was a jammed-together higgledy-piggledy
collection of hundreds of houses, each of which, as in Noklak,
seemed to be vying to sit on the highest piece of ground. They
didn't see any women, apart from the wives of the *gaonburas* in
their houses, but the men of the village were welcoming and eager
to show their visitors around. When questioned, they insisted that
no slaves remained in the village. All had been released back to
their homes except one, who had been sold into Burma. With the
vastness of the village, there was little that Mills could do but believe

them. They were disparaging about Noklu, and it was apparent that they would have liked nothing better than for the British to travel to burn their powerful neighbor too.

Late in the evening, after Mills had lost hope that the men of the Noklu *morung*s would obey his instructions to meet him at Panso, they turned up. The scraps of the *Statesman* that he had sent had done their job in persuading the village *gaonbura*s to travel to Panso in order to make their peace with the sahib of Mokokchung before their village was set upon and burned like Pangsha. "I interviewed them by lantern light," Mills wrote. "All went well." They insisted that they had returned their two slaves to their homes, although another had died and a fourth had also been sold into Burma. Without marching on their village Mills had little choice but to accept their stories. The fact that they had turned up in large numbers to make obeisance to him demonstrated that, for a while at least, the white man's strange injunctions against slave trading would be obeyed. Now, with the images of Pangsha burning on the distant hillside, they feared the consequences of disobedience. Mills was relieved. "Noklu having come to terms, we have been able to shorten our tour a little," he wrote to Pamela. "We shall all be glad to turn our noses towards home."

On December 6 the column began its homeward journey, its mission of war over but that of diplomacy not yet complete. Undoubtedly they did so much to Noklu's relief. Leaving Panso, they retraced their steps to Chentang, which they had left six days before. The journey entailed the long, steep climb back up to Sangpurr, passing through the village of Yukso and camping near Sangpurr at an elevation of 7,600 feet. The campsite prepared for them was shaded from the sun and icily cold, whereas at Sangpurr, after a short walk to the summit, they were able to bask in the sun's warming rays. There were some benefits of living at such an altitude, but the welcome that Mills and Fürer-Haimendorf received was a grudging one. Visitors were rarely seen here, and white ones never. The houses were shut up, with the occupants cowering inside and women and children dispatched to safety in the jungle farther down the slope. Signs of fear and hostility were all around them, as during the march to Chentang the following day *panji* littered the paths and caught two porters unawares, piercing their feet to the extent that they had to be carried in litters. Somehow they managed to climb down the tree trunks over the path and had an easier time of it than they had when they had begun the climb to Sangpurr a few days earlier.

At Chentang, where the column rejoined the porters and guards they had left behind to guard the camp while the Panso party was away, a pleasant surprise awaited them. Pangsha had kept its promise, and the final slave child had been returned. The slave was accompanied by a fine of five *mithan* cows and message from Pangsha that Fürer-Haimendorf abbreviated thus: "They are very proud to be considered 'sons' of the Government, but beg us not to return, for as it is, they have a difficult enough time with their wives, who refuse to allow them to rebuild their houses as long as we remain in the neighborhood. We send them all the necessary assurances, for we understand that even bold Pangsha men may have difficulties with their own wives." To the slaver-hater Mills it was a particularly proud moment, as he told Pamela: "After the show I feel I have not lived in vain. I have actually found and got into our own hands 5 children and 2 adults and have caused 2 more children to be returned to their parents. All have been saved from a life of drudgery and disgrace and very likely from human sacrifice." All this war and diplomacy had a purpose, he considered, and it was scenes such as the family reunion at Chentang that made the exhausting marches, endless politicking, and brief moments of fear during the running battle at Wenshoyl worthwhile. While Fürer-Haimendorf snapped photographs of the slaves, and of Mills sitting in their midst, by some extraordinary combination of circumstance every slave was reunited with a member of his or her family:

The child was the son of a man called Pangting [from Kejok] who was here simply beaming. The child is dumb, but an absolute little lamb. The poor hangdog little wretch had become a laughing baby. He came and sat with me and played. "Girly's" parents [from Saochu] were supposed to be dead and weren't, they were here as large as life. Even the unutterable "Girly" herself looked quite attractive with happiness. Her mother was almost speechless. We mustn't forget "Bert." It appears that that incredibly ugly youth has a wife whom he thought had been killed in the raid, but now she is alive and well, even *he* smiled. Just before the little party set off ahead of us to their home, "Girly's" mother told me that the slave we have been trying to get back from Burma was also her daughter, and begged me to get her back. I could only say I would do my best. Two hours later a real life drama happened. The poor little slave girl from Burma was brought in. *How* glad her mother would have been! But they will meet in a few days. I do feel rather proud of getting her back from miles inside Burma.

The bagpipers of the Assam Rifles happily played their Scottish airs in celebration of the event.

It was here that their journey home took a different path from the one they had taken from Mokokchung, for instead of returning to Helipong they marched northward directly to Tuensang, the homeland of the Chang people. It was a long, hard march, beginning at 6 a.m. on the morning of December 7. Tiredness now replaced the elation of the previous day, and tempers frayed, Mills again finding fault with Smith's organization of the porters. Lunch was called at 2:30 p.m. Afterward the column began the daily climb to habitation, again to 7,000 feet. Eventually Tuensang—"an enormous village" in Mills's words and the Chang's "great mother-village" in Fürer-Haimendorf's—came into sight. The column marched through its cramped streets and then dropped a good distance to camp on the northern side—at a height of about 4,000 feet—where eleven bamboo structures had been built for it. Tuensang had been visited several times before by tours setting out from Mokokchung, including by J. H. Hutton, and the white man and his laws were well known in these parts. The area was also relatively

peaceful: Pangsha's depredations and those of warlike villages to
the northeast were restricted to the area farther east. It didn't stop
the *panji* appearing on many of the tracks, however. One of the
porters stepped on one and severed an artery, nearly bleeding to
death.

To Mills's delight, a great pile of mail awaited the column at Tuensang, where letters had been accumulating for days. A rare repast
of tinned salmon, bully beef, cold chicken, potatoes, baked beans,
and cheese filled their hungry bellies, and fines against various villages for what Mills described as "contumacy" enabled the entire
column to feast off *mithan* beef that night—to Pangsha's four cows
had been added four from Ponyo and several from other villages.
Mills spent the evening under a hurricane lamp meeting deputa-
tions from an array of villages who came to see him to discuss their
grievances or to give an account of some misdemeanor or other.
The great joy for Mills the next afternoon was catching up with the
little party of freed slaves and their families, whose journey home
from Chentang meant a first stop at Tuensang. He told Pamela, "I
forgot to tell you the little girl from Burma was restored to her parents today, and I saw them all together. Another absolutely miraculously transformed child, a little smiling imp. Pangting's little boy
was too busy stuffing food into his mouth to play, but he gave me a
beaming smile. 'Girly' and the little one are the oldest and young-
est of four sisters, the two middle ones lost [in the original attack]."
The sojourn at Tuensang was for two nights to enable the column
to reorganize and for Mills to conduct business as the deputy commissioner. He toured Tuensang and was struck by its considerable
size, perhaps two miles from end to end, he estimated. Ever the
anthropologist, he scouted out material to send back to Balfour at
the Pitt Rivers Museum. These duties complete, and after saying
farewell to the freed slaves as they made their own way home, the
column packed up camp and headed northwest on December 10.
The journey was to take them another three days via the villages
of Hgabu, Longtang, and Loksan. The farther they headed back
toward administered territory, the more relaxed the Naga villages

became. It was obvious to the entire column that this was because they didn't fear the attacks of violent aggressors such as Pangsha and felt more secure the closer they were to British protection.

The 500-strong column now began to prepare for home, to relax, and to lose some of the tension it had exhibited when marching into the badlands of the eastern Patkois. At Longtang on December 10 Mills recorded singing and feasting, the Changs chanting, and everyone enjoying a full belly: the Nagas of roast pigs; the Gurkha sepoys of goat; and the Europeans of chickens, *mithan*'s tongues, and a little goat's milk for breakfast. It was at Longtang, after a hard march that Williams described to Mills as "blood-stained," that Chingmak, whom Mills described as his "old friend," turned for home. He had insisted on accompanying the column with his own retinue of Chingmei warriors until Mills had safely left Chang territory. It was an emotional parting. Mills had formed a personal and political alliance with this giant of the eastern hills, a man who had decided to ally himself and his village with the distant Raj and who was to prove loyal to it through thick and thin. "I am afraid we shall never meet again in this world," Mills lamented. "He is a very fine type of man, and without him we should never have got our slaves back. He nearly broke down when the moment came, and I hated it."

For the porters, each forward step brought them one step closer to home, and on the evening of December 11, from Loksan, they were able to gaze on the Dikhu Valley, the great green gouge in the earth that separated the Control Area from the Administered Area. They had begun the day with a very steep descent to a stream, of which they had taken advantage for a wash—the first for some days—before a steep climb of some 2,500 feet to Loksan. That night the festive spirit continued, with the sepoys having a party and keeping everyone awake until late with a din that drove Mills "nearly silly. Discordant raucous Hindu songs are bad enough but the tom-tom is the crowning evil. They have a huge fire burning and there is a fellow dancing in front of it." At every stop the local *gaonburas* would come and pay him their respects, which would keep him busy for most of the evening, but for virtually all others on the expedition, home was nigh, spirits were high, and the serious intent of the expedition now lay far behind them. They were returning as victors, even those who had been engaged merely to carry loads.

The following morning they began their descent into the valley, where they camped on the Dikhu River. Williams took the opportunity to fish, and they were met with mail from Mokokchung and a fresh set of newspapers from New Delhi. Horrifyingly, for Williams, Smith, and Mills, the papers were full of depressing news about the constitutional crisis in London. They now found it difficult to hide this news from Fürer-Haimendorf, and the representatives of the king-emperor on the edge of the world's greatest empire now felt embarrassed beyond words for the behavior of a king who didn't practice what they, as his emissaries, had to do every day of their professional lives as colonial servants: self-effacing and self-denying subservience to the imperial ideal. Edward VIII was failing to behave in the way that his own servants believed he should and to give full and proper dignity to his role as monarch. It was deeply unsettling and disturbing. "We are all utterly miserable," wrote Mills to Pamela. "We've no news yet of what finally happened, whether the King abdicated, or whether he gave the woman up. It is not easy to gauge public feeling properly from the many extracts in *The Statesman* but here I think we would prefer him to abdicate: his reputation will be so terribly damaged in any case." The crisis in London didn't prevent Williams from landing seven or eight *mahseer* and all enjoying a fish supper, but the following day it was all over. After a long, hard climb into Mokokchung they reached home, passing a number of welcoming villages—and cups of the ubiquitous *zu*—on the way. The march into the hills from Mokokchung took four hours, but much of it was undertaken with rice beer pressed into their hands and the cheers of Nagas welcoming back their triumphant army, returned from teaching the "savages" of the Patkois a painful but necessary lesson. In the Ao village of Longmisa long rows of *zu* were laid out to quench the thirst of the porters, and the village allocated a pig, which, as Fürer-Haimendorf reported, "Nakhu, as the oldest and most esteemed Naga of our column, kills with the lower end of his spear. Such is the old Ao custom of greeting the home-coming warriors."

At Smith's bungalow, where the Europeans retired for a final meal together, was a message for Mills. It was now December 13. A telegram from Shillong reported that on December 11 the king had abdicated and that the Duke of York had been proclaimed George VI. Long live the King! Even Fürer-Haimendorf was caught up in the gloom of his British friends, no longer attempting to hide their embarrassment and shame at the behavior of their former king. "The world and its troubles have caught us again," the Austrian observed.

Fürer-Haimendorf was facing his own problem. Although the sepoys could quite legitimately claim to have killed some of the enemy, all of the Naga porters were returning with tales of glory but no physical evidence of their manifold victories. Importantly, they had no heads. How could they return to their villages as warriors without such practical evidence of their martial credentials? Resourceful jurists among the porters, he observed, came up with the solution of substituting Fürer-Haimendorf's four Pangsha heads "for those of the killed enemies left lying on the field."

It is argued that since they were fairly fresh and had hung only on the head-tree, and not been stored in the morung, it is plausible to assume that their inherent "virtue" has not yet been finally absorbed in Pangsha's store of magical power. By this interpretation the value of my heads suddenly mounts, and it is soon apparent that they will never reach any European museum.

By no means all the porters take this point of view. The Lhotas and Rengmas recognize the heads as valuable trophies, and are burning with impatience to receive their share, but the Semas and the Sangtams stand on their dignity. A head that has not been severed from an enemy's body is to them useless for ceremonial purposes. . . .

I hand over one of the heads to the Lhotas and Rengmas, telling them to divide it, so that each village should receive a small piece. It is not only the men who have been with us on the Pangsha tour who will thus gain the right to the dress of the head-hunter, but all those who touch the small piece of head with their dao. Excitement runs high among the porters; their fellow-villagers will acclaim them as heroes, and the bringing in of the head will be followed by days of feasting.

With little more than a puff and a fizzle, the 1936 punitive expedition was over. In Fürer-Haimendorf's collection a photograph remains of the four Europeans, standing together outside Smith's bungalow following lunch, self-consciously showing to the camera the sangfroid that defined their roles as lawgivers in this lawless land. They stood in a semiformal, self-conscious pose, full of restraint and awareness of their position. All but Smith wore jackets; Fürer-Haimendorf and Mills wore ties. Smith was to remain in Mokokchung, Mills and Williams to return to Kohima, and Fürer-Haimendorf to walk back into the Konyak country, from whence he had first started out on this unusual adventure. The evening ended in typical fashion over gin and bitters and shared stories of hardship, excitement, danger, and triumph.

Sir Robert Reid, the governor of Assam, forwarded Mills's report on the successful expedition to Pangsha to New Delhi on January 30, 1937. He was pleased with the outcome of their adventure: "The expedition completely achieved its objects in effecting the release of several slaves taken as captives and in inflicting on Pangsha a well merited punishment not only for its participation in the slave trade but for its head hunting raids on its neighbors. The Deputy Commissioner, Naga Hills, has been asked to submit proposals for the constitution of a Control Area to include Pangsha and other villages." Mills's report argued that the Control Area should be extended to include those villages for whom slave taking had been allowed to fester for want of the exercise of effective restraint. "The proposed extension of the Control Area covers the approaches to the only known pass into Burma through which slaves are taken, and the whole of the country in which we know that slave-raiding has survived to the present," he wrote. The government of India agreed and in January 1938 extended the Control Area that ran alongside the British Administered Area, but not so far as to include Pangsha. This didn't mean, however, that the empire was creeping forward, only that the area in which Britain claimed an interest was now closer to its colony in Burma. The gap between the formal Control Area and the Burmese border, which looked so illogical on the map and equally irrational to colonial administrators frustrated by their inability to exercise the necessary influence over anyone outside the general purview that these categories denoted, was thereby reduced but was frustratingly not eliminated entirely.

Any self-congratulation by Britain was short-lived. Reports began filtering in to Mokokchung that the impact of the expedition remained limited to the villages that had been visited: towns within the region that had not received a visit continued to behave as they had always done. One such was the Kalyo Kengyu village of Nokhu, and another was Sanglao, which had previously been a victim of Pangsha's despoliations. The new deputy commissioner in Kohima, Charles Pawsey, was concerned by this state of affairs, as it was apparent that these villages were attempting to thumb their noses at British authority and to ignore the warnings that Mills and Williams had hoped would be spread far and wide by virtue of their recent visit. It was clear to Pawsey that the remote villages were counting on Britain not returning to their region anytime soon. He pressed Shillong for further action at the end of the wet season (after October) for a follow-up punitive expedition if these remote villages refused to give up the slaves they were reported to be holding; the government could find no grounds to refuse. Accordingly, in 1937 Pawsey, accompanied by the new subdivisional officer at Mokokchung, Hari Blah, set out with 174 officers and men of the Third Assam Rifles under the command of Major Bernard Gerty of the Ninth Jat Regiment. Unfortunately, no detailed accounts of this expedition appear to remain. Sir Robert Reid subsequently considered the expedition to have been a success in that slaves were recovered and recalcitrant villages punished: "The expedition left Mokokchung on the 1st November 1937 and by the end of the month all the slaves known to be in the unadministered area were set free without any casualty on our side. Nokhu was reached on November 12th, 4 slaves were released and a fine was exacted: Sanglao was reached on the 15th and was overwhelmingly friendly: Pesu was reached on the 17th and burnt and slaves recovered." Reid noted, nevertheless, that as soon as the expedition left the area stronger villages took advantage of the weakened state of those recently punished. While Pesu was being rebuilt, for instance, after being burned to the ground, Panso broke through the village's weakened defenses and killed six, taking their heads.

Any hope that Pangsha would not return to its old ways was dashed when during the dry season of late 1938 and early 1939 Mokokchung continued to receive reports of its trespasses and those of neighboring villages who were working in alliance with it. The target of considerable cruelty that year was the village of Agching. Early in 1939 the villages of Yungkao, Tamkhung, and Ukha grouped together to attack Agching, killing twelve people and removing their heads. In June that year, during the monsoon, they attacked again, this time accompanied by Pangsha, killing ninety-six. All these villages were now well within the recently extended Control Area. Action by Shillong could no longer be delayed because of the excuse that the villages sat outside the British area of influence, and another punitive expedition was dispatched. Guns were provided for the endangered villages for their protection. Led again by Charles Pawsey and supported by the new subdivisional officer at Mokokchung, Philip Adams, the expedition was supported by three platoons (100 men) led by Major A. R. Nye, Fourth Prince of Wales' Own Gurkha Rifles. Like the two previous expeditions to the region, it was considered a success. There was no opposition. Both Pangsha and Ukha, the two most bloodthirsty and aggressive villages, were burned, and those that were deemed to have played only supporting roles, such as Yungkao and Tamkhung, were fined. Practicalities continued to dominate the application of the law in these parts. The villages were sternly admonished for their activities and advised that they were not to use guns or take heads within the Control Area. The implication was that they could continue to hunt outside the Control Area, that is, into Burma. One of the aims of the 1939 punitive expedition was to arrest both Mongu and Mongsen, the two paramount chiefs of Pangsha. It is not clear what Pawsey had in mind for these two troublemakers, although a public trial at Mokokchung, followed by imprisonment, seemed the most likely plan.

Three large-scale punitive expeditions in four years crossing the eastern territories of the Naga Hills constituted a significant change in the experience of British-Naga relations in this northeastern region. Philip Adams led a further punitive expedition to Nian and Yungya, burning the villages in April 1943 following a year of violence. These expeditions, however, seemed to have minimal long-term effect, or indeed any real impact outside the villages specifically targeted for retribution. They did, nevertheless, make villages such as Noklak and Pangsha acutely aware that the government seemed willing now to act against slavery and head-hunting in a way it had previously been unable to and was serious about its prohibitions in both the Administered Area and the Control Area, of which they were now (unknowingly) a part. Armed action of this kind made the subdivisional officer at Mokokchung more than the paper tiger he had been in the old days, when missives from so far away could be easily ignored. It also made the British acutely aware of those in the region who were responsible for fanning the flames of civil disturbance—men such as Mongsen of Pangsha—so that they could mark their cards accordingly.

12

ERIC AND THE HEADHUNTERS

Fighting to retain control of himself, Sevareid stumbled uphill, heading for the site of the wreckage, where he presumed he would find the others. Clambering through the bush, he fell repeatedly, cutting himself on the sword grass and branches. In the short period of time during which he had dangled from the parachute he had spotted a village on a distant hillside, and a jumble of ill-connected questions bubbled to the surface of his mind. Panic was close, incoherent thoughts racing through his brain in no clear, logical fashion: "I have no food. There are berries here. Where are the Japs? Who lives in that grass village? I have no weapons. I have a penknife. A razor . . . That boy from Minnesota. He lived forty days in the New Guinea jungles. Maybe I can, too. No, this is too bad—no, cannot do it." Bloodied and emotionally exhausted, he at one point rested where he fell, entirely accepting the prospect of death. He thought of his wife and twin sons and attempted to calculate what his death benefits would be if his insurance company paid out when he didn't return. He tried to call out, but nothing more than a mumble emerged from his lips. He then heard shouting. Ned Miller and a blond-haired serviceman whom he didn't recognize from the plane—who turned out to be Sergeant Francis Signer—emerged from the undergrowth. Bloodied too, the three men sat for a while, saying nothing, as if attempting to restore their reserves of both physical and emotional energy.

Before long another shout was heard, this time for help. Walking slowly uphill, they came across a parachute caught in the branches of a tree, beneath which was sitting Sergeant Walter Oswalt, clearly in pain. One leg was crossed over the other. He groaned and told them that he had hurt his leg in the fall. Taking off his boot, Sevareid saw that the ankle was red and swollen, but his limited medical experience could not tell him whether he was looking at a sprain or a break. Then out of the bush stumbled Harry Neveu, complaining of a broken rib. After a few moments Neveu suggested that they move to the crash site, as it would be the natural rallying point for any other survivors. They, the last to jump, would surely be joined in due course by those who had jumped before them but who were now much farther away. Neveu judged that they were some 300 yards from the wreck, but that distance was covered in thick, chest-high brush. Sevareid placed a splint as best he could on Oswalt's ankle, wrapping it with parachute silk, and he and Signer helped Oswalt move along the path that Miller and Neveu managed to cut through the undergrowth.

Eventually they reached the blackened edge of a great pit gouged out of the earth in which the mangled remains of the plane still smoked fiercely. A plume of black smoke rising high into the air marked the half-acre of burned hillside scorched by the fierce fireball produced by the burning aviation fuel. They stared disconsolately at the scene of devastation before them, lost in silent contemplation of the recent events and the prospects for their salvation in this desolate land. Sevareid recalled Neveu muttering something about whether Felix had managed to get out of the aircraft, nervously concerned lest his friend had not made it, given the last-second rush to evacuate the plummeting plane. Neveu also stumbled through an apology for not getting them home; when interviewed years later he was convinced that Sevareid had misheard him and thought that Neveu was admitting to a personal failure to keep the aircraft in the air and that therefore he was somehow responsible for the crash. Such were the surging emotions of the moment. Happily, Sevareid made no such claim in his memoirs. To the contrary, he had commented, "So far as we could see, both pilots had done their duty to the utmost and had got us away from enemy territory. Neveu felt very badly, but it never occurred to any of us to hold him responsible; indeed, we were more inclined to be grateful that he had kept us in the air as long as he had."

The fire was still too hot to approach. A strange-looking lump of molten metal in the grass was recognized by Sevareid as his type-writer. Sitting down amid the wet brush on the outer rim of the circle of fire-blackened earth, the men attempted to work out what to do. A river ran through the valley half a mile below them, and a village could be seen on the same slope of the mountain, although in the far distance. It now seemed clear that Oswalt's leg was broken, and he lay on the wet grass uncomplainingly, yet in agony. They decided to stay where they were for the time being to wait for any stragglers and because they could not carry the injured Oswalt on their own. He was a giant of a man and would require at least four fit men to carry him to a place of safety. It was also an opportunity to gather their wits and think through how they might survive the onset of night. Neveu had a map, which he pulled out of his flying jacket. Unfortunately, the area into which he believed they had crashed was denoted by a white area marked "Unsurveyed." The nearest British outpost, Neveu knew, was Mokokchung, which was at least eighty-five miles as the crow flew but many miles farther if they were forced to walk there through these intimidating, corrugated mountains. Of any inhabitants the survivors were blissfully ignorant.

While they were miserably contemplating their plight, the distinctive and unmistakable sound of a C-47 Skytrain appeared separately in each of their consciousnesses. Unwilling to believe what they were hearing, they ignored it for a while until the reality of the drone in the distance was confirmed. Then, amazingly, the aircraft appeared down the valley and approached their position rapidly, flying low overhead, waggling its wings as it saw the men on the ground, who jumped up—except for Oswalt—in a frenzy of screaming and ecstatic joy. Oswalt's frantic distress messages to Chabua had been heard and sufficient information provided for the crew of the C-47 to find the thin pillar of smoke marking the spot of Flight 12420's demise. With a start Sevareid realized that the time was 10:15 a.m. It was only an hour after the crash, and here was the USAAF in the sky above, like a ministering angel. It was almost too good to be true.

Although searches for downed aircraft and their crews were not yet on an organized or systematic footing in the early days of the Hump airlift, the news of a downed aircraft would often lead to the first available crew being sent up to search for it. Useful innovations had already been developed, such as the creation of standard rescue packs bundled together with canvas and rope and attached to parachutes that were opened by use of a "static line" attached to the aircraft. They contained essential necessities for the preservation of life such as first aid equipment, knives, a rifle or two, and ammunition as well as food and blankets. The canvas cover and attaching cords could be used to make a shelter.

When the SOS messages came streaming in to the operations center at Chabua shortly after 9:00 that morning, a C-47 was tasked with the search within minutes of the receipt of Oswalt's distress signals. The ATC operations officer was Colonel Richard Knight. Tracking Oswalt's last radio signals, he gave the rescue aircraft an approximate location for the crash. After that the crew members were on their own and would have to use the "Mark I Eyeball" to locate the exact position of the crash on the ground. The US-AAF missing air crew reports (MACRs) from the time demonstrate that the crew of this rescue aircraft—pilots Captain Hugh Wild and George Katzman and radio operator Staff Sergeant Glenn Arbuthnot—were vastly experienced in searching for downed aircraft in what was already known to crews as the "aluminum trail" stretching between Assam and Yunnan. On this occasion the same problem that had faced Mills and Williams in 1936—the fact that the entire area was unsurveyed—meant that they would have to reach the general area and then search with the naked eye. It entailed flying slowly and methodically along every valley in the area of the last position provided by the doomed plane in the hope that evidence of the remains might be identified from the air. This was not always possible in areas of heavy vegetation, where the jungle canopy could easily hide wreckage from view. Many scores of aircraft were never discovered. On this occasion, however, the burning aviation fuel provided an unmistakable marker for the searchers. After traversing a number of valleys, they turned into the one that led directly to the plume of smoke under which they could see the ecstatic survivors jumping up and down close to the wreck.

After the rescue plane had circled the site several times, Neveu suddenly realized that the crew was trying to get them to an area of open ground where they could safely dispatch a parcel from the plane. The crew of the C-47 clearly didn't want to drop anything on the still burning wreckage. The survivors could see a patch of cleared ground higher up the hill that looked suspiciously as though it had once been cultivated. Scrambling uphill as quickly as they could, Neveu, Sevareid, and Miller found a track that took them directly to the open space. Sevareid could not help noticing footprints in the mud, and they passed other unmistakable signs of human habitation: a bamboo spout, for instance, thrust into the side of the hill to divert a small watercourse. Had it been placed here by the inhabitants of that distant village he had seen when swinging under his parachute, or were there Japanese soldiers about? Reaching the clearing, the exhausted men waved to the plane, and Neveu laid out his parachute as an aiming mark. Sure enough, a bundle was pushed out, swinging wildly under its parachute to fall virtually at their feet. In the bundle were an ax, machetes, blankets, cigarettes, army rations, mosquito netting, and two old Springfield service rifles, one of which had a broken stock. A further pass by the plane brought with it a small weighted bag in which the men found a typewritten note: "Remain at wreckage until rescue party reaches you. You are safe from enemy action there. Give some sign of life to searching aircraft by building a fire or displaying unusual signs by parachute panels. Further provisions coming by air tomorrow including a radio. Your location: 26°25' N.–95°20' E."* Yet

_____

*This was not correct. Pangsha is located at N 26°15'35", E 95°5'57". The original location provided by Hugh Wild was in fact seventeen miles northeast of the wreck's actual location as the crow flies, farther along the Patkoi Range inside Burma.

another pass, however, delivered two additional packages containing the radio. One held the receiver, but the transmitter in another package under a bright orange parachute was broken in the fall when the parachute failed to open. The equipment was collected and carried to the area where Oswalt sat, silently uncomplaining despite the pain in his leg, and he twiddled with the radio knobs in an effort to make contact with Chabua. One of the items was a set of ground-signaling panels with instructions for sending messages to the plane by arranging the letters on the ground for the air crew above to read. After completing several more circuits, the C-47 turned to the north. Within minutes the comforting drone of its engines drifted to silence, and it passed out of sight.

The absence of the noise of the aircraft above them enabled the men to hear sounds for the first time that unequivocally confirmed the existence of other human beings in the area—close by. Suddenly standing to listen, they heard the rhythmic sounds of many voices in unison, an eerie and slightly unsettling noise that sounded like a chant or marching song. It grew rapidly, and before they had much time to do anything other than shove Miller into the bush with the unbroken rifle and a handful of cartridges, a war party of muscled, spear-wielding men wearing little more than loincloths and singing a cadenced chant came trotting into view over the nearby ridge. The warriors ran up to them and formed a rough semicircle in front of the Americans. The chanting stopped. Sevareid wrote, "They had straight black hair, cut short around the head so that the effect was that of a tuft of trimmed thatch. Some had faded blue tattoo markings on their chests and arms. All carried long spears with splayed metal points, and some also held wide-bladed knives a couple of feet long, heavy and slightly curved, almost like a butcher's cleaver." For the five Americans, the sight of their sudden visitors was profoundly shocking. Sevareid grabbed a knife and stood protectively over the injured Oswalt. With the exception of the injured Oswalt's holstered Colt .45 and Miller's ancient Springfield, they were unarmed. The two groups stood looking at each other. The atmosphere was tense but was one of silent inquiry rather than of hostility. Then, surprising both himself and his comrades, Sevareid stepped forward, raising his palm in a sign of peace, and said instinctively, "How!"

It could have been a comic moment. The only word that came to his mind was a long-forgotten product of youthful reading of the stories of America's frontiers. But it seemed to do the trick. Placing their spears in the ground and slipping their *daos* back over their shoulders, the tribesmen moved forward calmly and began to smile. They were clearly intrigued with their unexpected visitors and fascinated by the Americans' equipment and clothes. Touching their boots, weighing the ax, and feeling the parachute silk, they sized up the extraordinary sight before them. Here were the inhabitants of the machines they had seen repeatedly in the skies above their mountain homes over the past year or more, come unexpectedly to earth. In fact, they knew exactly who these men were but had never seen them close up. During the previous six months Philip Adams had sent messages as far as Pangsha, via Chingmak and his sons, with instructions that if any men fell to earth from these *kepruo*s* they were to be looked after and not killed. Villagers would be rewarded with 500 rupees' worth of salt for their protection of any white men who might inadvertently parachute into their territory.† Adams could have had no absolute confidence that these white men, whom the Kalyo Kengyu would consider mortal enemies, would be entirely safe if they fell into their hands. As the minutes passed, however, it was clear to Sevareid and his colleagues that these inquisitive natives intended them no immediate harm. The villagers could see the power that the white men represented, with their beautifully machined equipment and the aircraft that had just spent thirty minutes circling the crash site above them, and appeared interested in their welfare rather than their demise. That was good enough for Sevareid. Although knowing nothing about the near-naked and fierce-looking men, the survivors could

---

Kepruo is the Angama Naga word for "airplane."

†The equivalent of US$500, a vast fortune at the time.

see that they were not Japanese and appeared friendly. It was a good start. Then, in a further gesture of comradeliness, the Americans were offered food and drink. A bamboo container and gourd were passed around, dispensing a sickly-sweet alcoholic beverage of some kind and a sticky maize paste that reminded Sevareid of pig feed. Each American endeavored, for reasons of diplomacy, to partake of the revolting substances.

By now Miller had emerged cautiously from the brush where he had been hiding. Indicating by sign language to their visitors that a package from the plane remained to be collected, a number of the men rushed off to fetch it, returning triumphantly a short while later with the container holding the broken transmitter. They touched everything, Sevareid noticed, but didn't attempt to steal any of it. Neveu attempted to communicate with the natives by reading a number of phrases from a language card he had in his pocket for such eventualities. Unfortunately, the phrases were in Kachin, and blank stares were the only response. During this time other survivors made their way to join the small congregation around the embers of the plane, entirely accepting of the goodwill of the natives whom they saw standing there. Most flopped down, exhausted, to rest on the wet ground.

Then, suddenly, the atmosphere changed. Trotting up the hill came another warrior, alone. The warriors in front of them tensed noticeably. Dropping into a walk, he cautiously approached the group. He looked different from their present company, Sevareid noted: "He was a beautiful specimen of manhood with long, rippling legs. But he was different. His hair was long and tied in a knot behind his head. His face was longer, and his appearance was very much that of a Sioux Indian of the American plains." Looking around, the man singled out Sevareid and presented him with a piece of paper. It was the note from Jack Davies. Sevareid scribbled a reply, and the man, with the gift of the orange parachute silk and a silver dollar, turned and trotted back in the direction from which he had come.

Pleasantries and introductions concluded, the next move was to get Oswalt to a place of shelter. The village lay perhaps a mile farther on, and with Oswalt in a makeshift litter formed by two army jackets buttoned together, the tribesmen seemed happy enough to lead the little procession to their home. On the way Sevareid described passing through cultivated fields full of millet growing in rough terraces on the hillside. The village appeared to be made up of fifty or sixty thatch-covered bamboo houses nestling "in a planless huddle along a ravine halfway up the mountain ridge." The fronts of the houses were raised on stilts, with verandas running the width of each house. In the distance, across a deep gorge, were other houses. This appeared either to be a suburb of a bigger village or an outpost of it. As they approached, and to their intense relief, five passengers—Bill Stanton, Colonel Wang Pae Chae, and three American enlisted men—emerged from one of the houses. "Come on in," one young American shouted; "the chicken and eggs are swell!" It appeared that they had all landed close to the village and had each been brought in by villagers and provided with shelter and hospitality. As with Davies's experience at Ponyo, the survivors were taken to a large building in the center of the village, which appeared to the men to be a central dormitory. What Davies and his colleagues at Ponyo had seen was a *morung*, a prominent—and often grand—building usually sited at the entrance to the village designed as a place where the postpubescent children in the village lived communally and where they were taught what it meant to be an integrated member of the village, learning its culture, traditions, and customs. Boys and girls lived in separate dormitories, sleeping on a raised wooden platform that ran down each side of the building, with a circular stone fire pit in the center.

The survivors stepped between scuttling pigs—ubiquitous in every Naga village and useful for their ability to ensure that the ground remained clear of human and animal excrement—and were ushered into the imposing *morung*. Sevareid was impressed with the extensive bamboo piping system that carried water around the village. What he was not to know was that these systems had been designed primarily to ensure that the women and children were not exposed to the threat of losing their heads when collecting water at the nearest stream. As at Ponyo, they saw women. Had they known it, this was a good sign, as it indicated that the villagers expected no threat from their visitors. When potentially dangerous strangers were nearby, women and children would be safely kept out of sight.

The men had arrived in the Pangsha colony of Wenshoyl. The last time white men had been seen here, they had been involved in a battle that had cost a number of Pangsha men their lives. The survivors had barely reached the *morung* before the beautiful sound of the twin C-47 engines sent them scurrying outside once again, joined this time by the squealing pigs and children in a mayhem of excitement. Along the valley toward them flew the majestic aircraft, turning tightly above the village and dropping by parachute a dozen large bundles. The startling arrival of these gifts from the heavens caused a flurry of excitement in the village as eager young men rushed to recover the bundles and take as personal booty the rope and canvas covers in which they were wrapped. Despite some angry pushing and shoving—and noisy waving of *daos*—violence was averted and the bundles recovered. Among the parcels was another message:

> The most important thing is for you to remain where you are. This is absolutely imperative for several reasons. Do not go to the native village, as they probably are not friendly. Also be on guard for any natives that may approach you; as they may or may not be friendly. An effort is being made to inform the village chief that you are friendly, but this information will take some time to reach him. Do not antagonize any natives. We will drop you anything you may need, and if it is not in the code-groups of the air-ground liaison code we dropped with the panels, use the alphabet code-groups. . . .
>
> Again, do not leave the area you are now in, and keep the party together. If you follow instructions we will get you back to

the base much quicker. Be assured the entire wing is working on your rescue. Enclosed is a more complete air-ground liaison code.

It is clear from this message that from the moment the team at Chabua were able to plot the crash location they knew that the survivors were in danger. The wing intelligence officer, Major St. Clair McKelway, a celebrated journalist with *The New Yorker* in civilian life who knew Sevareid well from before the war (although he had no idea that Sevareid was in the CBI theater at the time), had almost certainly been briefed by Philip Adams at Mokokchung on the relations that existed between the British and the various peoples of the Naga Hills. He must have been told explicitly of the situation in the Patkoi Hills, given the specificity of the typewritten message dropped to the survivors. As intelligence officer, McKelway made it his task to seek out all relevant information about the nature of the country over which crews of the ATC would fly and in which they might find themselves if anything went wrong with their aircraft. At some stage that day or the following day McKelway spoke directly to Philip Adams. There was a telephone at both Kohima and Mokokchung, linking them to Shillong, that might have been utilized to elicit information about the area of the crash, and there was a radio telephone at Chabua in a "shack," as McKelway described it, which could connect the base with either of these locations. It was not secure, however, and all conversations were held in code to prevent Japanese eavesdropping. McKelway knew, therefore, that the survivors were in the midst of the lion's den and sought to warn them without panicking them unduly.

Sevareid read the note, looked around him, and shrugged his shoulders. They were inside the village, the locals seemed hospitable enough, and in any case Oswalt needed protection from the rain that threatened to arrive in the next few hours. Sevareid watched a group of important-looking tribesmen gather in a neighboring house, wearing elaborate headdresses to signify their rank, talking animatedly. He was too tired to think much of it. While he was contemplating these issues the C-47 made a wide sweep of the area as if awaiting something. Fortunately, the men cottoned on, quickly read the ground-signaling panels, and, using the code that had been sent, spelled out "Medical assistance needed." With a waggle of its wings the C-47 departed for the north, and within half a minute its comforting drone was but a memory.

As dusk began to fall the fourteen survivors in the village—they had no idea of its name—had sorted themselves out, stacked the gear dropped by parachute, and settled to rest in the *morung*. Oswalt's leg was by this time in a bad way. Clearly broken, it was badly swollen, and the skin around the break was dark blue. He would need medical attention soon if the leg were to be saved.

When it departed for home Wild's C-47 had radioed forward to Chabua the information that the survivors had asked for medical assistance. When it landed back at base nearly an hour later the aircraft was met by a delegation of four men on the apron, all wearing parachutes. As he approached the airfield Hugh Wild was instructed by control to refuel and prepare to return for his third trip over the Patkoi Hills that day.

The ATC wing surgeon at Dumbastapur was Lieutenant Colonel Don Flickinger, a Stanford-trained surgeon who had considerable experience of flying on search-and-rescue missions. As soon as Wild and Katzman had radioed to say that they had found the survivors, Brigadier General Edward Alexander had had Flickinger brought into the operations center. The men on the ground had indicated that they needed medical assistance. But what sort? Would it be sufficient to merely drop medical supplies to them and issue instructions by radio? It was agreed that Flickinger and two of his medical assistants would return in Hugh Wild's Gooney Bird and assess the situation from the air. As they were discussing the options Alexander—fearful of losing his wing surgeon, given all of the other medical needs at Chabua—gave Flickinger an explicit order: "You are not to parachute in there. That's official!" Without committing himself either way, Flickinger replied that he would let Alexander know what he came up with when in the air.

Flickinger had in fact decided that he would parachute in to join the survivors and administer the medical help that they had requested. No one else could do it, and he had no way of assessing from a distance how serious the injuries on the ground were. It was an extraordinary decision. As the ATC wing surgeon Flickinger had no need to risk his life in such a manner, but he unhesitatingly decided to jump. He indicated to his two assistants in the sick bay at Chabua that they didn't need to accompany him, but he would be pleased if they decided to do so. Flickinger had parachuted before— in Hawaii before the outbreak of war, and had torn the ligaments in one of his knees in so doing—but neither Sergeant Richard Passey nor Corporal William McKenzie had ever done so. They nevertheless accepted the challenge. The fourth man on the plane was Major St. Clair McKelway. He wanted to accompany the flight to see the terrain at first hand and to brief Flickinger during the journey on the nature of the people among whom the survivors had landed. Knowledge of the true nature of the Nagas of the Patkoi Hills, as described to him by McKelway on the flight, made Flickinger's decision to jump even more admirable. He knew he would be jumping directly into danger but was not to be diverted from his course. They agreed that at first light one of the ATC C-47s from Chabua would return and drop weapons and ammunition for the survivors as well as gifts for the Nagas.

Dusk was now settling over the Patkoi Hills when the weary survivors, resting in the *morung*, heard the sound of the C-47 yet again. "What could they be dropping now?" Sevareid thought grumpily as he struggled to his feet, his body feeling all the aches, abrasions, and strains of the parachute jump: a sore throat (caused by the jolt of the opening parachute—although he did not know this); bruised legs and shoulders from the ill-fitting straps; and cuts, bruises, and sprains from landing in the trees and chest-high brush. As he came out of the building and looked skyward he saw the C-47 at a much higher altitude than it had flown at earlier in the day and three parachutes descending in a neat clump. It took a few seconds to realize that each of the packages had legs. Flickinger had jumped quickly and calmly when Hugh Wild had turned in the cockpit and signaled him to do so and had been quickly followed by the slightly less sanguine Passey and McKenzie, who later admitted to much nervousness about the prospect of leaving a perfectly good airplane and committing themselves to parachutes without ever having received any training.

On the ground Sevareid was astonished at the sight, instantly recognizing the significance of what he was watching. Men were coming, of their own volition, to help them! He had not considered, in his wildest dreams, this outcome to their predicament and was humbled by the personal commitment men were making to those whom they didn't know, yet who needed their help. Running excitedly out of the village, he met Don Flickinger as the surgeon landed. Unlike Sevareid, Flickinger was the epitome of calm, as Sevareid wrote:

> I got to the crest of the steep slope as the first jumper floated past, missing the summit by a scant few yards. I could see the insignia of a lieutenant colonel on his jacket shoulders. He grinned at me and I shouted foolishly: "Here! We're here in the village." He held up a finger in a crisp gesture, like a man strolling past on a sidewalk, and said in a conversational tone: "Be with you in a minute." Half weeping, half laughing over the wonderful absurdity of the meeting, I scrambled down the slope and slid to a halt before him as he was brushing dirt from his clothes and beginning to unwrap protective bandage from his knees. He was a slim, closely knit man of about thirty-five, with cropped hair, and vivid dark eyes in a brown, taut face. He smiled easily as we introduced ourselves. "I'm Don Flickinger," he said. "I'm the wing surgeon. Saw you needed a little help."

It was a bizarre, deeply melodramatic moment, and in a heartbeat Sevareid realized that here was the man who would take charge of the party, not just bind up Oswalt's leg. Before long they were safely in the *morung*, Flickinger setting Oswalt's leg with bamboo splints by the light of a torch, surrounded by curious natives while most of the survivors lay on mats, mentally and physically exhausted by what had turned out to be an extraordinary day. In the center of the building a fire burned, villagers eating the remains of an unidentifiable animal whose remains lay on the embers. Sevareid looked around him, his composure recovered. All was well with the world—or so he thought.

13

MONGSEN

One of the local men watching Flickinger set Oswalt's leg, unknown to his visitors, was Mongsen, one of the fiercest warriors of the tribe whose previous encounters with white men had not been happy ones. He had been at the wrong end of the massed Lee-Enfield rifles of Williams's sepoys in 1936 and Gerty's in 1939. Now he squatted with a child in his arms, patiently waiting for the American doctor to finish his ministrations. After leaving the uncomplaining Oswalt, Flickinger needed no persuading to examine an ugly abscess under the little girl's ear, a large growth that not only disfigured her but potentially threatened her life. Showing Mongsen how to break an antibiotic tablet in his mouth and spit it into the child's mouth, he gently refused the egg that Mongsen offered in payment. This act of kindness easily disarmed the hostility of one potential enemy. It precipitated a makeshift surgery for Flickinger, however, as he treated the ailments of survivors and villagers alike in the torchlit darkness of the *morung*.

It was in Flickinger's nature to be generous—after all, he had just risked his life to parachute into Pangsha (although he too had no idea of the actual identity of the village or its violent history)—but he intuitively understood the need for gentle measures to win over the confidence of the Nagas, about whom he had been briefed in general terms by McKelway, and to wear down any residual hostility that might exist against the newcomers. The night had now closed in with an intensity not before experienced by those used to the pseudodarkness of electrically fueled towns and cities across

America. And it was raining. The dark blue clouds Sevareid had
spotted late that afternoon had arrived on cue with the onset of
darkness to tip their contents out in vast torrents across the mountains. The monsoon period between April and October brought
nightly drenchings of often fearsome intensity that made the men
wonder that the thatched roof over their heads could contain the
volume of water that fell upon them. It was cold too. At a height
of 6,000 feet above sea level the temperature during the hours of
darkness dropped to just above freezing. At night the villagers each
wrapped him- or herself in a single blanket, which seemed the only
concession they made to the cold; they spent their waking hours
otherwise, male and female, apart from a tiny loincloth, entirely
naked.

Silence settled over the *morung*. By common agreement all—
villagers and visitors alike—determined that the time had come to
sleep. There would be more talk and more medical consultations
in the morning, no doubt. Several of the survivors, Sevareid noted,
needed no excuse, exhausted bodies lying stretched out on the mats,
fast asleep, in the smoky interior of the building. There didn't appear to be a chimney. Sevareid dozed off with the others and before
long was in a deep sleep. Then suddenly he was awake again, with
a start, as the sound of massed voices approached and two armed
natives jumped into the *morung* over the sleeping bodies of those at
the door. After a heart-stopping moment in which he thought they
were being attacked he heard, to his great relief, Davies's voice calling out his Livingstonian welcome. The party from Ponyo had arrived. Now wide awake, the two parties greeted each other warmly,
and while the fire was restoked, all began to share their stories of
what had been—for all of them—the most eventful day of their lives.
Duncan Lee handed around his bottle of Carew's gin, and they celebrated its survival along with their own. Nineteen men now shared
the *morung*, the only two missing being Corporal Basil Lemmon
and Second Lieutenant Charles Felix. Perhaps they were in the jungle, separated from their fellows. The natives most surely would find

them in the morning and bring them in safely. It was after midnight before they were all able, finally, to drop off to sleep.

The cold dawn arrived all too quickly. Shivering, wrapped in blankets, the men stirred the embers of the fire and ate an unappetizing meal of cold tinned meat from the rations dropped the previous afternoon. Before long the comforting drone of the C-47 was heard again, and it was soon circling the village, dropping bundles of supplies, swinging down under their parachutes, accompanied by the excited squealing of the children and the shouting of the men as they rushed to collect them all. With the drop came a note from McKelway: "The British political agent* is with us this morning, trying to identify your position from the air. The land party will start out as soon as we know where you are. Important that you stay where you are until we get to you. The agent is sure there are unfriendly Nagas all round you. They will have to be fixed before you can go through them safely. It may take a week or more to get to you. Let us know your needs."

Understanding flooded Sevareid's consciousness. So these were the famous Nagas! He knew of them, of course, not least from his conversations with the British tea planters at Chabua, but for some reason in the excitement of the previous twenty-four hours his mind had not registered that they might be guests of these fearsome people. Sevareid looked around him. The Nagas had been hospitable and civil so far, but how long would this last? He had already noticed some near-ugly scenes that morning as young men had fought over the bundles dropped from the skies, threatening each other with their vicious *dao*s and scowling at Sevareid, who had attempted to assert his authority among the melee.

The morning—it was now Tuesday, August 3—was clearly one for decisions. The first was made for them by one of the Naga leaders, a man wearing a richly woven red blanket and a red conical

---

*The local political agent was headquartered in the town of Dibrugarh, seventeen miles from Chabua. It is clear that he was in communication with Philip Adams in Mokokchung.

hat, adorned with boar's tusks and a large hornbill feather with a black stripe. By means of sign language he demonstrated to Flickinger, Davies, and Sevareid, the recognizable leaders of the American-Chinese group, that they would have to move out of the *morung* and away from the village. Sevareid suspected that the Nagas were none too happy with the fact that the falling parachutes were knocking great holes in the village's fields of maize, and it made sense that the guests move to an area dedicated to them; there wasn't space in Wenshoyl for nineteen newcomers. Flickinger's view (which he kept to himself) was that separation from the village made it easier for them to be attacked, if the Nagas decided to turn on their visitors.

The man pointed to a grassy ridge back in the direction of the wrecked plane where he evidently wanted them to stay and gave a few instructions to those around him. The young men of the village rushed off to cut bamboo. Within what Davies recalled as three or four hours, three substantial shelters had been erected—Neveu estimated that each was about twenty-five feet long and twelve feet wide—one of which was allocated to the civilians and officers, one to the enlisted men, and one to storage for the supplies. Neveu was horrified at this forced segregation but said nothing to Flickinger about it. To his mind they were all in it together, and ensuring the group's survival meant mucking in together rather than re-creating the hierarchies of a different world. It is clear that Flickinger, who had unobtrusively taken charge, had a different view, however, believing that the structures of military discipline needed to be maintained even in a survival situation.

The consignment received that morning had included enough lightweight M1 carbines for each man to have one, together with ammunition. At least they would be able to defend themselves in the event of an attack, either by Nagas or Japanese. On seeing one of the weapons a Naga nervously imitated the sound of a rifle report, which indicated that although the villagers didn't possess weapons themselves, they knew precisely what they were. It was good, the Americans considered, that the Nagas now knew their visitors were armed. Although their northern neighbors did have weapons, the Pangsherites didn't, although it was clear that they had been trying to secure them. A report from Mokokchung dated August 6, 1940, noted that two guns sent to Pangsha by the village of Ukha had been confiscated by Sangbah of Chingmei, working on behalf of the government.

During the morning a small group of men from Ponyo arrived at Wenshoyl, distinctive because of their long hair tied in ponytails. Using sign language, they explained that they had discovered another survivor, but chopping movements to the leg indicated that he was injured. Sevareid, together with Richard Passey, Sergeant Glen Kittleson, and William McKenzie, immediately set off with the group, carrying a stretcher that had been dropped that morning. During the journey Sevareid nervously wondered whether in fact this was a trap by the Nagas to separate the group and kill the rescue party when they were away from the camp. But his fears were allayed when they arrived at the still-smoking wreck of the aircraft. Ponyo men were beating strips of aluminum from the ruins and carting away anything they could salvage. Lying next to the blackened pit was the body of Charles Felix. He had not survived the crash after all. One of his legs had been severed on impact. McKenzie and Passey dug a grave for him, and, with the intrigued Ponyos looking on, McKenzie committed him to the earth with a reading of the Lord's Prayer. Somberly they returned to their newly built camp outside Wenshoyl. Now that the sad fate of Charles Felix had been determined, where was Basil Lemmon?

While the rescue party was away, Don Flickinger had organized the encampment. It was clear that rescue might take some time and that it would entail walking out through the green mass of formidable mountains, which currently held them captive, toward India. In the meantime, the survivors would need to organize themselves to ensure that they remained a coherent military party. Sevareid was right: Flickinger was a natural leader and took to the task effortlessly. His right to lead the group was never questioned, and all settled comfortably under his calm authority. A bamboo fence was built around the camp (for psychological security only, as it would not have served as a protective palisade), and young men of the village were induced to cut down the long grass around the camp by the offer of the much-prized tin cans that when full contained American rations. The survivors were all given duties, and a night guard was instituted, with a man undertaking sentry duty for two hours at a time during the hours of darkness. Jack Davies was responsible for organizing the retrieval of the C-47 loads when they fell; Duncan Lee managed the supply tent and its contents; Bill Stanton would take charge of signaling the aircraft when they were overhead; Oswalt operated the radio; Sevareid was diarist and chaplain; Giguere was cook; Neveu was responsible for the guard roster. After a few days the two Chinese officers took over the cooking of the rice, which they did superbly.

One of Jack Davies's additional duties was to oversee bartering with the villagers. Flickinger was concerned lest bartering get out of control and create animosity or squabbles, a situation that could quickly destroy trust between the two groups and lead to hostility. Whatever happened, diplomatic relations with the Nagas needed to be maintained at a careful equilibrium. The members of the American-Chinese party were not servants or masters of the villagers; neither were they overlords or in any way to be considered a threat. They were to exist in a degree of peaceful equanimity until such time as arrangements could be made for them to leave. Already all sorts of material, much of which the Americans regarded as rubbish—such as string, waste canvas, tin cans, and the like—had become prized targets for acquisition by the Nagas. A carefully controlled trade would ensure, Flickinger hoped, that blood was never drawn in arguments over who got what and for what price. In exchange the visitors were offered firewood, eggs—many old and rotten, though something of a local delicacy—scrawny chickens, and sometimes other meat such as pig and goat. So passed Tuesday, August 3.

On the following day Sevareid noticed a number of new Nagas in the village. Who could they be? The early-morning C-47 drop

brought a new message from McKelway and the news that the local
British political agent was in the aircraft.

> You are within eight miles of what is called British control terri-
> tory, some sixty miles southeast of Mokokchung. There is British
> sub divisional officer there. Try to get word to him by the natives,
> but don't leave the place you are in now. He is known to the na-
> tives as the Sahib of Mokokchung. Our land party will start from
> there tomorrow or next day according to present plans. British
> political officer flying with us advises you to be as friendly as pos-
> sible with natives but not to relax vigilance. To stay together as
> much as possible and not to wander about singly. You know best,
> being on spot, but he thinks display of arms will make them sus-
> picious and perhaps cause them to attack you. . . . Reason you
> shouldn't start out before we give the word is that there are sav-
> age Nagas between you and Mokokchung who have to be fixed
> by the British first. . . . Try to contact the head man of Chingmei,
> six miles due west of you. He is said to be a good fellow, loyal to
> British.

Sevareid was able to ascertain that the new Nagas who had appeared during the day were no less than the headman of whom
Adams had spoken—Chingmak—together with his two sons, Sangbah and Tangbang. The message that they were to oversee the
safety of the survivors had reached Chingmei from Mokokchung
in less than two days, an extraordinary feat. The message had been
rushed from village to village, and when it had reached Chingmei,
Chingmak took it upon himself personally to enforce the sahib of
Mokokchung's wishes, knowing as he did the danger that the unsuspecting white men would be in. If the survivors had known this,
it would have considerably settled their nerves. In fact, Chingmak
and his sons did much more than make their presence felt in the
village, which undoubtedly had a sobering effect on any hotheads
in Pangsha who might have thought of taking revenge on the white
men for their humiliation at the hands of Adams. They also placed

protection parties of Chang warriors north and south of the village along the Langnyu River to warn of any intruders. In his diary Sevareid described Chingmak as "old man, slightly bent, not unkindly, rather intelligent face. Red blanket, white cowrie shells as ear ornaments (how did they get up here from sea?). Ornate red-feather headdress and heavy chest tattooing. . . . Squats and smiles by hour, pleased to puff cigarettes. Doesn't seem to have any suggestions." The red blanket was his sign of office as a British-appointed *gaonbura*. Sangbah, whom Sevareid estimated to be about thirty-five years of age, also wore a red blanket. Sevareid didn't at the time realize that Sangbah was Chingmak's son. He had noticed that Sangbah's presence, however, had made a distinct impression on the Pangsha Nagas. Sangbah had a natural air of authority, and though he appeared to speak a different dialect than the locals, they obeyed his calm injunctions with alacrity. What is more, he understood a few words of English, and by speaking of Mokokchung—where of course he had gone to school—he was able to make Sevareid understand that he was there as the survivors' protector. Sevareid was able to deduce his loyalties soon after meeting him when, smilingly, he pointed to the Pangsha villagers and drew his hand across his throat.

The days that followed began to fit a pattern as the survivors organized their existence, maintained friendly but careful relations with the Pangsha villagers, regulated the trade in bartered goods to prevent price inflation, and received regular gifts from C-47s flying south from Chabua. The intense rain that fell every night required daily repairs to the thatched roofs of their *basha*s, and the camp was gradually improved with benches and other structures made with bamboo. The natives seemed content to accept the presence among them—albeit in their own encampment—of these uninvited guests, and Sevareid noticed over time a variety of different Nagas who came to have a look at these strange people who had descended on them so suddenly, bizarrely floating down under canopies of white silk. Apart from those they had glimpsed during Mills's, Pawsey's, and Adams's previous expeditions, these were the first white (and Chinese) men the Nagas of the Patkois had ever seen. The survivors were a little like exhibits in a zoo and accepted their status as such with good humor. A permanent gaggle of wide-eyed children sat at the bamboo fence, peering through at the fascinating and otherworldly specimens on the other side. In addition to the Changs from Chingmei, a small group of Ponyo men appeared to be in the Pangsha camp almost permanently, possibly because they were traditionally hand-in-glove with Pangsha but also perhaps because they felt some ownership over "their" small party of parachutists.

There was loot too. In addition to the leftovers and bartered goods now flooding into Pangsha—not to mention the aluminum and other salvage stripped from the wreck of Flight 12420—Brigadier General Edward Alexander also met Adams's request for provisions to be dropped to the Nagas to pay them for their protection of the survivors and to buy their continued support on the basis that greed would trump any residual hostility that might otherwise flare into violence and even murder. At noon on Thursday, August 5, the daily C-47 dropped bags of rice for the village, an exercise that came close to rebounding on the survivors, as the bags were dropped by free fall from 200 feet and nearly struck a number of the villagers who had rushed out to ensure that they grabbed them first. The arrival each day of the C-47 from Chabua almost became a problem in itself as villagers scrambled and fought for possession of the ropes, wrapping, and parachutes, which had become prized possessions. The Pangsha elders tried to maintain discipline, but it was an uphill battle. Davies and Sevareid overcame the problem by appointing twenty Naga "retrievers," giving them armbands and rewarding them with cotton parachute cloth at the end of each drop. The survivors didn't complain about the extent of the largesse that their comrades at Chabua loaded into the C-47 each day. There was clearly a degree of guesswork at the air base about each load. What would be useful either to the survivors or the villagers? Two large boxes of tea had no use to the Nagas, so the tea was used as a rather fragrant form of bedding, but no rationale could be found for the three and a half pairs of socks, two pairs of underpants, and 110 undershirts that arrived that day. It looked as if the Chabua quartermaster was having a clear-out. One of the many items dropped on the men that astonished Jack Davies was canned water—American drinking water canned somewhere in the United States. It was a nice thought but entirely inappropriate in what must have been one of the wettest parts of the world. "Never mind that it was the monsoon season, that we were camped 100 yards from a sparkling mountain stream, which flowed into a cascading river at the bottom of the valley. I assume that the rescue routine prescribed dumping American water on American boys downed anywhere in the world."

Each day that passed enabled the survivors gradually to relax about their hosts' intentions. Curious children became a feature of the camp, watching their guests' every move. Jack Davies recalled waking every morning to the studied observation of "a squatting Naga or two intently watching me gather my wits. From dawn to dusk we were under observation, objects of endless wonderment." The children particularly enjoyed listening to the strange sounds of music on Oswalt's radio receiver, broadcast all the way from another world—San Francisco. Oswalt's was a sorry task, as during the days of their sojourn in Pangsha he heard the desperate calls from a number of aircraft going down (most with no survivors) somewhere over the Hump.

Flickinger was by this stage running daily surgeries for the villagers. Many suffered from ulcerated sores, which they allowed Flickinger to treat with sulfanilamide powder, an early antibiotic powder in widespread use by US forces in the period before penicillin went into mass production. This appeared to work spectacularly well, and "sulfa" tablets were also given for intestinal complaints. Jack Davies noted, however, that Flickinger was allowed to treat only "men, boys, and infants. Even in illness the women were kept away from us."

All the while pieces of baggage thrown from Flight 12420 during the desperate attempt to lose weight when the port engine failed were brought in, including Jack Davies's briefcase, with its contents miraculously intact. During the air drop on August 5 a copy of instructions regarding the rescue party was also dropped to keep the survivors informed about the progress of events. It read:

> [Rescue] party, led by Lieutenant LaBonte of radio air-warning station, will proceed to Mokokchung. Here large party will form and start for scene of wreck. Porters and guards will be ready and have been arranged for. Mr. Adams, accompanied by Lt. La-Bonte, will lead rescue party. Meantime, thirty guards have started to stranded party for protective purposes if necessary. Coolies to carry stretcher cases, if any, will be available. Trip in and out from Mokokchung will require between two and three weeks. Advisable to put a plane or two a day over the stranded party for moral effect on natives and to pick up messages. Two thousand silver rupees have been furnished Mr. Adams. One half-ton of salt should be dropped on village where stranded party is as reward to Nagas.

On August 5 a pig was slaughtered for their guests by the villagers, and the following day, despite relentless rain and cloud that prevented an air drop, a young *mithan* bull was hauled reluctantly into the encampment, bellowing nervously as if it understood its fate. It was slaughtered after some ceremony by the Nagas, and Don Flickinger then proceeded to skin and gut the carcass expertly. It was the cause for a joint celebration. Sevareid recorded in his diary:

> Our camp given two quarters. Vast audience, festive spirit. Natives bring in two bamboo poles, tie bull's hoof to one pole, and after another long speech thrust it upright in ground. Then Colonel [Flickinger] asked plant second pole, tying one our hoofs to it. Flick tries make speech: "We who came to you from skies . . . oh, hell, let's sing them a song." We gathered and sang "I Been Working on the Railroad," "He's a Jolly Good Fellow," and as

afterthought the national anthem. They listened solemnly, much impressed. A gaudy ceremonial spear with dyed clusters of bright red hair on shaft stuck upright before camp. We now appear to be officially friends by treaty. Feel much more secure.

During the festivities, they suddenly found another cause for celebration. Corporal Basil Lemmon came limping in, his arms around two Ponyo men. He was exhausted. Only after a day or so of rest was he able to tell his story. Coming down alone, he had been fearful of being in territory occupied by the Japanese and so avoided contact with humans. He had no idea where he was or of how to survive in such a hostile environment. Without food, shelter, or protection from either insects during the day or the freezing elements at night, he stumbled into a Ponyo field shelter and was found there by men working in the maize fields. He was kindly treated, warmed by a fire, fed with rice, and carried the three miles or so to Pangsha.

14

THE SAHIB OF MOKOKCHUNG

As each day passed the men gradually learned more of the efforts being made to rescue them. On Saturday, April 7, they received another typewritten note from McKelway stating that the rescue party, traveling overland from Mokokchung, would arrive on or about August 15. Sevareid wondered about the guards dispatched for "protective purposes," not suspecting that, under Sangbah's control, they were already in place. Sangbah ordered that new shelters be built in good time to prepare for the arrival of what looked likely to be a large rescue party. On Monday, August 9—a full week after the crash—a number of new faces joined the encampment, settling in with Chingmak and Sangbah and disdaining the Pangsha Nagas. One distinctive member of this group wore a leopard skin, obviously the prize of a previous encounter in the wilderness that denoted his prowess as a hunter. Unknown to the men, this was Tangbang, Sangbah's brother, who delighted in demonstrating his skill with the crossbow. It was a powerful weapon, its foot-long arrow astonishingly accurate out to seventy-five feet and so powerful that it required the user to lie on his back and cock it with his feet. Tangbang had been managing the "protective" party along the Langnyu River, positioned there to act as an early warning of an enemy approach. The Japanese were as close as three days' march away in Burma; if they found out about the survivors and determined to pursue them, the Nagas would have very early knowledge of their approach.

Otherwise, life settled into something of a routine. It could even have been enjoyable if it weren't for the fleas that plagued some of the men at night, the endless rain, and the nightly temperature drop. On August 9, in a letter to his wife, Jack Davies captured something of the situation:

> It is afternoon and it is raining, as it does most of the time, for this is monsoon season. I am sitting on a piece of a parachute on a blanket on a ground sheet on the ground and leaning against a sapling post which forms one of the uprights to our palm and weed thatched hut. I can hear the stream 100 yards back of me rushing down the steep side of the mountain. Across the valley strata of India-silk mist are drifting along the face of the opposite slope, whose peaks are lost in the pale gray overcast. Duncan [Lee] is sitting opposite me with one shoe off and one shoe on reflectively scratching his leg. Eric [Sevareid] lies rolled up in a blanket fast asleep at the other end of our nine-man basha.

One night, under a clear, cold moonlit sky, the men sat around the campfire singing songs from home. "At such moments," Sevareid admitted, "I love it here, wouldn't be elsewhere." The place was beautiful and atmospheric. Despite their predicament, the men felt that they were among friends. "Layers of white mist would creep over the dark hills like glaciers in motion, and once at midnight we were transfixed by the sight of a perfect rainbow by moonlight." Feeling something of a fraud, as he hadn't stepped inside a church for years, Sevareid led the "Church Parade" on Sunday, April 8, fashioning it as a memorial service for Charles Felix, who was now known, since the rescue of Lemmon, to have been the only casualty of Flight 12420.

On one occasion a high-flying Japanese reconnaissance plane flew overhead; on another a flight of what they thought were Zeros went racing down the valley. The survivors' obsession with their own predicament didn't allow them to consider that the Japanese would not be interested in them: with the massive American effort along the Brahmaputra and the Ledo Road, the Japanese had bigger fish to fry, but the flights nevertheless caused them some anxiety. A further cause of anxiety was an article in the *Statesman*, published in New Delhi, that was dropped to them. It described their predicament and mentioned some of them—including Seva-reid—by name. If the Japanese were close by and looking out for downed fliers, this was a security breach of an entirely unnecessary kind. A slit trench was dug so that if they were attacked, Oswalt at least would be protected from bomb blasts. A message from Brig-adier General Alexander at Chabua asked them to keep an eye out for Japanese activity, but the truth was that there was precious little to see, hidden away as they were in this mountain vastness. The closest Japanese presence to Pangsha was at the Naga village of Khamti, thirty-eight miles as the crow flew to the southeast on the Chindwin. A number of scattered villages lay in between, but Japanese patrols from the Eighteenth Division rarely ventured into these hills. A determined patrol, with Naga help, would take three days to cross the hills to reach the survivors. Flickinger nevertheless got the men to rehearse preparations for an attack.

When the weather allowed, the daily air drop began to equip the survivors for the next stage of their journey: the strenuous march over the mountains. Socks and boots swung down under cotton parachutes—silk was too scarce to use for the supply bundles—and although the 'chutes worked reasonably well, a number of Naga young men were nearly injured by these loads, which fell unexpect-edly faster than those attached to their silken cousins. Flickinger, to the great amusement of the watching Nagas, tried to organize calis-thenics for the men in an attempt to prepare them physically for the long march to come. To relieve any latent boredom he also orga-nized a spear-throwing contest with the Pangsha men. Amazingly, Richard Passey turned out to be an athlete of note (a ski champion in his native Utah, Sevareid believed) and very nearly won the con-test, almost beating the Pangsha warriors at their own game. Sat-isfactorily, for political reasons at least, a chuckling Naga won and scuttled away with his prize—three tin cans—clutched to his chest.

Sevareid observed that they had by now been able to iden-tify a range of personalities among the Pangsha Nagas. Most, he considered, were "very friendly, laugh loudly, love practical jokes." He was particularly struck by the man they all called "Moon-sang," whose child Flickinger was treating with antibiotics. He clearly was a leader who generated considerable respect in the village. Sevareid described him as a man with a cultivated face and "expressive, intelligent eyes." It would have been no surprise to Sevareid to learn that this was the man who had led Pangsha for many years to head-hunting glory. He was not intimidated by the white men, merely intrigued by the power of their machinery, the efficacy of their medicine, their determination of purpose, and their self-confident representation of a new and extraordinary world outside the borders of Pangsha's self-contained green kingdom. As a man who knew about power, he was impressed with that which these men epitomized: the masses of material goods that fell almost daily from the sky; the skill of the hands that had so lovingly and perfectly shaped the great silver *kepruo*s in the sky (even if they were occasionally to crash, which signified only that, great as these men were, they were not infallible); and their obvious unity of purpose.

Mongsen was an intelligent, inquisitive, and pragmatic man. He wanted to learn about the outside world, one that had forced itself on him so astonishingly six years before. Before then stories of the white man, of guns, of medicine, and of the trappings of civilization that had washed into the far reaches of Assam in the late nineteenth century had been merely apocryphal: heard and talked about but never seen. The extraordinary effort that the white men in the sky were making to sustain the survivors on the ground and the quick arrival of Chingmak and the Chingmei Nagas, obviously under instruction from the sahib of Mokokchung, demonstrated to him that he and his fellow villagers were spectators in a much bigger and fascinating story. He was convinced, correctly, that his family and the wider tribe were honorable participants in this narrative by virtue of the care they had provided for their uninvited but welcome guests and their obedience to the instructions he had received months before to protect—rather than to behead—any parachutists who floated down from the skies. He was content that this should be so. Quietly and patiently, Mongsen awaited the arrival of the sahib of Mokokchung, whom he had last had cause to meet, in different circumstances, in 1939.

Then, without warning, as Friday, August 13, was drawing to a close, after nearly fourteen days in the wilderness (and two days before they had been told to expect deliverance), the noise of a large approaching group of Nagas, made distinctive by the cadenced chant of their marching song, could be heard rising and falling in the far distance, penetrating across the valley and through the low-hanging mist to the ears of the startled survivors. The noise grew gradually louder. The survivors gathered together and stood in quiet expectation. Out of the valley emerged their deliverers, climbing strongly and purposefully, their war chant announcing their arrival with gusto and immense pride in their authority and self-evident power. Sixty Naga warriors in their native accouterments, but brandishing ancient shotguns, led a train of forty Naga porters carrying their distinctive matted conical packs on their backs. At their head, in a blue polo-necked shirt, long, dark blue flannel shorts, and heavy brogue walking shoes, carrying a thin bamboo cane, was the sahib of Mokokchung himself. It was at once impressive and humbling. The chanting died down, and all was momentary silence. Even the chattering Pangsha children stood still, hushed by the spectacle before them, drinking in a scene of wonderment. It was another Livingstonian moment. But it didn't last long. With a splurge of self-conscious energy the 100-strong column spilled into the survivors' encampment, taking over and asserting their authority noisily and pompously.

Sevareid, for once in his life, had nothing to say. Standing in front of him was a slim, fair-haired young man, quiet and calm in demeanor, who was "king of these dark and savage hills." He had a natural authority, derived as much by his calm intelligence as by his position as the emissary of the king-emperor and the small army he had brought with him. "Adams was unforgettable," he was to tell *Reader's Digest* in 1944. "Soft-spoken and with a genuine Oxford accent, he came with savage guards, with scores of coolies, with peppermints and a chess set. He had the air of one dropping in for tea. He was the 'sahib of Mokokchung' whom Sangbah had often mentioned to us in reverential terms as the real king of these wild hills." Sevareid, for all his contempt for the British Empire and his disregard for British colonialism, could not but wonder at a system that was able to transplant a young man from the fields and villages of Sussex, via the University of Cambridge, into a situation where he was responsible for administering life on the edge of the world. It was almost surreal, but in fact very real.

With Adams came a handful of emissaries of the other great empire to which most of the survivors themselves belonged, the United States of America. These were men who were part of the USAAF's aircraft warning scheme in the Naga Hills far to the south of the Patkoi Hills a hundred miles east of Kohima, which watched over the Chindwin for Japanese aircraft en route to Allied targets farther north. Lieutenant Andrew "Buddy" LaBonte had come with a radio, with which the survivors for the first time could talk to the world they had left behind on August 2. He was accompanied by Staff Sergeant John Lee DeChaine.* These men were already vastly experienced in looking after themselves in the Naga-inhabited hills above the Chindwin (albeit in territory that was on friendly terms with the British administrators), having been part of the aircraft warning unit since it had been established in late 1942. Adams's Mokokchung-based factotum, Emlong, who had accompanied the first expedition in 1936, was described by Sevareid as a potbellied and powerful man "who wore a leopard skin, spoke a few words of English, and was a famous tiger hunter." The Naga guards were mercenaries recruited from the Konyak people in the villages close to Mokokchung; most were desperate for a piece of martial glory. They all knew, of course, of the previous expeditions

---

*Some accounts include Captain J. J. Dwyer, Sergeant Joe Merritt, Sergeant Kenneth Coleman, Corporal Anthony Giota, and Private Frank Oropeza. Sevareid, however, who captured every detail of the rescue, was explicit that Adams was accompanied only by LaBonte and DeChaine.

to these parts and wanted to be part of the opportunity to demonstrate their superiority over those distant "savages" in the Patkoi
Hills. Managing them was going to be a task in itself. Unlike the
situation in 1936, when a full company of the Assam Rifles was able
to accompany Mills and Fürer-Haimendorf, no disciplined troops
were available in 1943. The Assam Rifles were scattered across the
eastern Naga Hills, supporting the Assam Regiment in protecting
the approaches to India from the Japanese across the Chindwin
in Burma. Eager but relatively ill-disciplined bands of young Naga
men recruited from the western hills for the duration of the expedition would have to suffice.*

The arrival of the marching column was managed in a way that
seemed designed to demonstrate its unassailable authority. The
Naga guards exerted their superiority over the Pangsha Nagas by
contemptuous looks and a haughty swagger, fingering the shotguns
that denoted a power far beyond anything these Pangsha creatures
could ever consider or attain. By their association with the sahib
of Mokokchung they were a breed apart, and they made sure that
the men of Pangsha were aware of it. The porters immediately set
to work cutting bamboo to build a proper palisade around the encampment, as if to assert their role in providing protection to the
air-crash survivors and to demonstrate distrust of the perfidious
Pangsherites. A *basha* was quickly assembled for Adams's use and
his portable camp table opened outside it and laid for supper. The
separation of Adams from the rest of them and the attention paid
to him by his Naga factotum and his servant Shouba all delivered
a series of positive images with regard to his position and prestige
to the Pangsherites—if, that is, there was any doubt. He dined alone
that night, both Nagas and survivors keeping a respectful distance.
The dignity of the king-emperor in faraway London was reflected
in no small part by the behavior of the sahib of Mokokchung, and

---

*It was across these hills that the Japanese invasion of India would come in March
1944. It wasn't turned back until June, in bloody fighting at Kohima and Imphal.
See Lyman, *Japan's Last Bid for Victory*.

Adams was acutely aware of this simple though profound reality. Watching all this palaver, Jack Davies quipped that he was disappointed that Adams didn't dress for dinner.

While the new column settled into the encampment in a fury of activity, and before it got too dark, Philip Adams introduced himself to the survivors in an almost shy, diffident way. He was far from the ignorant, bumptious colonial administrator of Sevareid's imagination. Here was an intelligent, cultured, and empathetic man. He wore his authority lightly, but it was clear that he was immensely respected by those who knew him personally as well as those who had only heard of him by reputation. As they had heard already from Major McKelway, Adams had been sure that Mongsen and the Pangsha leaders would obey his injunctions about looking after air-crash survivors, but he wasn't entirely sure what the men of Ponyo would do, given that they remained outside Mokokchung's jurisdiction and no longer had any British influence from within Burma now that it was under the control of the Japanese. He had accordingly made haste to get here, the column leaving Mokokchung on Saturday, August 7. The column had made the journey across the mountains in six days and five nights. In the meantime, he had asked Chingmak to assert a strong presence in the encampment to ensure the immediate safety of the survivors.

Adams quietly explained the recent history of both Pangsha and Ponyo, and for the first time Flickinger, Sevareid, and the other survivors were able to appreciate the potential predicament into which they had inadvertently fallen. But all, so far, was well. The Pangsha Nagas would be recompensed for their care of their visitors by a substantial gift of salt, a precious commodity that was rare in these hills. Adams was able to tell them something of Chingmak and his sons. Sangbah, now back in Chingmei recovering from a fever, had spent a short time in Mokokchung at a mission school at the urging of his father, who wanted him to understand the ways of the British. His brother Tangbang was a considerable character in his own right, a celebrity perhaps in modern parlance, who had seventeen heads to his name and a reputation as a warrior even greater than that of Mongsen. The crossbow arrow they had seen him fire was normally tipped with poison. Adams had himself been injured in the shoulder the year before by one such weapon during a skirmish and had survived only because the poison was old.

The primary weakness of the column was the fact that the Naga guards recruited for the purpose of escorting Adams to Pangsha were themselves a volatile lot and caused him more worry, Sevareid observed, than did Pangsha. It took all his powers as a leader simply to ensure that the guards remained in order. They had come, so they thought, to join with the British to punish the men of Pangsha, and they wanted a slice of the action, as their fathers and brothers had had—with much glory—in 1936, 1937, and 1939. Two young guards, overcome by greed, snatched some tin cans from Corporal Stanley Waterbury and refused to return them. It took the threat by Adams of the confiscation of their *daos* before the guilty parties submitted and were punished by demotion to the ranks of the porters for two days. Adams was quiet and gentle, Sevareid observed, but was able to exercise an iron fist when required.

Final preparations were being made for the march to Mokokchung. The daily C-47 drops provided boots and stores for those undertaking the trek—ordered through Lieutenant LaBonte's radio (operated by a crank handle)—and salt for the people of Pangsha: one and a half tons of it in forty-pound bags, seventy-five of them in total. Again, death or permanent injury was avoided only by serendipity, as the bags came down by free drop and some close shaves were recorded among the eager young men who were tempted to run out and catch them as they fell. The Chinese officers fashioned a chair from bamboo for the immobile Sergeant Oswalt; another reluctant bull was slaughtered for a farewell feast; and by the evening of August 17 the entire party—some 120 men—was ready to leave the encampment in Pangsha the following morning. The people of Pangsha had behaved in an exemplary manner to the survivors and perhaps had enjoyed the sojourn among them of their heaven-sent guests. Jack Davies observed that "instead of decapitating us, the savages adopted us. I suppose it was because of

the manner of our advent into their midst. If we had not come bil-
lowing down to them from above, if we had entered their territory
on the ground, across fiercely contested territorial boundaries, we
would have been ambushed and our skulls added to the village's
collection of trophies. The same might well have happened had
we tried to stay on at the long house after the first night of hospitality." One man in particular had reason to be grateful for the unexpected visit. Sevareid wrote, "As we sat on our blankets for a last
smoke before retiring, a visitor came in to see Colonel Flickinger.
It was Mongsen, the warrior with the gentle eyes, whose baby the
Colonel had saved from death. At the Colonel's feet he laid a beautiful crossbow of polished red wood inlaid with pieces of yellowing
ivory. It was without doubt his most precious possession."

Jack Davies expressed genuine sadness at saying farewell to
Pangsha and Ponyo:

> I left my headhunting brethren not without a twinge of regret,
> certainly with appreciation. They had received us with hospitality
> and consideration. They had been honorable in their dealings
> with us—they found my dispatch case and kukri and brought them
> to me, the case badly dented, but all the contents there. And as a
> spontaneous gift, one of them presented me with a scabbard for
> my kukri. It was made of two concave slabs of bamboo, bound to-
> gether with plaited thongs of bamboo and decorated with a line
> drawing burnt into the slabs: an airplane, below it a parachute,
> and dangling from the chute, a man.

15

THE LONG WALK HOME

The manna from heaven that had served to sustain the survivors during their sojourn in the bamboo encampment outside Wenshoyl, and which had served in part to buy the acquiescence of their hosts, came very close to derailing Adams's plans on the morning established for their departure. The superabundance—even embarrassment of riches—that had rained from the skies during the previous twelve days had created raging torrents of desire for the Americans' material possessions amongst the people of Pangsha that the survivors—in the midst of the naive obliviousness often common to those who have too much—had failed to recognize. Despite the recent emergence of their country from the Great Depression, the young Americans had no concept of just how rich they appeared to the Pangsherites, nor indeed to Adams's mercenaries. Just as they were about to leave the survivors nonchalantly threw their trash into a pile in the center of the camp. It was an attempt to clean up after themselves, but it had untold and nearly catastrophic consequences. The pile comprised rope, tins, cloth, bottles, paper, parachute silk, and any other accumulated stuff that could not be carried out or was simply no longer wanted. These items, however, represented a considerable treasure to the men of Pangsha. Adams's mercenaries were horrified that the Patkoi "savages" should be allowed to profit from the white men in this way and wanted the detritus for themselves. An ugly confrontation resulted that, observers such as Sevareid and Davies believed, nearly resulted in bloodshed.

Adams became aware of bickering between some of the watching Nagas and of increasingly raised voices. Suddenly, men began shouting at each other, *dao*s were unsheathed from back scabbards, and angry insults were exchanged. Realizing what was happening, Adams immediately took control, walking boldly into the midst of an animated swarm to pull people apart. Tangbang and Emlong likewise rushed into the fray to remonstrate with the angry mob, shouting, warning, and cajoling. After what seemed like an age tempers cooled, but it had been a close thing. "Nearest we have come, I think, to general massacre," recorded Sevareid in his diary:

> Suddenly natives were yelling, threatening us and one another with knives, one old man brandishing knife and leaping up and down exhorting others to attack. I stood by nervously holding rifle and umbrella, could see Adams gravely worried. He moved like lightning, snatching Headhunters by the hair, tossing them right and left without looking back, got guard around junk until passions cooled and he could share it out to the chiefs. A near thing, I am sure. Think if he had shown indecision or fear we would have had bad fight. Believe Adams sore at us for leaving so much stuff.

Adams managed to calm the excited crowds by dividing the refuse and apportioning it to the leaders of Pangsha in the same way that he had already allocated the salt that had arrived as a reward for allowing the survivors to retain their heads. It was a solemn and somewhat subdued crowd that eventually began to weave its way gently down the slopes toward the Langnyu River, a little later than anticipated, for the first stage of the journey. The first night's stop was to be at Noklak. Rain began to fall, cooling martial ardor even further.

Almost immediately Sevareid began to feel his lack of fitness. The extraordinary supermarket-in-the-sky from Chabua had dropped fresh pairs of heavy British military boots (after first requesting the men's individual sizes), into which the survivors had been busy hammering metal studs (thirteen to each sole) to give them better purchase on the rough terrain. But the boots were hard and not worn in, and chafing and blisters began to emerge within the first few miles. That night Sevareid had two large blisters—each the size of a silver dollar—on the balls of his feet, and the uncomfortable boots were made even worse by an errant stud nail somehow piercing his foot.

The column, in single file, stretched for nearly two miles. From the outset the survivors, weakened by their long wait and in any case ill-prepared for the physical demands of this wild country, struggled. The march on that first day was a mere eight miles but was cruelly demanding of all their mental and physical energies. Sevareid would later conclude that although tough physically, the march demanded much more of the men mentally. He was a prescient observer of how each of his fellow travelers dealt with his first exposure to the march. Some were better able than others to cope with the psychological demands of the seven days they would experience together on the trail: "Colonel [Flickinger], who was near end of convoy, slowly drew past us, looking pale, jaws clenched, muttering to himself—sheer triumph of will, he determined to come in ahead of party, preserve his leadership. Colonel Wang collapsed two miles from Noklak, was carried rest of way. He now having coolies build him bamboo chair, seems have plenty rupees besides jewels for payment. Colonel Kwoh ashamed, feels this great loss of face for Chinese. Flick sitting head in hands when I pulled in, said: 'This will separate the sheep from the goats.'"

The arrival of the column was regarded as a significant occasion for the people of the sprawling village of Noklak. The largest number of white men they had seen previously was the handful of men who accompanied the previous punitive expeditions, the first of which had been in 1936. Adams's expedition had bypassed the village when it had arrived in the area the previous week, marching directly from Chingmei to Pangsha for reasons of speed. But the news of the parachutists had traveled like wildfire around the hills, and people were eager to see what the fuss was all about. Many of the Noklak *khel* elders had journeyed to Pangsha to view the white men in their encampment at Wenshoyl, like specimens in a zoo. The survivors had realized that they were objects of ethnological interest to the Nagas and had noticed the almost daily arrival of new observers from ever more distant villages, eager to see what the skies had delivered into their midst. The people of Noklak, including (unusually) all the women and children, now crowded the balconies of their stilted houses to watch the column slowly wind its way through the crowded walkway that provided Noklak's main street. The parachutists must have seemed a pitiful sight to these fit mountain people, and Oswalt's elaborate Chinese-built bamboo litter, carried high by ten Nagas, must have seemed a quite remarkable contraption.

The overnight respite was an opportunity for the survivors to recuperate after what had been a long but not overly demanding day—they didn't know it yet, but much worse was to follow—and for Adams to undertake his functions as magistrate. Noklak was spread along a north-south ridge on the western edge of the broad valley that looked across to Pangsha, in the far distance, nestled on the edge of the Patkoi Hills. While Sevareid looked after his feet (and threw away his British hobnailed boots, to be replaced by the softer American shoes he had been wearing when the plane had gone down), Adams met with the Noklak elders and heard a complaint about an encroachment on their land by their neighbor, Panso, the elders of which had been instructed to meet him at Noklak. Sevareid saw the elders in the village, offering gifts of eggs, pigs, and hens to the sahib of Mokokchung. Panso, a traditional ally of Pangsha, remained an unknown quantity to Adams, despite its protestations of loyalty and public subservience to the emissary of the Raj. Mills's interaction with the village in 1936 had been brief, not long enough to determine whether its civility was genuine cordiality or a ploy in response to the presence of superior firepower. Sevareid had heard Adams discuss a potentially dangerous pass through the hills between Chingmei and Kuthurr that was a well-known site for ambush. A disaffected village, such as Panso, could cause much trouble for the column and was evidently much on Adams's mind. But so far as Sevareid could see, the Panso delegation was dutifully obedient at this point in time, with no evidence of hostility, despite the fact that Adams, after hearing the facts of the case, ordered Panso to relinquish the land that it had taken from Noklak.

That night the exhausted men ate their food—carried on the backs of the porters from the stores dropped to them at Pangsha— and soon after the sun went down collapsed onto the wooden cots in a bamboo encampment just outside the village, constructed for them on Adams's instructions. The porters and Naga mercenaries organized the stores and sat around their campfires sharing— and exaggerating, no doubt—their stories of the confrontation that morning with the uncivilized "savages" of Pangsha. This encounter was something to tell the women and children at home. The survivors, to a man, slept through the hubbub.

The following morning, as the dawn rose, a hot breakfast of bully beef and tea fortified the Europeans before the column was once again on its way. The objective this day was Chingmei, not many miles distant but across hills far steeper than they had encountered so far. It was now August 19. The scenery was stunning, Sevareid recalled, for those not too exhausted to appreciate it. Real "Metro-Goldwyn-Mayer," he wrote. Thick jungle filled the bottoms of valleys, with spectacular waterfalls spilling from high, rocky clefts in the mountainside. But this beauty had a sting in its tail: the tracks over the hillsides were so steep that they required, on occasion, the assistance of ropes made from vines and tied to tree trunks. For the last two miles the survivors, climbing steeply up to Chingmei's hilltop position, required some pushing and pulling by the Naga mercenaries. It was an exhausted group that flopped down at Chingmei late that afternoon, although Adams was pleased with their progress and determined that they would not need to take the rest day here that he had anticipated.

Chingmei, home of Chingmak, Sangbah, and Tangbang, provided a warm welcome that some of the men were to regret. They were accommodated in Naga houses and the *morung* and thus shared their quarters with many thousands of preexisting inhabitants: scurrying rats and the ubiquitous flea inside and rooting pigs, squabbling hens, and unctuous roosters underneath. But the hospitality was warm and genuine. Sangbah, lying in bed with fever—probably a recurrent bout of malaria, prevalent in the lowlands so in all likelihood picked up during a long-distance foray down to the Brahmaputra or Chindwin—was determined to ensure that his village entertained its visitors royally. "Afraid we are in for an evening of pub-crawling," Adams warned Sevareid as they, together with Don Flickinger and Richard Passey visited Sangbah in a house that Sevareid noted for its cleanness. Sangbah was being looked after by a wife whom Sevareid described as having a "really lovely face, air of refinement." It was an emotional meeting. Flickinger now recognized, from his conversations with Adams, that the safety of the survivors on the hillside at Wenshoyl had been guaranteed by Sangbah and his men, judiciously placed in the hills around Pangsha. Bedridden, Sangbah apologized for not accompanying the column to Mokokchung. His incapacity didn't hinder him, and his visitors, from drinking a considerable quantity of *zu*, an activity that made them all somewhat maudlin: "Flick thanked him for all he has done for us. Sangbah shook head, said he not done enough, gave Colonel his brass head-hunter ornament, highest gift his possession. . . . Both Flick and Sangbah deeply touched at parting, both close to tears. We shall send him gifts from Mok[okchung]."

Leaving Sangbah's house, they went to Tangbang's, where Adams was due to receive respect—and gifts of food—from elders from neighboring villages. Sevareid's staccato account in his diary humorously captures some of the characteristics of the encounter:

Drank much *zu* in Tang-bang's place which much dirtier, his young wife much coarser, behaved like gangster's gun-moll trying do well before the quality. Wore dozens brass arm rings. Each time she served us, breasts hung in front of our faces, embarrassing Passey, who is proper, religious type.* Then, all somewhat drunk, we climb to Wang-do's basha in upper khel. His wife giggled constantly, filled cups every sixty seconds. Wang-do is Arabic-looking, very strong face, gather he has rather supplanted chief Chingmak. Adams mischievously tells Wang-do he disappointed that Wang-do has but one child, means he been on trail too much, neglecting his household duties. All laugh, find keenest pleasure in jest. Flick gives his wife his silk parachute scarf, and Adams says this will ensure twins and that the "Colonel Sahib" will be part father. More giggling.

The third day of the march began the following morning, August 20, with the march to Kuthurr. This was the part of their journey for which Adams had been concerned about the possibility of ambush by malcontents from any of the villages who may have harbored continuing grudges against his authority. A long stretch of dark, close jungle had to be navigated, with multiple opportunities for sharpened *dao*s or crossbows to surprise the unwary. But every man in the column was on his guard. The Naga mercenaries, denied a fight so far, eagerly clutched their fighting *dao*s, and the survivors all watchfully gripped their M1 carbines. Before long the last men of the column had wound their way out onto the hillside and into the bright sunshine. The tension of the jungle dissipated and allowed the men to think of their physical infirmities. The sun beat down for the first time during their sojourn in these hills. Blisters caused increasing agonies for most, although many of the survivors were proving to be strong walkers and custodians of American prestige.

Who might have been a strong marcher had not been obvious at the outset of the trek, Sevareid mused. Those whom he had thought would be able to cope easily, especially those who were younger and fitter, were not necessarily those who made it through

---

*Richard Passey was a Mormon, a direct descendent, Sevareid believed, of Joseph Smith.

uncomplainingly or without help. He was impressed with Giguere and Passey, for instance, who were both fit and eager and kept up with Adams at the front of the column. They had what Sevareid described as "that extra something which makes a man superior—in addition to powerful legs." Likewise, Colonel Kwoh, not accustomed to boots, kept plodding on regardless of his feet, which were wrecked by bleeding blisters. He was perseverance personified—a man, Davies suggested, who demonstrated why China would never be beaten. Bill Stanton, Duncan Lee, and Jack Davies were also impressive in different ways. None of them ever complained, demonstrating that the issue was as much "mind over matter" as much as it was physical strength. Davies was a tower of strength, made light of the difficulties they were facing, and amused the Nagas with his impressions of their dirgelike chants: "Davies and I limp along, rifle one hand, spear as walking stick in other, discussing State Department and U.S. foreign policy as though strolling down F Street [in Washington]. John has great reserves moral courage." Davies hid his discomfort well. In a letter to his wife he wrote, "Most of the time on the trail has been busy—breaking camp, watching the scenery, the porters and the tough savage scouts, engaging in conversation with the rest of the party, wishing to hell the day's hike were over, making camp and shooting the breeze after supper." Duncan Lee also appeared to be enjoying himself. The others groaned in mock irritation when he jumped out of his bed every morning, eager for the day's march. He "seems take pleasure whole affair," observed Sevareid, "looks rather like cultured, bespectacled pirate with bandanna around head, knife and pistol on hips."

All the while the USAAF was following their progress like an aerial mother hen. During the march to Kuthurr a note was dropped to the column, along with supplies of food, from General Alexander: "Good luck and good going. I will send you everything you ask for except pianos and violins. I take it the morale is good. We are much relieved at the safety of your party. Let us know if you need anything." The only thing they needed, Sevareid quipped, were new feet.

The fourth day of the march—Saturday, August 21—was by far the worst as they clawed their way through tangled valley bottoms before climbing into the clouds for three hours to reach Helipong. Even the Naga porters, with their heavy loads, found the going tough: at one rest Sevareid noticed one porter's bloodied back. They were carrying the expedition's heavy loads while the Americans walked free of encumbrance. It was hard enough climbing the mountainside under the jungle canopy, where everything was cold, dark, and slippery, using vines to haul themselves upward, but when they climbed out of the tree cover they were hit by an unrelenting sun, although still surrounded by vicious head-high sword grass. Even proximity to this grass seemed to induce deep, painful cuts. There was no water. Each step for Sevareid was one of pain and exhaustion. "I could not do it again," he wrote later. Somehow Oswalt's litter was brought up the mountain—Sevareid could not conceive of how—as upward they staggered. Sevareid's head began to swim, and he felt close to losing consciousness. He rested by the trail while Davies went on ahead to get help from Don Flickinger. It was sunstroke. Cutting some of the tall grass away from the path with their *dao*s, the others created an area where he could rest. Flickinger's arrival with two cans of apricot juice revived him, as did some water a porter had brought half a mile down from Helipong itself, called for by Davies. Meanwhile, Neveu struggled with a painful sore on his left leg and was helped along by some of Adams's near-naked mercenaries.

At long last the column wound its way into the cold embrace of Helipong. The Americans' first experience of the village was just like that of Mills and Fürer-Haimendorf seven years before: at nearly 8,000 feet the temperature was cold, but at least the sun was shining and the views magnificent. In the far distance they could see, shining, the glistening, snakelike Brahmaputra, winding its way from the Himalayas to the sea. It was perfect weather for aerial resupply from the circling C-47s from Chabua, although the tightly constrained terrain meant that the first dispatch of free-dropped supplies of salt for the local Nagas landed directly in the village, demolishing the roofs of a couple of the houses and causing the corralled cattle to stampede. Using his hand-cranked radio, Sergeant LaBonte shouted instructions to the crews, and a second attempt resulted in yet more destruction, but this time to their own temporary *basha*s. To Flickinger's great upset the *basha* collapse destroyed the knife, together with its intricately carved scabbard, that had been given to him by Mongsen. But at least no one was hurt, and the gifts dropped from the sky went some way toward restoring friendly relations with the villagers.

The fifth day's march was, in comparison with the previous day's exertions, an easy ramble. The journey to Chongtore entailed a long, winding climb down from the heights of Helipong before a gentler and shorter incline into the village. It was at Chongtore on Sunday, August 22, that Sevareid was able to transmit his first account of his adventure to the outside world, using LaBonte's radio set, which required hand-cranking for power. The process took an agonizing three hours, but the professional journalist in him pressed him to persevere. Albert Ravenholt of UPI sat above in a circling C-47 and transcribed Sevareid's story, and then pushed it through the notoriously difficult British censors in New Delhi. It was transmitted from India on the following day. Five days later it was published across the United States, front-page news in most papers. One can forgive some of the ethnological inexactitudes in the finished article: the censor in India was unwilling for the story to give too much away by describing the Nagas specifically. They became, therefore, "Burmese Headhunters." "I am grinding this out on a hand-crank wireless set dropped to us by one of the rescue planes of the air transport command," ran Sevareid's report. "We are in the middle of a village of Aborigines perched atop one of the 6,000 foot mountains. In another four days we hope to reach civilization." He didn't say that it was now raining steadily, the oppressive heat of the previous day fortunately only a memory. For the sake of positivity he allowed himself a degree of exaggeration:

Ahead of us, however, lie more mountain peaks and tortuous valley trails, but our party is in good shape, physically and morally,
and we know we can make it. . . .

Many of us are covered with insect bites and sores, but it is
nothing serious. Yesterday I became a victim of the heat and exhaustion, but I'm quite alright now. All in all, the civilians of the
party seem to be standing up to it as well as the soldiers.

Throughout, what Davies described as their "Celestial Catering Service" dropped supplies whenever the weather allowed. At
Chare it had included a case of canned beer: Pabst Blue Ribbon.
Colonel Flickinger was forced to quash the rumors circulating that
the immense effort the USAAF was undertaking on their behalf
was only because of the presence in their midst of "big shots" such
as Davies and Sevareid. There seems little doubt, nevertheless, that
having celebrities such as Sevareid in the mix accelerated efforts
to professionalize the search-and-rescue capacity within the ATC.
"It works like telephoning the local grocery store for extra sugar,"
reported one of the pilots nonchalantly in a report filed by Albert
Ravenholt on August 24. Lieutenant Craig Jones had dropped rations and boots to the column that day, all ordered in advance.

The rain continued that night and into the next day as the long
column wound its careful way down once more into a deep river
valley and then climbed uphill again to Chare. The men walked
a total of fifteen miles, utilizing for the first time the black umbrellas that had been dropped to them at Pangsha. It was almost
comical, the effectiveness of the umbrellas not quite removing the
feeling of incongruity the men felt in carrying them through the
jungle-matted Naga Hills. It could have been Madison Avenue or
Piccadilly Circus, they thought, but they knew enough of the Nagas
by now to know that they prized these "bumbershoots" for their
pure utilitarianism. The rain, of course, made the jungle trails all
the more treacherous, and at one point Sevareid fell and broke the
Naga spear for which he had bartered with the Ponyo natives back
at Wenshoyl. He was more furious with himself for losing his prized

spear than for the fact that he had badly wrenched his shoulder in the fall.

The men now observed a changing cultural landscape as they neared Mokokchung. The closer they came to civilization, Sevareid observed, the less noble the Nagas looked. They wore mixtures of European and native clothing; they were more prosperous and settled and had less of the savage about them. Danger no longer lurked around the next corner; this part of the world was far less wild than that from which they had just come. The new world they were entering seemed all the less attractive. "In a way, rather a disappointment," he recorded. But there were other potential excitements. They were now in tiger country; there were still some of these beautiful creatures that Emlong and Tangbang and their like had not yet removed from the face of the earth. There was also a herd of wild elephants, which tended to roam the lower reaches of the valleys in the interior of the Naga Hills. With the end in sight, the men began to notice their extraordinary surroundings: astonishing rivers; jungle-covered hills; exotic birds and flowers, especially the orchids. Davies tried to capture some of this beauty in a letter to his wife: "The mists were lovely on the mountains and trailing through the valleys. We stopped by streams and waterfalls to drink cold sweet water and look at Rousseau-like foliage with small bright orchids—moist and vivid pink." But the most exciting thing was that at Chare the local people were able to point out the men's immediate destination on the other side of the valley: Mokokchung.

16

BACK TO CHABUA

From across the valley their destination didn't look too far away—and indeed it wasn't, even when calculated in terms of long climbs down and up mountains. With "civilization" in sight, the men were spurred to a final effort, even though they knew that there was at least a full day of walking to undergo beyond Mokokchung before they could meet the vehicle transport that would take them back to Chabua. Once past Mokokchung the survivors would meet the press: the US Army cameramen, with cameras clicking, and the few accredited journalists in the region. The men peer out from the photographs of that day with tired smiles, exhausted satisfaction rather than exuberance being the main emotion.

For Sevareid, that prescient commentator on both politics and the human condition, the moment entailed consideration—again—of Britain's extraordinary empire. He still couldn't understand it. As the column wound its tired way into Mokokchung the following afternoon—Tuesday, August 25—he was astonished to see Naga men and women saluting. Even more incongruously, a number started singing the British national anthem, "God Save the King": "It made no sense, but one could not help being somewhat awed. There were sandbags in the chill gloom around Buckingham Palace, and London was brazen with stiff upper lips; here, on the other side of the world, brown men with tattooed faces and spears smiled in the sun and suggested to the white men's great spirit, wherever he was, that he take care of their Great Sahib—wherever he was. The British Empire makes no sense, but there it is, an imposing, ubiquitous feat which will not be denied."

Few of the others concerned themselves with such considerations. The sun was shining, and a clean-shaven, immaculately
uniformed American soldier stood by the trackside taking photographs. Bizarrely, he said not a word of greeting as the exhausted
men trooped past. The native population of the village had turned
out in strength to welcome the returning column—and the survivors of Flight 12420—with *zu*. To all intents and purposes, the survivors had made it. To whom did they owe their salvation? In the
immediate sense it was "the unbelievable" Philip Adams, the local
emissary of a far-distant power who ruled by notebook and judg-
ment far more than he did with rifle or jail. Over lunch in Adams's
neat bungalow, surrounded by the ordered gardens that Sevareid
imagined were a direct translation from Adams's native Sussex, Sevareid questioned the subdivisional officer about the benefits of
civilization for the people of the Naga Hills. One gets the sense that
Sevareid was taken with the entire romanticism of his recent experience. The so-called "Headhunters" had behaved perfectly civilly
to him and his fellow travelers. They had not demanded his head in
exchange for his dropping into their territory unannounced, and
it seemed a shame that the trappings of "civilization" should be
forced on these simple people against their will.

But Adams's view was as unequivocal as Pawsey's, and Mills's
before them. The Nagas in their native state lived fearful lives,
dominated by daily concerns about security that limited their human experience to one not much better than survival. Sevareid
got Adams wrong. His conclusion was that Adams believed "that
the savages back in the hills were happy people. They were strong,
cheerful, keenly intelligent, more straightforward and healthy both
in mind and in body than the Indians of the tepid plains. They were
men of honor and instinctive dignity. What frightened him was that
up to now, wherever 'civilization' and its ways had crept in among
the Nagas, it had harmed and debased them." From an ethnological and cultural perspective, Sevareid was right: the colonial administrators had little time for the culture-changing impact of the
missionaries and were afraid of the effect of opening up the hills to

newcomers from Assam and Bengal. But in all other respects Sevareid misjudged the British colonial administrator. Adams didn't possess any romantic notions of the noble savage living a happy and uncomplicated life if unmolested from the outside. Adams was ultimately fearful of what life without the rule of law meant for the people of the hills when the only law was power, and the utilization of such power was evidenced through the use of brutal force against those unable to protect themselves.

Adams and his colleagues had a Hobbesian vision of a lawless future for the Naga Hills if the villages were not taken in hand by benevolent authority. They understood from their own experience that only strong, undivided government could provide an alternative to the state of existence that characterized the lives of many powerless Nagas. Without such intervention life in the Control Area and the unadministered areas would remain one of "continual fear and danger of violent death, and the life of man, solitary, poor, nasty, brutish, and short," as Hobbes famously described an ungoverned world. Adams and Pawsey could see every day, as had Mills and those who had followed, the benefits that the prohibition on head-hunting and human sacrifice had had for the Nagas of the Administered Area. Despite his respect for the traditions, ancient history, and developed cultures of these people, Adams wanted more than anything else to enable them to live in peace. It was this imperative that he shared more than anything else with his predecessors and peers. When questioned in more recent times about what heritage the colonial experience had brought the people of the Naga Hills, a single response was emphatically expressed: *the rule of law.* This was the greatest legacy of the British colonial administrators in the Naga Hills from the time of Dr. J. H. Hutton until independence in 1947.

| | |

In a celebration of their rescue the USAAF dropped the men an extravagant cooked lunch while they were resting at Mokokchung. It was an extraordinary effort by the men at Dumbastapur, who were eagerly following the travails of their countrymen as they safely emerged from the Naga wilderness. They knew that any of them could easily have been among the survivors. Davies described the event in a letter to his wife: "The boys wafted to us by parachute the kind of Sunday dinner that mom used to cook: hot tomato soup, hot fried chicken, gravy, mashed potatoes, peas, hot biscuits, and for dessert, ice cream with chocolate sauce, coconut cake and coffee. This touching extravaganza represented considerable effort, coordination and skill, and what's more, warmth of spirit."

That day, as they rested on the grass in front of Adams's bungalow, feasting on an unimaginably sumptuous meal from aluminum containers prepared in a canvas-covered kitchen 100 miles to the north and dropped from the skies, they reflected on their good fortune. They still had two more days of walking as they made their way down to the Brahmaputra Valley, but they were safe, and they had accrued memories for a lifetime. Emlong proudly showed Flickinger and Sevareid photographs of himself after the 1936 punitive expedition—taken by Fürer-Haimendorf—proudly posing with a group of heads, which, despite what he insinuated, must have been those snatched by the anthropologist from the slopes of Wenshoyl. The Pangsha dead of 1936 hadn't had their heads removed on the battlefield by the British or any of those in the fighting column. But it made a great photograph, and Emlong's prestige among his American friends now reached a new height. The officers and civilians clubbed together to purchase a blanket each to be sent back to Chingmei for Sangbah, and Sevareid sat down to type out a new story for UPI. It was never printed in the newspapers but formed the basis for a long article in *Reader's Digest* that was published a few months later.

On the following day blisters and tiredness were disregarded as the men began the final part of their journey. They hobbled down the bridle path from Mokokchung in the direction of the plains, walking eighteen miles to their overnight stop at one of Adams's inspection bungalows, used for his tours into the Administered

Area, situated on the road to Mariani between the Naga hamlets of Aliba and Changki. The march was made no easier by the fact that they were now walking downhill most of the time on the broad bridle path that dropped out of the mountains toward the Assam town and railway stop of Mariani. Their objective was the airfield at Jorhat, from whence they would be flown back to Chabua. The day was unseasonably wet, and the men were glad of the welcoming sight of the corrugated iron roof of the bungalow, especially Duncan Lee, who during the twelve-hour march had been startled by a tiger dashing through the bush next to the track; Roland Lee, who had to be carried because of a foot infection; Sevareid, who had caught a cold; and Harry Neveu, who had fainted and had to be revived on the trail.

On Friday, August 27, 1943, the men walked the remaining 14 miles of some 140 that they had covered over the preceding ten days. As they emerged from the bush Sevareid had a pang of regret. It had been an extraordinary, even moving, experience. He had survived an air crash that had claimed the life of the airplane's copilot; had lived among a tribe of people with a reputation as notorious headhunters; had made friends with Nagas such as Sangbah and Tangbang, whom he would always remember with warmth and affection; had come face-to-face with the practical reality of imperialism at work on the edge of empire through the work of Philip Adams; and had marched to safety, protected on the ground by a crowd of Naga mercenaries armed with spears, *dao*s, and shotguns (and in the air by the ever-present Gooney Birds of the USAAF), across a range of hills that would have defeated most men. It was almost like a dream, but as he looked back at "the jagged blue lines of the mysterious mountains" from which he had just emerged, he realized how real, and yet at the same time surreal, his and his fellow survivors' experience had been. Then civilization was upon them:

> We heard the muttering of automotive engines ahead, rounded a bend in military formation with the colonel walking at our head,

and came upon a line of parked jeeps and command cars and a small crowd of smiling officers and men and newsreel photographers. The sun was crushing, and after an hour of posing with the others and trying to speak into a microphone for the film sound track, I felt as limp and exhausted as I had on any day of the long march. Within two minutes my command car had slid off the trail. After another half-hour of backbreaking work I rode on, bouncing from side to side, clinging to my seat, becoming violently sick at my stomach, feeling that my head would split. The road flattened out, there were water wheels and tired buffalo, drooping, torpid Hindus, soiled houses and heavy smells. One sweated, and the muggy air was hard to breathe. We were back in India, the India the world knows.

In his article in *Reader's Digest* Sevareid acknowledged that their rescue had been brought about by the determined efforts and sacrifices of many people, and at considerable cost. What had the Nagas thought of their unexpected guests? Sevareid didn't know but mused that they now knew what Americans looked like and perhaps as a consequence would look after future air crews and passengers who were forced to jump for their lives over their ancestral lands. One night on the walk back to Mokokchung, one of Adams's Naga mercenaries had said to Private William Schrandt, "India, there." He pointed west. "China, there." He pointed north. "America, there." And he pointed *up*.

The happy convoy moved slowly and bumpily across the rutted Assamese roads to the dusty railway stop of Mariani and then the final ten miles to the airfield at Jorhat. Their arrival at the long concrete pan with the waiting Gooney Bird brought them back into a world from which they had been absent for only a month, though it seemed several lifetimes:

A smiling Texas army nurse stood by the steps of the hospital plane as we climbed into the cabin. We sat again in the two rows of aluminum seats, mopping our scraggly beards with our filthy bits of silk, looking again across the narrow space at one another. The same bad joke occurred to everyone: "This is where I came in." Neveu, the pilot, looked around with a pale face and suddenly got very sick and was made to lie down on one of the suspended stretchers. I listened nervously to the engines and sweated despite the cool rush of air.

17

BLACKIE'S GANG

Captain John "Blackie" Porter, a twenty-seven-year-old ATC pilot from Cincinnati, Ohio, based at Jorhat, heard of the crash of Flight 12420 first with anxiety and then with relief. By means of enormous effort twenty men had been rescued from one of the most inhospitable places on earth. But the ATC effort had been pulled together in an ad hoc fashion, using volunteers, to the detriment of the airlift to China. When aircraft went down over the Hump the crews' friends were sometimes allowed to look for them. But the regular flights didn't have the equipment or training to do much more than make a token attempt to find a downed aircraft lost under a canopy of green. What if rescue efforts were planned and used specially trained men and appropriately equipped aircraft?, Porter mused. He decided to lobby Alexander to set up a discrete team to search and recover downed air crews. After several weeks of waiting, permission was finally granted, along with the allocation of two ancient C-47s and two sets of dedicated air crew specially recruited for the task. The small team was soon known across the ATC in Assam as "Blackie's Gang." What Porter established in 1943 as a result of the crash of Flight 12420 proved to be the forerunner of the sophisticated search-and-rescue mechanisms adopted by US forces during the remainder of the war and into the postwar world. Whereas 62 percent of personnel missing from flights over the Hump were rescued in 1943, this number would increase to 77 percent by mid-1944 as a direct result of the achievements of Blackie's Gang. By the end of the war the percentage was even higher.

At the time of the crash of Flight 12420 Blackie Porter had been flying for only two years, but he had completed over 2,250 flying hours on a wide variety of aircraft and was very well acquainted with the dangerous vicissitudes of the Hump. Blackie's Gang was fully operable by October 23, 1943, flying from Chabua, and a month later the two C-47s were joined by two B-25 Mitchell bombers and a few L-5 light aircraft. Sergeant Bill Blossom was operating a crash rescue vehicle at Chabua when he was approached by Porter to join his "gang." Trained as a parachute rigger, Blossom leaped at the chance to escape the monotony of base support duties. He was impressed by Porter. A quiet, even shy man, Blossom considered that Blackie "came by his nickname honestly, with his thick black hair and dark eyes.... There was an inherent goodness and whole-someness about him, but once airborne, he changed. He reveled in that environment and became a fearless dare-devil. His courage was admirable. It was easy to identify with him and he was the most informal officer I ever encountered, yet the utmost respect from his men was there for him, always. He gave us a singleness of purpose! He raised our sights."

Porter's search-and-rescue team began to see immediate success. He tried to have at least two aircraft available for operations each day, and ground-crew mechanics worked through the night under floodlights to ensure that no day went by without aircraft available to fly. Procedures were developed to professionalize the business of search and rescue, and the crews began to train to operate in this distinctive new role. Porter recruited Oswalt to his team. Pilots began to fly routinely just above treetop level, with everyone on board looking for the telltale signs of a crashed aircraft—signs that from a greater height would be impossible to see against the backdrop of continuous vegetation. Once the general area of a crash had been identified, and if the crash site was not immediately visible, crews learned to conduct pattern flying, checking the ground below in a systematic fashion, section by section, with all eyes in the aircraft looking hard at the ground for signs of disturbance that might reveal the place where a stricken aircraft had entered the jungle canopy. The low flying terrified Blossom, who complained one day to Porter that they had flown too close to the surface of the Brahmaputra. "It seemed to me that the props were just a few inches above the water and I knew the consequences if they would just touch." Porter's response was "We want to live too, Bill."

— Many of the procedures that had been employed at Pangsha were refined further. Once survivors had been found, notes providing initial instructions were dropped to them on yellow streamers, followed by radios, weapons, and survival equipment. Where possible rescuers were dropped by parachute in order to provide aid to the injured and guide the survivors in the direction of friendly villages or to places where the light aircraft could recover them, a couple at a time. In 1944 the first helicopters were deployed in this role. The USAAF had ordered its first production helicopter, the Sikorsky R-4, in January 1943 and deployed a small number in Burma in early 1944. The first use of the new aircraft for search and rescue took place between April 22 and 23, 1944, when the composer Carter Harman, a helicopter pilot in the US Army, rescued the pilot and three wounded British soldiers from a downed L1 light aircraft. Don Flickinger's selfless act in parachuting in to help Oswalt at Pangsha became the inspiration for a new procedure that involved dropping specially trained volunteer medics to survivors whose injuries could not be treated without expert help, including plasma and blood for transfusions in the field.

Back at Chabua Blackie's Gang was given its own warehouse, which the men filled with material they could drop to downed air crews. It was "run by a former New York nightclub operator named Joe Kramer," observed Theodore White. Kramer organized the dropping of material required for immediate survival—"food, medicine, bandages, boots, clothes, compasses, maps, signaling panels, playing cards, books, Bibles and goods to barter with natives." Thereafter, as the survivors walked or were led to safety, Kramer would organize the loads that were dropped to them on daily supply runs until they had returned to a place of safety.

While Porter and his gang had to take constant care in flying because of the obvious dangers of the mountainous terrain, another continuing danger were the predatory Japanese fighters operating from Myitkyina Airfield. At low altitude, lumbering along the treetops looking for crashed air crews, the search-and-rescue aircraft were especially vulnerable to the pack-hunting Zeros that daily patrolled these angry skies. For self-protection the gang's aircraft were armed with British Bren light machine guns, which they poked out through the aircraft doors and windows. Porter himself used a Bren on one occasion—November 6, 1943—to destroy a Japanese fighter on the ground. With the copilot flying the plane, the unwieldy C-47 flew past the Japanese plane at its slowest speed, firing thirty-round clips of .303 ammunition into the enemy aircraft. After several passes they left the enemy fighter a wreck and its pilot dead.

Porter was not averse to attacking Japanese ground positions when he saw them. The ATC daily tactical summary for December 9, 1943, recorded that Porter's B-25 had come under machine-gun fire. Porter had turned to look for the enemy: "Sighting two Jap emplacements, Porter and his crew strafed and silenced both positions. Sometime after a Japanese encampment . . . and three trucks were spotted. The trucks and party were thoroughly strafed." But the Japanese got Porter in the end. On December 10, 1943, Porter's B-25 was shot down by a clutch of Zeros near Fort Hertz. Only one man managed to parachute to safety before the aircraft crashed. Yet the system Porter had begun to establish continued to flourish. In the three months before his death Blackie's Gang had found and recovered 127 Allied air crews from 58 downed planes. By the end of the war search and rescue had contributed significantly to the 1,171 lives saved from 590 crashes in this theater of war.

| | |

What of Pangsha? On November 26, 1943, a mere four months after the crash, the region in which Harry Neveu's aircraft had been lost erupted once more in violence. This time, however, a strange alliance took shape. The villages of Chingmei, Nokluk, Pangsha, Ponyo, Tsaplaw, and Tsawlaw, along with a number of smaller villages, all found common cause in attacking and destroying Law Nawkum, farther north along the Patkois in Burma. Between 250 and 300 men, women, and children were killed in the fighting, their heads taken to adorn the villages of their attackers. Nothing was done in response by the British authorities in faraway Mokokchung. There were now permanent USAAF watch stations in the Patkoi Hills, guarded by men of the Assam Rifles, but because no harm was threatened to them, this internecine violence was ignored despite its scale. Other American airmen who came down over the Patkois in the months that followed were treated kindly and returned to Mokokchung, the government paying in salt (to the value of 400 rupees each) for the return of downed airmen. The truth was that not much could be done about these occasional bouts of warfare, even if Shillong had had the resources to send men into the hills to put them down by force of arms. During the World War II years Britain could mount only occasional forays into the Control Area to enforce its authority in extremis. Nothing much more was possible, especially when the principal focus was on defeating the Japanese. The Nagas in the Control Area and farther afield—despite the personal desire of both Charles Pawsey and Philip Adams—were no match for the harsh realities of power and fear. The truth was that Naga villages such as Chingmei, Noklak, and Pangsha had local power over their neighborhoods, and the British didn't. Even occasional Jovian descents from Mount Olympus such as Mills's punitive expedition in 1936, the deputy commissioner's and subdivisional officer's occasional "tours," and Adams's 1943 rescue mission could not change the long-term reality of power on the ground.

Charles Pawsey had been advocating the extension of the British prerogative in the Control Area for years. He was constantly frustrated that the government of Assam appeared willing to turn a blind eye to the deliberate flouting of the 1933 ban on using weapons in intravillage disputes inside the Control Area. In Pawsey's view, the law was made a mockery of by not being enforced. It was particularly invidious that in large swaths of the eastern Naga Hills, up to and including the Patkoi Range, systematic raiding and headhunting were allowed to continue because of government inaction. He argued repeatedly that the Control Area be extended all the way to the Burma border (thereby including Pangsha, for instance) and that the deputy commissioner be given carte blanche to enforce the law by means of punitive expeditions in event of its serious breach. On November 11, 1941, Pawsey laid out his proposition in a paper prepared for the government of Assam in Shillong.

1. Burma now administers up to the Patkoi [Range]. We can't allow our villages to raid Burma administered villages, nor is the idea that Burma should be allowed to take action against villages on our side of the Patkoi a pleasing one.
2. In practice the area up to the Patkoi is controlled politically. The first Pangsha expedition in December 1936 was undertaken when Pangsha was not in the control area. This year the Rotongre column will be operating outside the control area. The survey column in 1936 was operating as far as the Patkoi in the Chen area. Practically every village from Tamkhung near the Patkoi due east of Mokokchung southwards to the point where the district boundary meets the Patkoi near the Tizu has now been visited.
3. No new commitment will be involved by the extension of the Control Area.
4. The use of guns in the Control Area in tribal warfare is forbidden [and had been since 1933]. We can't tolerate the present position under which villages outside the area are more advantageously placed than those who carry out our orders.

His argument, made repeatedly in the years that followed, was based not on territorial aggrandizement—he was a colonial civil servant, not an imperialist—but on the principles of security and good governance that had already been shown to be beneficial to the villages that lay near the Administered Area. Head-hunting in the Control Area was endemic, but the evidence of many years of experience in the Administered Area was that people became more prosperous and secure even when they had been forced by the authorities to dispense with the ancient custom of head-lopping.

Of course it was not just head-hunting that villages in the Control Area wanted to preserve but their own prerogatives of power, a desire that in large part originated in the fear that they themselves would be subject to force by others. Fear of their neighbors created perverse behaviors: villages sought to protect their own independence by deliberately seeking the subjugation of others. Fear therefore bred fear. It was an age-old conundrum, a common feature of the human condition. The adage "killed or be killed" described the problem. Pawsey realized that the only way to remove the fear of another village's domination was to provide security for all villages but argued that this could be achieved without the wholesale application of colonial authority:

I am not in favor of the whole of the present Control Area being taken up. As villages in the control area get more civilized there comes a time when they realize how far better off and happier the administered villages really are. The outstanding example is the Sangtam villages just to the east of Mokokchung which were first administered in about 1927. . . . At that time they were so poor that they used to work for the Aos during the harvest, and other busy seasons, and in their external relations across the frontier were dominated by the Changs. Now Chare, the largest Sangtam village is one of the chief sources for the supply of rice to Mokokchung Station. Instead of the male population spending half their time on sentry duty they can work in the fields and trade and work in the plains in the cold weather.

The rest of the Sangtam tribe is continually clamoring for administration and accordingly the proposal . . . was submitted in 1939.

In a report of a tour in January 1942 Pawsey made an observation entirely at odds with the one that Sevareid was to make nearly two years later: Nagas in peaceful areas lived healthier and wealthier lives than those in territories dominated by traditional structures of village-by-village control. "What struck me on this as on other tours was the superiority in every way of our administered villages and villages of the trans-frontier people. They are much better nourished and have better physique and they look more contented. It is quite time that Sampure and Longmatrare and the villages in that area were administered. They are continually pressing for this step to be taken." Pawsey added a caveat by noting that any extension of the Control Area would need to be with the agreement and acquiescence of the people concerned. He didn't advocate enforced occupation: "I would be strongly opposed to the taking over of areas not fit for administration. For instance if we took over the Chang area we should have to put at least a platoon in the village to preserve peace between the khels who are bitter enemies. Any extension of the administered area should only be with the consent of the people concerned."

Pawsey's arguments were based firmly on facts. The title "Control Area" was an embarrassing oxymoron. It should more correctly have been called the "Uncontrollable Area" given the extent of gun-based lawlessness that characterized the sections that were effectively beyond the reach of British retribution. It was the old story: villagers would pay fines for misdemeanors if they had to, but it didn't make any difference to the tribal way of life, in which head-hunting was an important feature.

One of the problems of this policy for managing the Administered Area, for colonial administrators and Naga villages alike, was how to apply it practically. What could the villages do, or not do? Was all head-hunting banned, or was it just large-scale massacres that were forbidden? Was individual murder allowable but large-scale transgressions not? On January 20, 1936, the subdivisional officer in Mokokchung captured this moral and political dilemma with regard to the Yungya shooting of a Hukpong man:

"The transfrontier men of this area would like either to be given a free hand to wage their wars or else to have a clear order from Government that every village which takes a head will be burnt by Government." This suggestion, of course, hinged on the villages' expectation of the consequences of committing an infraction against distant rules that were indifferently (it appeared) applied.

Head-hunting had romantic connotations for some Europeans, and the phrase "heads taken" or "taking heads" has the tendency then and now to diminish the moral impact of what was, in plain speaking, murder. In the Administered Area, of course, head-hunting was prohibited by law, and on the whole resources were available to punish perpetrators. But in the Control Area men such as Pawsey and Mills had no choice but to turn a blind eye to murder because there was nothing that they could do about it. All they could do was respond to grievous breaches of regional stability by the sending of punitive expeditions. Some degree of hypocrisy was allowed in this environment. For instance, the "loyal" village of Chingmei was used to enforce Mokokchung's injunctions against widespread lawlessness while accepting that it could take an occasional head when the situation allowed. Indeed, it seems as if there was official sanction of some head-taking. The reports record an occasion in 1940 when Sangbah, enforcing Mokokchung's law against Ukha, didn't receive the fine that Philip Adams had demanded and so took an Ukha head instead. The report noted drily, "Ukha paid rest of the fine."

On March 27 and May 30, 1943, the troublesome village of Ukha (northeast of Tuensang) attacked two villages in the Control Area, Shakchi and Aghching. Ukha was beaten back on both occasions but used guns in the second attack—expressly forbidden in the Control Area since 1933—and Philip Adams was fearful that both villages would be exterminated. It was certainly not helpful for a large, aggressive, and armed village, friendly with Pangsha, to be allowed untrammeled freedom to exert its will in this manner. Accordingly, on June 26, Pawsey asked for a punitive expedition to be mounted against Ukha. He calculated that this village alone had caused the loss of 279 heads in this troubled area. Shillong refused permission. The village had previously been burned in a punitive expedition in November 1939 because it had joined with Pangsha and others to exterminate the village of Aghching, which had lost ninety-six heads. Guns had been used in this attack, and in 1936 Pangsha had been expressly ordered not to use guns and had taken an oath that it would refrain. Pawsey repeated his request on August 13, 1941, but again it was refused. Ukha was never pacified and continued its local reign of terror for years. In July 1944 Ukha took a head from Tobu, a village three miles south of Ukha, and followed this murder with other raids. Pawsey yet again asked for permission to march on the village but yet again was refused. The situation continued to simmer. On March 24, 1945, it was reported that the transfrontier villages would themselves resume raiding if Ukha was not stopped. Before long the entire village of Tobu had been wiped out and 400 men, women, and children killed. "This dreadful massacre was entirely unnecessary," recorded Pawsey angrily, "and could have been easily avoided if the constant requests of the Deputy Commissioner and the sub-Divisional Officer to be allowed to interfere had been granted."

Pawsey continued to argue the case for outlawing head-hunting entirely in the Control Area. On May 30, 1947, he wrote to Philip Adams, now secretary to the governor, "I am assuming that the stony silence which greets most of the proposals submitted to Shillong is the equivalent of non-acceptance. All proposals to extend either the administered or the control area are of course designed solely to establish law and order, the pre-requisite of which is the prohibition of head hunting." The return of the rescue mission from Pangsha in late August 1943 energized Adams and Pawsey once again to ask Shillong to countenance an extension of the Control Area. Without it there was no way that the British could "stop head hunting, and [they] would be forced to allow the local insecurity that encouraged this practice to fester without check." It is clear that the colonial administrators were of one mind, but it is also clear that no amount of cajoling would persuade the government of Assam,

or of India, to extend its responsibilities even for humanitarian reasons. At the point at which the empire was about to shrink, and to
do so rapidly, not even the humanitarian impulses of anthropologically minded colonial administrators would be allowed to expand
Britain's commitments beyond those it already had. Eric Sevareid's
head-hunting friends were on their own.

| | |

What became of the participants in these Naga dramas? Philip
Mills was appointed adviser to the governor of Assam for tribal
areas and states in 1935. He had been awarded the Rivers Memorial Medal the previous year "for anthropological fieldwork among
the Nagas" as well as receiving the Gold Medal of the Royal Asiatic
Society of Bengal for "contributions to the study of cultural anthropology in India." He retired in 1947 at the age of fifty-seven (he
had joined in 1913 and served for thirty-four years in India) after
suffering increasing ill health due to heart disease and because of
repeated exposure to malaria (he had nearly died from the disease
in 1924). The following year he began teaching anthropology at the
School of Oriental and African Studies (SOAS) in London, building up the Department of Cultural Anthropology alongside his old
friend Christoph von Fürer-Haimendorf until ill health forced his
retirement in 1954. He died in 1960.

Charles Pawsey became famous for his involvement in the Battle of Kohima between April and June 1944, for which service he
was knighted. All accounts of Pawsey's contribution to the British
victory at Kohima speak of the significant role he played in securing and maintaining Naga support for the British in their struggle
against the Japanese. His friend Christoph von Fürer-Haimendorf
observed that one of the reasons why the Nagas remained loyal to
Britain was the popularity of Pawsey and his administrators, men
such as Philip Mills. One of the historians of that great battle, Arthur Swinson, remarked, "It is doubtful . . . if the Nagas would have
undertaken any of this difficult and dangerous work if it had not

been for the extraordinary character of Charles Pawsey, the Deputy Commissioner of Kohima. The Nagas trusted him completely; they knew that in no circumstances whatsoever his word would be broken." He died in 1972. Philip Adams replaced Mills as secretary to the governor of Assam, Sir Andrew Clow, and remained as secretary to the first governor of Assam, Sir Akbar Hydari, in postindependence India. Bill Archer stayed in India until independence in 1947, after which he became keeper of the Indian section at the Victoria and Albert Museum in London. He became a noted expert on the subject of Indian art and died in 1979. Following a lifetime in India and Nepal, Dr. Christoph von Fürer-Haimendorf became professor of anthropology at the SOAS in London. He revisited Pangsha in 1970. Fürer-Haimendorf died, aged eighty-seven, in 1995. Major Bill Williams returned to the Seventh Gurkha Rifles from his secondment to the Assam Rifles in April 1938 and retired to Britain at independence in 1947.

On November 4, 1943, the American press announced that Eric Sevareid had passed through New Delhi en route to the United States after completing his slightly delayed visit to Chungking. He had been in China only a month, time enough for him to be unequivocally persuaded that Stilwell was right. Yunnan under Kuomintang control was a sink of graft and official turpitude in which the only winners were those who had access to US-supplied riches and the losers—the vast majority—wasted away as a result of starvation, neglect, and brazen criminality. Despite the millions of dollars being poured into China by the United States and the hundreds if not thousands of American lives being lost to keep the Kuomintang in the war by the miracle of the Hump and the new Burma Road, millions of neglected Chinese—mostly rural peasants—were dying of starvation, not the product of poor government but rather of deliberate neglect. It was as clear as day to Sevareid that the Communists had won the battle for hearts and minds and would eventually triumph. It was the commonsense view held by most rational observers of the China scene in 1943 and 1944 but not by the armchair strategists and ideologues in Washington, who didn't have the wit to see beyond the Kuomintang propaganda and their own political (and sometimes financial) self-interest. Sevareid's suspicions of Kuomintang perfidy were confirmed when, in Kunming, Chiang Kai-shek refused to meet him. His return to the United States offered even greater disappointment. No one in FDR's administration seemed interested in his conclusions, and a long article that he prepared lies dormant in his archives because the War Department refused to allow anything disparaging of its gallant Chinese allies to make its way past the censor.

Sevareid reported the remainder of the war for CBS, including the Italian and Northwest European campaigns. He went on to become one of the most famous American broadcasters of the twentieth century, commenting nightly on CBS alongside Walter Cronkite before retiring in 1977. He died, aged seventy-nine, in 1992. His account of the war was published in 1946 as *Not So Wild a Dream*, and Raymond Schroth wrote his biography in 1995. His role as one of Murrow's boys has been brilliantly documented by Stanley Cloud and Lynne Olson.

By contrast, Jack Davies's diplomatic career was egregiously destroyed by a McCarthy-led witch hunt in 1954, and he was not exonerated until 1969. He was awarded the Medal of Freedom for "exceptional and meritorious service in China and India from March 1942 until December 1944." This included his involvement in the Pangsha affair. The citation noted that "the passengers on the plane in which he was flying en route from India to China were forced to bail out in territory inhabited only by savages. Mr. Davies' resourcefulness and leadership were in large measure responsible for the eventual rescue of the party. His conduct during this period was in the highest traditions of the Service." He died, aged ninety-one, in December 1999.

Captain Duncan Lee never got to meet General Dai Li (who died in an aircraft crash in 1945). Dai Li had the Americans neatly and tightly entangled around his little finger, helped by the egotism of Captain Milton Miles, who resolutely refused to come under any form of in-country authority. Davies always considered

Miles a lackey of Dai Li, who used the American for his own nefarious ends—primarily the acquisition of equipment—without actually giving anything of substance in return. In Davies's view, Miles and SACO, over which he presided, were little more than a state-sponsored smuggling organization, completely subservient to Dai Li, in which American expertise and equipment were subverted to selfish Kuomintang ends without any form of American control. Wild Bill Donovan, Davies concluded, "was unable to bring Miles under control because Mary was both a protégé of Admiral King's and a captive of Tai Li's." He could well have mentioned that Miles was in an entirely different league than Dai Li and had no notion that he was being played like a puppet on a string. Dai Li was able to persuade a gullible Miles to accept his account of what was happening inside China with US training and equipment, and Miles appeared to accept this unverifiable propaganda lock, stock, and barrel. It was clear to those, like Davies, working in China that Dai Li was at the heart of all the intrigue and corruption in Chiang Kai-shek's court. To his diary on July 6, 1943, Stilwell complained of Dai Li taking "graft" from the management of traffic and vehicles using the Burma Road.

The purpose of Lee's visit to Chungking, on Donovan's instructions, was partly to interrogate Dai Li in order to answer the questions that Jack Davies had raised about Miles's unaccountable operation. It is debatable how much Lee would have got out of Dai Li, had he been able to meet him, given Miles's protection of his Chinese master and Dai Li's complete control of information about his operations to the Americans. Lee returned to the United States, where he continued to spy for the Soviet Union until 1945, when fear of exposure and the threat of execution forced him to drop his connections with Moscow and cover his tracks. The revelations to the congressional House Un-American Activities Committee of the ex–Soviet spy Elizabeth Bennett in 1948 (she had turned herself in to the FBI in 1945) made public the claim that Lee worked for Moscow, or had done so during the war. Lee energetically and publicly refuted all accusations of treachery. He was supported throughout by his friends and ex-colleagues, including Donovan, none of whom could envisage this all-American patriot ever doing anything to harm his country. They were wrong. It was only with the 1995 declassification of the Verona Project, a US counterintelligence program, and material subsequently presented by the notebooks of the Soviet Committee for State Security archivist Alexander Vassiliev that the US spy in the OSS, "Koch," was identified as Lee. He was never indicted for treason, however. He continued to practice law until his retirement in 1974. He died, in Canada, aged seventy-five, in 1988.

Walter Oswalt was killed soon after returning to Chabua, when he died along with Blackie Porter on December 10. Some weeks later William McKenzie found his unarmed plane under Japanese attack. He parachuted to safety and marched out of the jungle for the second time. Harry Neveu died, aged sixty-eight, in 1991. Hugh Wild retired as a general in 1970, following service in Vietnam. He died in 2013 at the age of ninety-four. Buddy LaBonte was awarded the Legion of Merit for his part in the rescue. He died in 1981 at the age of sixty-three. John Lee DeChaine died, aged seventy-eight, in 1996. Don Flickinger was not rebuked for ignoring Alexander's orders not to jump in to administer medical aid to the survivors of Flight 12420. He became a space physician of note, choosing the first American astronauts in 1959 for the Mercury program, which led to the United States' first orbital flight in 1962. He retained a lifelong interest in parachute rescue, developing aircraft-ejection equipment that included a small supply of oxygen for the initial descent and a barometric-release mechanism to ensure that the parachute didn't open until it was in air that was thick enough to breathe. He died, aged eighty-nine, in 1997.

Joe Stilwell struggled on, fighting a losing battle against history. His determined protection of what he perceived to be America's true interests excited the intrigues of those in Chiang Kai-shek's camp—the Generalissimo included—who clamored both publicly and privately for Stilwell's dismissal. He survived the intrigues of 1943, however, for a short period of time, and even enjoyed the support of the Generalissimo, particularly leading up to the Cairo conference in November 1943. It wasn't until 1944 that the reality of China finally hit home among the US Joint Chiefs of Staff. In a strongly worded memorandum from the Joint Chiefs to President Roosevelt, the strategic situation in the CBI theater was laid bare. It was clear that Chiang Kai-shek had managed to deliver nothing of substance in the two and a half years of war apart from what Stilwell had achieved with his Chinese forces; that the Chennault Plan had been an expensive mistake and had achieved none of what had been promised; that the Japanese still roamed at will in eastern China as a result of Chennault's provocation; and that none of this would have happened if Stilwell's advice had been taken in the first place. It was a clear vindication of Stilwell's position and arguments regarding the relative roles of China and the United States in the war. On July 6, 1944, Roosevelt wrote to Chiang Kai-shek, setting out the conclusions reached by the Joint Chiefs of Staff: Stilwell must be appointed to overall command of the Chinese armies. But Roosevelt continued to underestimate the Chinese leader's ability for dissimulation, and a long period of high-level dialogue ensued, during which lend-lease supplies continued to be poured into China (which Chiang Kai-shek worked feverishly behind the scenes to control). An impasse was finally reached when Chiang Kai-shek refused to deal further with Stilwell and demanded his removal as the price for further cooperation. Roosevelt reluctantly agreed, and Stilwell was recalled on October 18, 1944. He died of stomach cancer in 1946 at the age of sixty-three. His nemesis, Major General Claire Chennault, who helped Chiang Kai-shek to convince President Roosevelt to remove him in 1944, died in 1958 at the age of sixty-four.

Insofar as the written record is concerned, the fates of the others who were part of this story have been lost to history.

EPILOGUE

During the time of this story the village of Pangsha was considered part of India's orbit, and after independence in 1947 it became part of the new country. However, the arbitrary line drawn across a map in the previous century by some anonymous colonial bureaucrat clearly placed Pangsha in Burma, a fact that became more evident as digital and satellite mapping technology now demonstrate. For this reason the village and its various *khels* were handed over to Myanmar in 2015. It remains remote from the world and physically looks quite different from the thatched conglomeration found by Mills in 1936 and the air-crash survivors in 1943. Houses remain on stilts but are now made of rough-hewn clapboard and corrugated iron and painted brightly.

When India gained its long-awaited independence in 1947, the Naga Hills were part of Britain's political settlement, much to the chagrin of many Nagas, who felt no affinity with India and desired their own independence. The ICS men in the Naga Hills during the run-up to independence, however, were convinced that this decision represented the best outcome for the Naga people, Charles Pawsey for instance arguing that Naga independence outside a new India would inevitably result in "tribal warfare, no hospitals, no schools, no salt, no trade with the plains and general unhappiness." Both Mills and Adams contributed to the preindependence debate in then-secret papers written for the governor of Assam, outlining the options available for the Nagas to survive within a political environment in which Britain was absent. Both unequivocally supported the idea of the hill tribes retaining semi-independent status in an independent India. These pleas fell on deaf ears, however. Sir Andrew Clow, for whom James Mills wrote "Note on the

Future of the Hills Tribes of Assam and the Adjoining Hills in a Self-Governing India" in 1945, dismissed the idea of keeping the Naga Hills outside an independent India as "grandiose," arguing that they should become part of a federal agency within a new India. Even the idea of a temporary solution whereby Britain retained political control after independence for a period of, say, ten years, was "a chimera."

But it was by accident of history, brought about by the speed with which independence was secured—rather than by political design—that the Naga Hills became part of the new India on August 15, 1947, despite the efforts of people such as Philip Mills to secure some form of semi-independent status for Nagas and others. Few outsiders were able to visit the remote Patkois (now generally referred to as the Patkai Ranges) in the several decades following independence, when many across Nagaland (so called since becoming an independent state within the Indian Union in 1963) fought against the Indian state for the right to Naga independence. These agitations rumble uncomfortably on, despite the desire of many for a permanent, sustainable peace. In 2006 the Kohima Educational Society (KES), an organization established in Nagaland to act as the Naga partner of the British-based Kohima Educational Trust (KET), was approached by local Naga people about building a hostel in Pangsha in order to support the education of young children who would otherwise need to walk many miles to the local mission school, then in the process of construction, and who found it impossible to undertake this journey every day. The KET had been established in 2003 by surviving British veterans who had fought alongside their Indian comrades in the tumultuous Battle of Kohima in 1944 to turn back the Japanese invasion of India. At their annual gathering in York in 2003 these men decided to create a formal and enduring memorial of their gratitude to the Naga men and women who had assisted them to overcome their enemies during those desperate days, forming a charitable organization to aid the advancement of education across Nagaland. An initial report by the prominent Naga writer and newspaperman

Charles Chasie identified Pangsha as an area of extreme poverty, so it was decided to build the hostel near the newly built Straightway Mission School just outside the village. The purpose of the hostel was to provide accommodation during the week for some of the children who would have to travel up to thirty miles to attend the new school. Without living accommodation during the week the school would struggle to sustain a viable pupil population. Immediate support came from Mr. P. Longon, the Nagaland minister for soil conservation, who had been born in Tuensang, and in 2008 he escorted KET trustee Sylvia May to the village. May described her trip with Longon; her husband, Rob; KES trustee Pfelie Kesiezie; and KES manager Bendang Ozukum:

> It was the most astonishing trip that I have ever made. The road was tortuous. It took 15 hours from Kohima, the last two hours on mud and only passable because . . . [Longon] had organized bulldozers from the nearest town of Noklak to make the road passable. Six months of the year this road is unusable. We made the journey in one day. Leaving Kohima at 4 a.m., we arrived at 7 p.m., and were greeted by a welcoming line of singing locals, performing a welcome song and dance. After a meal of hornet and chicken brought all the way from Noklak, we retired by candlelight. There was no electricity.
>
> Woken at 3.30 a.m. by the local cockerel, half an hour before dawn, we began to enjoy this rare and remote part of world. Villagers came from all over the area. Pangsha residents walked up and those from the Burma side also made the long journey. The terrain cannot be underestimated. Thousand-foot high mountains with jungle-covered sides which plunge into valleys at impossibly steep angles. It is incredible that any roads have been hewn out of this terrain at all. The villagers travel on foot and mostly barefoot. Some wore sandals and one or two have sneakers.
>
> As soon as the Minister had completed his meetings with the Burmese villagers, the party walked up to the top of the hill

following what had been a constant procession since dawn. There we were greeted by an amazing sight. A huge circle of around 60 to 70 Nagas in traditional clothes were gathered in a circle, singing. A further 100 or so looked on. Rob and I were thrust into the circle to join the festivities and once again we danced with the local people.

During their visit the Mays were told the story of Flight 12420 by the villagers and shown remnants of its wreckage. "One man," Sylvia May recalled, "who claimed to be 100 years old says that he remembers the British coming to his village and burning it down. He also remembers the plane crashing. . . . The villagers showed us where the plane came down and talked about rescuing the people who'd been on the plane."

The prospect of building a hostel here would perfectly suit the aims of the KET: the safekeeping of Eric Sevareid and the other survivors of the crash on August 3, 1943, was as much a cause for gratitude as was the support given by Nagas to Charles Pawsey and the Anglo-Indian forces fighting their life-and-death struggle at Kohima and elsewhere in the Naga Hills. So it was agreed: the KET would fund the building of a substantial hostel complex for the village. But the expectation of a two-year construction period proved to be fantastically overoptimistic. Building didn't get under way until 2010, and it was not until March 2014 that the years of planning, fund-raising, and construction finally came to fruition with the formal opening of the new three-building hostel. The KES, represented by its chairman, Dr. Phyobemo Ngully, together with KET trustee Hugh Young, formally presented the hostel to the village in front of an audience, recalled Young, of "some 220 school children and a lesser number of village elders, pastors, school and government officials." After a brief ribbon-cutting ceremony there followed prayers by the three village and International Trade Centre pastors and welcoming speeches by the leaders of the three village councils (Old Pangsha, New Pangsha, and Dan Village). The children recited Psalm 23 and sang a hymn before "grace before the feast" was said by the pastor of Old Pangsha. (Christianity has clearly entirely eclipsed the animism of the pre-European era.) This signaled the start of the inauguration feast, which included pork, chicken, and fish caught from the Langnyu River. It was, concluded Young, a deeply moving experience and augured well for the long-term future of these children, and indeed of their remote village.

What would Mongsen say? I have no doubt that he would chuckle and think, "First you burn me down, and now you build me up! Such is life in these parts. But at least we are now friends." I am sure that he would accept the work of the KET as partial payment for the care the men and women of Pangsha extended to the American and Chinese survivors of Flight 12420, and others in the months that followed, in those long-ago days. Perhaps, with the enduring poverty in that ancient community, what has been built there can not only contribute positively to the physical needs of its people but support the renewal of their spirit and enable them to hold their heads high among the people of Nagaland—and indeed farther afield.

MAP 1
The Administered Area

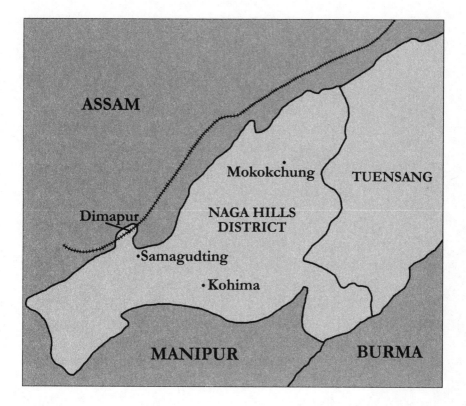

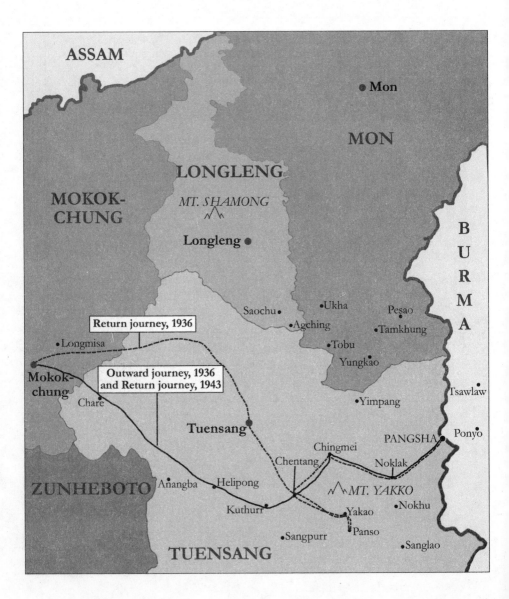

MAP 2
Routes Between Mokokchung and Pangsha, Including Those of the 1936 Expedition and the Survivors' Return in 1943

APPENDIX A
Weapons of the Patkoi Nagas

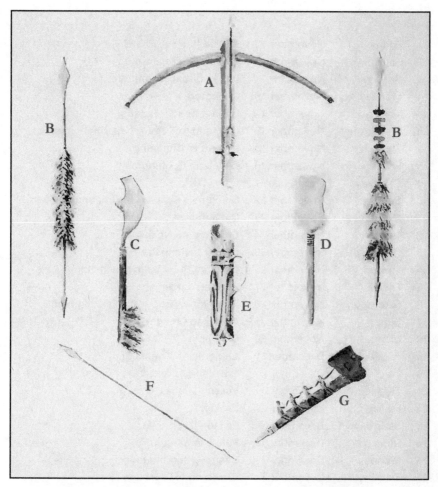

A. Crossbow used by Singphos Daphlas and Nagas on the Patkoi Range.

B. Spears used by the same with hair ornamentation. The circles denote the owner's rank.

C., D. Different kinds of *dao*s used by the Patkoi tribes. D is doubled-edged.

E. A bamboo drinking cup adorned with real "poker work."

F. The plain-shafted spear used for throwing.

G. Carved wooden pipe used on the Western Patkoi. The bowl represents a human head, and a row of monkeys stands along the stern.

Source: Art and descriptions from L. W. Shakespear, *A History of Upper Assam* (1914).

APPENDIX B

1936 Expedition Diary

1	Friday	November 13	Mokokchung to Chare
2	Saturday	November 14	Chare to Phire-ahire
3	Sunday	November 15	Phire-ahire to Chongtore
4	Monday	November 16	Chongtore
5	Tuesday	November 17	Chongtore to Helipong
6	Wednesday	November 18	Helipong to Kuthurr (via Chinguinen)
7	Thursday	November 19	Kuthurr to Chentang
8	Friday	November 20	Chentang to Chingmei
9	Saturday	November 21	Chingmei
10	Sunday	November 22	Chingmei (day walk to Yimpang and back)
11	Monday	November 23	Chingmei
12	Tuesday	November 24	Chingmei to Noklak
13	Wednesday	November 25	Noklak to Pangsha
14	Thursday	November 26	Langnyu River below Pangsha
15	Friday	November 27	Burning of Pangsha
16	Saturday	November 28	Battle of Wenshoyl; Noklak that night
17	Sunday	November 29	Noklak to Chingmei
18	Monday	November 30	Chingmei
19	Tuesday	December 1	Chingmei to Chentang
20	Wednesday	December 2	Chentang to Yukso
21	Thursday	December 3	Yukso to Panso
22	Friday	December 4	Panso
23	Saturday	December 5	Panso
24	Sunday	December 6	Panso to Sangpurr
25	Monday	December 7	Sangpurr to Chentang
26	Tuesday	December 8	Chentang to Tuensang
27	Wednesday	December 9	Tuensang
28	Thursday	December 10	Tuensang to Longtang
29	Friday	December 11	Longtang to Noksan
30	Saturday	December 12	Noksan to Dikhu River
31	Sunday	December 13	Dikhu River to Mokokchung

APPENDIX C
1943 Crash Diary

	Day	Date	Survivors	Rescue Party
1	Monday	August 2	Wenshoyl	
2	Tuesday	August 3	Wenshoyl	
3	Wednesday	August 4	Wenshoyl	
4	Thursday	August 5	Wenshoyl	
5	Friday	August 6	Wenshoyl	
6	Saturday	August 7	Wenshoyl	Mokokchung
7	Sunday	August 8	Wenshoyl	Mokokchung to Chare
8	Monday	August 9	Wenshoyl	Chare to Helipong
9	Tuesday	August 10	Wenshoyl	Helipong to Kuthurr
10	Wednesday	August 11	Wenshoyl	Kuthurr to Chentang
11	Thursday	August 12	Wenshoyl	Chentang to Chingmei
12	Friday	August 13	Wenshoyl	Chingmei to Wenshoyl
13	Saturday	August 14	Wenshoyl	Wenshoyl
14	Sunday	August 15	Wenshoyl	Wenshoyl
15	Monday	August 16	Wenshoyl	Wenshoyl
16	Tuesday	August 17	Wenshoyl	Wenshoyl
17	Wednesday	August 18	Wenshoyl to Noklak	Wenshoyl to Noklak
18	Thursday	August 19	Noklak to Chingmei	Noklak to Chingmei
19	Friday	August 20	Chingmei to Kuthurr	Chingmei to Kuthurr
20	Saturday	August 21	Kuthurr to Helipong	Kuthurr to Helipong
21	Sunday	August 22	Helipong to Chongtore	Helipong to Chongtore
22	Monday	August 23	Chongtore to Chare	Chongtore to Chare
23	Tuesday	August 24	Chare to Mokokchung	Chare to Mokokchung
24	Wednesday	August 25	Mokokchung	
25	Thursday	August 26	Mokukchung to the plains	
26	Friday	August 27	Chabua	

SELECTED BIBLIOGRAPHY

Primary Sources

Archer, W. G. "Trans-Frontier Raids 1920–1946," http://himalaya.socanth.cam.ac.uk.

Brookes, Stephen. *Through the Jungle of Death: A Boy's Escape from Wartime Burma.* New York: John Wiley & Sons, 2000.

Davies, John Paton, Jr. John Paton Davies Jr. Papers, Harry S. Truman Library, Independence, MO.

Macfarlane, Alan, ed. "The Films of Ursula Graham Bower in Nagaland, 1938–1944." University of Cambridge Streaming Media Service, http://upload.sms.cam.ac.uk/collection/1810528.

——. "The Nagas of the Assam-Burma Border." Cambridge Experimental Videodisc Project, http://æwww.alanmacfarlane.com/FILES/nagas.html.

Mills, J. P. Diaries, Pitt Rivers Museum, University of Oxford, Oxford, England.

——. J. P. Mills Papers, School of Oriental and African Studies, London, England.

——. J. P. Mills Papers and Correspondence, Pitt Rivers Museum Archive, University of Oxford, Oxford, England.

——. *Tour Diaries and Articles on Assam, 1924–1936.* Zug, Switzerland: Inter Documentation Co., 1970.

Mills, Pamela. Interview, 1981.

M1380. Missing Air Crew Reports of the US Army Air Forces, 1942–1947. Box 305256, National Archives and Records Administration, Washington, DC.

Sevareid, Eric. Eric Sevareid Papers, Manuscript Division, Library of Congress, Washington, DC.

Secondary Sources

Ao, Tajenyenba. *British Occupation of Naga Country.* Mokokchung, Nagaland, India: Naga Literature Society, 1993.

Barker, George. *A Tea Planter's Life in Assam.* Calcutta, India: Thacker and Spink, 1884.

Belloc, Hilaire. *The Modern Traveller.* London: Edward Arnold, 1898.

Bernstein, Mark, and Alex Lubertozzi. *World War II on the Air: Edward R. Murrow and the War That Defined a Generation.* Naperville, IL: Sourcebooks Mediafusion, 2005.

Blossom, W. R. "Capt. John. L. 'Blackie' Porter's Search and Rescue Squadron at Chabua in the Hump." In *China Airlift—the Hump*, vol. 3, edited by John G. Martin. Nashville, TN: Turner Publishing Company, 1991.

Bootland, Margaret Elizabeth. Recorded interview, Sound 19821. London: Imperial War Museum, 1999.

Bower, Ursula Graham. *Naga Path*. London: John Murray, 1952.

Bowers, Alva. *Under the Headhunters' Eyes*. Philadelphia, PA: Johnson Press, 1929.

Bowers, Peter. *Curtiss Aircraft, 1907–1947*. London: Putnam & Company, 1979.

Bradley, Mark. *A Very Principled Boy: The Life of Duncan Lee, Red Spy and Cold Warrior*. New York: Basic Books, 2014.

Brown, Anthony Cave. *Wild Bill Donovan: The Last Hero*. New York: Times Books, 1982.

Carton de Wiart, Adrian. *Happy Odyssey*. London: Jonathan Cape, 1950.

Channa, S. M., ed. *Nagaland, a Contemporary Ethnography*. Delhi, India: South Asia Books, 1992.

Clark, Mary. *A Corner in India*. Philadelphia, PA: American Baptist Publication Society, 1907.

Cloud, Stanley, and Lynne Olson. *The Murrow Boys: Pioneers on the Front Lines of Broadcast Journalism*. New York: Houghton Mifflin, 1997.

Cross, John. *Jungle Warfare*. London: Arms and Armour Press, 1989.

Davies, John Paton, Jr. *Dragon by the Tail*. New York: W. W. Norton, 1972.

——. *China Hand*. Philadelphia: University of Pennsylvania Press, 2012.

Davis, John, Harold Martin, and John Whittle. *The Curtiss C-46 Commando*. Tonbridge, England: Air-Britain, 1978.

Downie, Don, and Jeffrey Ethell. *Flying the Hump in Original WWII Color*. Minneapolis, MN: Motorbooks International, 2004.

Elwin, Verrier. *The Nagas in the Nineteenth Century*. Oxford and New Delhi: Oxford University Press, 1969.

Fenby, Jonathan. *Chiang Kai-shek: China's Generalissimo and the Nation He Lost*. New York: Carroll & Graf, 2005.

Fürer-Haimendorf, Christoph von. *The Konyak Nagas: An Indian Frontier Tribe*. London: Holt, Rinehart and Winston, 1969.

——. *The Naked Nagas*, 2nd rev. ed. Calcutta, India: Thacker, Spink & Co., 1962.

——. *Return to the Naked Nagas: An Anthropologist's View of Nagaland, 1936–1970*, 2nd rev. ed. London: John Murray Publishers, 1977.

Gallagher, O. D. *Retreat in the East*. London: Harrap, 1942.

Ghio, Bob. "Lost in Head-Hunter Country." *YANK: The Army Weekly*, December 31, 1943.

Graham-Bower, Ursula. *The Hidden Land*. London: John Murray Publishers, 1953.

Gribble, R. H. *Out of the Burma Night*. Calcutta, India: Thacker, Spink & Co., 1944.

Guha, Ramachandra. *India After Gandhi*. London: Pan Macmillan, 2007.

Ham, Peter van, and Jamie Saul. *Expedition Naga: Diaries from the Hills in Northeast India 1921–1937 and 2002–2006*. Suffolk, England: ACC Editions, 2006.

Hobson, Geraldine. "J. P. Mills and the Hill People of Assam." *Journal of the Indo-British Historical Society* 12 (1998): 61–70.

Hodson, T. C. *The Naga Tribes of Manipur*. London: Macmillan, 1911.

Hutton, J. H. *The Angami Nagas: With Some Notes on Neighboring Tribes*. London: Oxford University Press, 1921.

——. *Diaries of Two Tours in the Unadministered Areas East of the Naga Hills*. Calcutta, India: Asiatic Society of Bengal, 1929.

——. *Naga Manners and Customs*. Gurgaon, India: Vintage Books, 1990 (reprint).

——. *Report on Naga Hills*. New Delhi, India: Mittal, 1986 (reprint).

——. *The Sema Nagas*. London: Macmillan, 1921.

Jacobs, Julian, Alan MacFarlane, Sarah Harrison, and Anita Herle. *The Nagas: Hill Peoples of Northeast India—Society, Culture and the Colonial Encounter*. London: Thames and Hudson, 1990.

James, Lawrence. *Raj: The Making and Unmaking of British India*. London: Little, Brown, 1997.

Johnstone, Major General Sir James. *My Experiences in Manipur and the Naga Hills*. London: Sampson Low, Marston and Company, 1896.

Kahn, E. J. *The China Hands: America's Foreign Service Officers and What Befell Them*. New York: Viking, 1975.

Ltu, Khrienuo. "Nagas' Role in World War II." *Journal of North East India Studies* 3, no. 2 (July–December 2013): 57–69.

Lunt, James. *A Hell of a Licking: The Retreat from Burma, 1941–2*. London: Collins, 1986.

Lyman, Robert. *Japan's Last Bid for Victory*. Barnsley, England: Praetorian Press, 2011.

Macfarlane, Alan. "Mills, James Philip (1890–1960)." *Oxford Dictionary of National Biography*. Oxford: Oxford University Press, 2004.

MacKenzie, Alexander. *History of the Relations of the Government with the Hill Tribes of the North East Frontier of Bengal*. Cambridge and New York: Cambridge University Press, 1884.

McKelway, St. Clair. *Reporting at Wit's End*. London: Bloomsbury, 2010.

McKie, Ronald. *Echoes from Forgotten Wars*. Sydney, Australia: Collins, 1980.

Means, Gordon. "Human Sacrifice and Slavery in the 'Unadministered' Areas of Upper Burma During the Colonial Era." *Sojourn: Journal of Social Issues in Southeast Asia* 15, no. 2 (October 2000): 184–221.

Miles, Milton E. *A Different Kind of War: The Little-Known Story of the Combined Guerrilla Forces Created in China by the U.S. Navy and the Chinese During World War II*. New York: Doubleday, 1967.

Mills, J. P. "Anthropology as a Hobby." *Journal of the Royal Anthropological Institute* 83, no. 1 (January–June 1953): 1–8.

——. *The Ao Nagas.* London: Macmillan, 1926.

——. "The Effect on the Naga Tribes of Assam of Their Contact with Western Civilization." Paper delivered at Fifth Pacific Science Congress, 1934.

——. *The Lhota Nagas.* London: Macmillan, 1922.

——. *The Pangsha Letters of J. P. Mills,* edited by Geraldine Hobson. Oxford, England: The Pitt Rivers Museum, 1995.

——. *The Rengma Nagas.* London: Macmillan, 1937.

——. *Tour Diaries and Correspondence.* Naga videodisc, Department of Social Anthropology, University of Cambridge.

Myint-U, Thant. *The Making of Modern Burma.* Cambridge: Cambridge University Press, 2001.

——. *The River of Lost Footsteps—Histories of Burma.* New York: Farrar, Straus, and Giroux, 2006.

Neveu, John. *The Crash of a C-46; Tail Number: 41-12420.* San Francisco, CA: City College of San Francisco, 2012.

Olson, Lynne. *Citizens of London: The Americans Who Stood with Britain in Its Darkest, Finest Hour.* San Francisco, CA: Presidio Press, 2010.

Paananen, Eloise. *Pararescue.* New York: John Day & Co, 1964.

Peter, Walter. "Burma Hermits." *YANK: The Army Weekly,* April 6, 1945.

Plating, John. *The Hump: America's Strategy for Keeping China in World War II.* College Station: Texas A&M University Press, 2011.

Probert, Henry. *The Forgotten Air Force: The Royal Air Force in the War Against Japan 1941–1945.* London: Brassey's, 1995.

Puthenpurakkal, Joseph. *Baptist Missions in Nagaland.* Shillong, India: South Asia Books, 1984.

Rackmales, Bob. "Grace Under Pressure." *Foreign Service Journal* (July–August 2008): 8.

Randle, John. *Battle Tales from Burma.* Barnsley, England: Pen & Sword, 2004.

Ravenholt, Albert. "Rescue Party Leads 20 Men Thru Jungle; Airplanes Aid." *Coshocton Tribune* (Ohio), August 30, 1943, 3.

Reid, Sir Robert. *History of the Frontier Areas Bordering on Assam from 1883–1941.* Shillong, India: Assam Government Press, 1942.

Rooney, David. *Stilwell the Patriot: Vinegar Joe, the Brits and Chiang Kai-shek.* London: Greenhill Books, 2005.

Schroth, Raymond. *The American Journey of Eric Sevareid.* South Royalton, VT: Steerforth Press, 1995.

Sevareid, Eric. *Not So Wild a Dream.* New York: Alfred A. Knopf, 1946.

——. "Our Good Friends, the Headhunters." *Reader's Digest* (February 1944).

Shakespear, Leslie. *History of the Assam Rifles.* London: Macmillan, 1929.

———. *History of Upper Assam, Upper Burmah and North-Eastern Frontier.* London: Macmillan, 1914.

Slim, Sir William. *Defeat into Victory.* London: Cassell and Company, London, 1956.

Smith, William Carlson. *The Ao Naga Tribe of Assam: A Study in Ethnology and Sociology.* London: Macmillan, 1925.

Steyn, Peter. *Zapuphizo: Voice of the Nagas.* London: Kegan Paul International, 2002.

Stilwell, General Joseph W. *The Stilwell Papers*, ed. Theodore White. New York: Da Capo Press, 1991.

Stockhausen, Alban von. *Imag(in)ing the Nagas: The Pictorial Ethnography of Hans-Eberhard Kauffmann and Christoph von Fürer-Haimendorf.* Stuttgart, Germany: Arnoldsche Art Publishers, 2014.

Stowe, Leland. *They Shall Not Sleep.* New York: Alfred A. Knopf, 1944.

Swinson, Arthur. *Kohima.* London: Arrow Books, 1956.

Syiemlieh, David R., ed. *On the Edge of Empire: Four British Plans for North East India, 1941–1947.* Delhi, India: Sage Publications, 2014.

Tyson, Geoffrey. *Forgotten Frontier.* Calcutta, India: W. H. Targett & Co., 1945.

US Military Observer, Singapore. "Japanese Tactics and Activities in Northern Malaya." December 28, 1941. War Department, G-2 Regional File, Box 2146, File 6675, US National Archives and Records Administration, Washington, DC.

Vance, Charles. "Do You Remember Luliang, China?" In *China Airlift—the Hump*, edited by Harry Howton. Poplar Bluffs, MO: China-Burma-India Hump Pilots Association, 1983.

Wakeman, Frederic. *Spymaster: Dai Li and the Chinese Secret Service.* Berkeley: University of California Press, 2003.

Webster, Donovan. *The Burma Road: The Epic Story of the China-Burma-India Theater in World War II.* New York: Farrar, Straus, and Giroux, 2003.

White T. H. "The Hump." *LIFE* magazine, September 11, 1944.

Wragg, Alfred. *A Million Died! A Story of War in the Far East.* London: Nicholson & Watson, 1943.

ACKNOWLEDGMENTS

This book would have been impossible without extensive use of the published and unpublished accounts of many of the participants, including Philip Mills, Eric Sevareid, Jack Davies, Christoph von Fürer-Haimendorf, and Harry Neveu. One of these was the account in *The Naked Nagas* by Christoph von Fürer-Haimendorf of the 1936 expedition and also his marvelous photographs, digitized in 2008. Who would have thought that such wonderful history could be viewed in black-and-white today? I am grateful to his son, Nick Haimendorf, for permission to quote so extensively from his father's story and for permission to use some of the marvelous treasure trove of his father's photographs. I am indebted to Mrs. Geraldine Hobson for allowing me to use the letters written by her father, Philip Mills, to his wife, Pamela—*The Pangsha Letters of J. P. Mills*—during the expedition and for introducing me to her father's papers and photographs. I also wish to thank Suzanne St. Pierre Sevareid for permission to quote from Eric Sevareid's beautifully written account of his adventures in *Not So Wild a Dream*. I acknowledge the pioneering work of Mark Bradley in uncovering the secret story of Duncan Lee in his excellent biography *A Very Principled Boy* (2014). None of my story could have been told without the richness of these sources. My take on Joe Stilwell was first developed in *The Generals: From Defeat to Victory, Leadership in Asia 1941–45* (London: Constable, 2008), which owed much to my good friend David Rooney, author of *Stilwell the Patriot* (2005). A number of secondary sources have been invaluable in the telling of this story, all of which are listed, and gratefully acknowledged, in the bibliography. I am grateful also to the Japanese historian Dr. Kyoichi Tachikawa for information about the dispositions of the Eighteenth Division in northern Burma in 1943.

Finally, and by no means least, I wish to acknowledge the support of Philip Grover, archivist at the Pitt Rivers Museum, Oxford; Charles Chasie, author and member of the Kohima Educational Society, Kohima (and descendent of the Khonoma chief who killed G. H. Damant in 1879); Professor Alan Macfarlane; Robert Palmer; Khrienuo Ltu; the librarians of the Manuscript Division, Library of Congress; and Robert and Sylvia May for making this book possible.

INDEX

Naga names of individuals are indexed as single names. Names of Naga villages and tribes are identified as such.

A Million Died (Wragg), 24
Adams, Philip (sahib of Mokokchung)
  briefed McKelway on Naga situation, 169
  concern about Konyaks in rescue party, 193–194
  concern for survivor safety, 193
  convinced Mongsen to care for crash survivors, 189–190
  as ICS administrator and anthropologist, 98
  as leader of rescue party, 209
  letter from Pawsey about head-hunting, 224
  life after rescue, 226
  magistrate duties in Noklak, 199
  Nagas told to help survivors, 164–165
  perceptions of Nagas, 209–210
  punitive expedition (1943), 157, 158
  as representative of British king, 192–193
  respect shown by Nagas, 192
  responsibility to Naga population, 103
  on semi-independence for Naga Hills, 231
  stopped Nagas fighting over survivors' trash, 196–197
  unable to enforce authority in Patkoi Hills during war, 219
  visit to Sangbah's home, 201

Administered Area
  ambiguous rule enforcement, 222–223
  to be extended with consent of population, 222
  benefits of governance in, 210, 221
  bordering Dikhu River Valley, 152
  gaonburas in, 122
  lawlessness from outside, 93–94
  as only area of control, 93
  opposition to slavery, 156–158
Agching village, 157
air support for China decision, 43
Air Transport Command (ATC)
  aircraft accidents, 12–13
  ATC members on Flight 12420, 5, 58
  in crisis at Chabua, 14
  search and rescue capacity in, 206, 215
  Sevareid on Hump pilots, 7
  White on, 11
aircraft types at Chabua, 1
Alexander, Edward, 170, 182, 188, 203
Allies
  bomber crew tortured and beheaded by Japanese, 32
  Chennault's push for air capability in China, 49
  Chinese Army training by Britain, 7
  forced out of Burma, 26
  Germany as second front, 65
  support of China, 43–44, 47–48, 51, 53–54, 56
aluminum trail, 162
American Baptist Foreign Missionary Society, 89

American Society of Airplane-Haters,
    13
American Volunteer Group (AVG), 19
Anangba village, 115
Angami Naga tribe, 86–87, 90, 99
Angami territory, first flights over, 78
"Anthropology as a Hobby" (Mills), 101
anti-British nationalists aiding
    Japanese, 33–34
Ao Naga tribe, 91–92, 94, 153–154
The Ao Nagas (Mills), 99, 102
Arbuthnot, Glenn, 162
Archer, Bill, 98, 99, 103, 226
"Asia for the Asiatics" and Japanese
    militarism, 31
Assam, 3–4, 85
Assam Rifles
    firepower vs. local knowledge, 120
    as former Gurkha soldiers, 121
    formerly Naga Hills Military Police,
        94
    on guard at Chingmei, 139
    protecting India from Japanese, 192
    punishment expedition against
        Pangsha, 110–113
    Shakespear as commandant, 82
    unavailability for rescue mission, 192
    as USAAF watch station guards, 219
Assam tea, 85
Assam-to-Yunnan air-ferry route
    (Hump route), 2, 10, 43
ATC. *See* Air Transport Command
Aung San, 33–34
Aung San Suu Kyi, 34
AVG. *See* American Volunteer Group

B-25 Mitchells, 1
bail-out advice, 3
Baisden, Chuck, 20
Balbahadur, Subedar, 131
Barker, George, 85–86
*basha*s (temporary shelter), 5, 181
Bataan Death March, 30–32
Battle of Kohima, 225, 232

Belloc, Hilaire, 121
Bennett, Elizabeth, 228
Bert (slave), 144, 150
Blackie's Gang, 215–218
Blah, Hari, 156
Blainey, Geoffrey, 93
Blitz, London, Sevareid's coverage, 61
blood chits, 1–2
Blossom, Bill, 216–217
Boatner, Haydon, 73
Bootland, Alan and Beth, 24–25
boots for return hike, 194, 197–198
Bower, Ursula Graham, 101
Bradley, Mark, 63–65
Brahmaputra River Valley, 4, 43, 83,
    142, 211
Bren light machine guns, 218
Britain. *See* East India Company; Raj
British censorship of Burma situation,
    22
British East India Company (EIC), 4,
    83–85, 88, 91–92, 98
British Empire, Sevareid on, 208
British imperialism and control of
    Nagas, 85
British political agent, 176, 180
British surveying expeditions, 90
Brodie, T., 91
Bronson, Miles, 88
Brookes, Stephen, 23–25
Brown, Anthony Cave, 70
Burma
    British rule (1885–1942), 17
    ethnic and tribal frictions, 21
    exodus from, 20–25
    extended Control Area toward,
        155–156
    geography of, 16–17
    hill country tribes, 21
    Indian workers in, 21
    Japanese invasion, 17–18
    ongoing civil war, 34
    population exodus after attack,
        20–25

Stowe's reportage on, 19
villages raided from Patkoi Hills
   villages, 220–221
Burma Army, tribespeople recruited,
   22
Burma Independence Army, 34
Burma Road, 17–18, 24, 45, 47, 50–51
Burmese people, sided with Japan
   against colonial British, 21
Bushido, 31

C-46 Commandos, 1–2, 11–14
C-47 Skytrains "Gooney Birds," 1, 80,
   161–162, 168
C-54 Skymasters, 1
C-87 Liberators, 1
camp organization, 178–179, 181
canned water, 183
Carton de Wiart, Adrian, 55
CBI (China-Burma-India) theater, 50
"Celestial Catering Service." *See* rescue
   packs
Chabua USAAF air base
   ("Dumbastapur"), 1–2, 4, 217
Chakhesang village, 78–79
Chang expedition (1889), 94
Chang Naga tribe, 99, 107, 117–118
Chare village, 113–114, 206, 221
Chasie, Charles, 233
Chennault, Claire Lee, 5, 44, 49, 51–55,
   230
Chennault Plan, 53, 73, 230
Chentang village, 119, 122, 144, 149–150
Chiang Kai-shek
   demand for Allied resources, 56
   lobbied for American support
      against Japan, 43
   objectives and strategies, 46, 48
   promoted Chennault plan, 53–54
   refusal to meet Sevareid, 227
   relationship with Stillwell, 45, 48,
      229–230
   Yoke Force, 51, 53
   See also Kuomintang

Chiang-Chennault air offensive plan,
   73
Chicago Daily News, Stowe on Burma
   Road, 19
children, visibility of in villages,
   167–168
China
   Allied policy of support, 43
   Chinese intelligence and SACO, 66
   honest with US, 44
   manipulation of American views,
      72–73
   Mao's defeat as goal, 44
   political sense per Davies, 71
   Trident Conference plans for, 55–56
   US airpower in, 49
China National Aviation Corporation
   aircraft at Chabua, 1
China-Burma-India (CBI) theater, 50
Chinese Air Force, loan of P-43s, 5
Chinese Army, 7, 71–72
Chinglong village, 94–97
Chingmak
   emotional leave-taking with Mills,
      152
   fealty sworn to George V, 107, 138
   guide provided to expedition, 127
   as Mills's friend, 123
   as protector of survivors, 180–181,
      193
Chingmei village
   as advanced base camp for punitive
      expedition, 123
   attack on Law Nawkum, 219
   enforcing Mokokchung's
      injunctions, 223
   Matche sought sanctuary in,
      107–108
   return after punitive expedition, 138
   stop on return march, 200–201
Chingpoi village, 95
Chins (Burmese hill country tribe),
   21, 33
Chirongchi, 116

Chongtore village, 115–117, 205
Christian missionaries, 87–89, 104, 209–210
Chrysanthemum (Eighteenth) Division (Japan), 27–28, 33
Church Parade, 187
Clay, Joseph, 58
Cloud, Stanley, 59, 227
clouds' effects on planes, 8
Clow, Andrew, 102, 226, 231–232
Cockpit Joe ballad, 4
Coleman, Kenneth, 191
Communism in China, predicted by Sevareid, 226–227
Control Area
    bordering Dikhu River Valley, 152
    destabilizing effect of Pangsha's actions, 108
    head-hunting in, 222–223
    life without government intervention, 210
    opposition to slavery, 156–158
    Pawsey's concern, 219–222
    request to include Pangsha, 155–156
Corsica Daily Sun (Texas) on Martin as MIA, 22
Cross, John, 28
crossbows with poisoned arrows, 114–115, 186, 193–195
cultural anthropology, understanding Nagas, 99–100
Curtis-Wright aircraft at Chabua, 1

Dacca Military Police, 95
dacoits (bandits), 24
Dai Li, 6, 66–69, 227–228
Damant, G. H., 82, 90–91
daos (swords), 80, 96–97
Davies, John Paton, Jr. (Jack)
    on bail-out decision, 38–39
    on beauty of country, 207
    as celebrity in survivor group, 206
    in charge of bartering with Nagas, 179

on Dai Li and Miles, 66–69
fitness level on march, 203
as Flight 12420 passenger, 5, 15, 58
on leaving Pangsha and Ponyo, 195
on Lee, 6
life after rescue, 227
on lunch for survivors at Mokokchung, 211
met native men after parachute jump, 75–76
on Miles and SACO, 227–228
under Naga observation, 183
on Pangsha treatment of survivors, 194–195
parachuted from Flight 12420, 74
in party joining survivors in Wenshoyl, 175–176
retrieval of rescue loads, 179
and Stilwell, 43, 71–72, 73
survivor camp description, 187
Davies Papers, Truman Library, 76
Dayak (Iban) headhunters, Borneo, 83
DeChaine, John Lee, 191, 229
Detachment 101 (OSS), 34, 67–71
A Different Kind of War (Miles), 68
Dikhu River, 113, 152–153
diplomatic tour to Panso village, 143
dissonance between civilized imperatives and native culture, 104
dobashis (interpreters), 111, 132
Donovan, Leisure, Newton & Irvine, 65–69
Donovan, William "Wild Bill," 71, 228
Doolittle Raid on Tokyo, 32
Dorman-Smith, Reginald, 19–20
downed aircraft, finding, 162–163. See also Blackie's Gang
Downie, Don, 3
Dumbastapur, origin of name, 5
Dwyer, J. J., 191

East India Company (EIC). See British East India Company

education programs, current, 232
Edward VIII's abdication, 126, 139,
    153–154
Eifler, Carl, 67–68, 70–71
Eighteenth (Chrysanthemum) Division
    (Japan), 27–28, 33
elephants and tigers, 207
Emlong, 191, 197, 211
Ercolani, Lucien, 30–32
ethnological and anthropological
    studies, 104. *See also individual
    anthropologists*
evangelizing missions. *See* Christian
    missionaries

feast given by Nagas at survivor camp,
    184–185
Felix, Charles, 2, 175, 178, 187
ferry pilots, 4–5, 12–15
First Anglo-Burmese War, 85
Fisher, Herbert, 12
fitness of crash survivors, 202–203
Flickinger, Don
    camp activities organization, 188
    difficult first day's march toward
        Chabua, 198
    as forerunner of volunteer medic
        parachuters, 217
    gift from Mongsen, 195, 205
    as leader for survival group, 177–178
    life after rescue, 229
    maintaining equilibrium between
        Nagas and survivors, 179
    medical treatment of villagers, 174,
        183
    parachuting in to survivor group,
        170–172
    preparations for Japanese attacks,
        188
    visit to Sangbah's home, 201
    as wing surgeon, 170
Flight 12420
    attempted emergency route to
        Jorhat, 36

bail-out, 37–42
crash site, 160
engine problems, 15, 35–36
oil pressure gauge problem, 35–36
passengers, 5–6
preflight checklists, 1–2, 8
weight concern, 11
Flying Tigers, 19
Forsdike, Eric, 8
Fort Hertz, Burma, 9
France, Sevareid's coverage in, 60–62
Fuller, Joseph Bampfylde, 83–85
Fürer-Haimendorf, Christof von
    on crossbows with poisoned arrows,
        115
    on danger of solo travel in Naga
        Hills, 107–108
    donation of heads to Naga sepoys,
        154–155
    Emlong photographs with heads,
        211
    expedition photographs, 116
    on friendliness of Panso, 146
    life after rescue, 225–226
    on Mills's approach to Nagas, 101
    on Pangsha emissaries at
        Chimgmei, 140–141
    on punitive expedition to Pangsha,
        110–111
    search for Wenshoyl, 133
    study of Nagas, 98, 103
    study of Noklat, 136
    on views from Helipong, 117–118
    visits to uncontacted villages, 115

Gallagher, O. D., 22, 29–31
gaonbura (village headman appointed
    by British), 181
gaonbura system of Naga government,
    91–92
gasoline air transports to China, 2–3
Gauss, Clarence, 71
Geneva Conventions of 1929, 32
Germany, 60–62

Gerty, Bernard, 156
Gibb, Isabella "Ishbel," 64
gift exchange in Ponyo, 78–79
Giguere, Joseph "Jiggs," 58, 74, 179, 203
Gilbert, Henry, 22
Giota, Anthony, 191
Girly (slave), 144, 150
goat sacrifice, 80
Great Awakening, 88
guns, 220, 223. *See also* Lee-Enfield rifles
Gurkhas
   as Assam Rifles, 121, 226
   Burmese Army recruitment from, 22
   as Gurkha Rifles, 157
   J. Cross as, 28
   kukri (fighting knife), 38
   subdued Chinglong, 97

Ham, Peter van, 99, 105
Hamilton (Captain), 94
Harman, Carter, 217
head-hunting
   in Control Area, 221
   as cultural dissonance problem, 104–106
   heads confiscated at Yimpang, 125
   Inner Line System increases, 105
   as Naga practice, 83–84
   occasionally sanctioned, 223
   Pangsha and Yimpang rampage, 108–109
   prohibition, beneficial effects of, 210
   raids by tribes in nonadministered areas, 93–94
   Raj and missionary opposition to, 89
helicopters for search-and-rescue, 217
heliograph apparatus, 118
Helipong village, 117, 204
Helland, Edward, 58
Heppner, Richard, 67

hill country tribes as pro-British, 21
History of the Areas Bordering on Assam from 1883–1941 (Reid), 82, 84
Hobbes, Thomas, 210
Hobhouse Commission, 98
Holongba village, 115
hostel for distant-living school children, 232–234
Hukawng Valley, Burma, 9
Hull, Cordell, 22
human sacrifice, 108, 109, 142, 149, 210
Hump (Assam-to-Yunnan air-ferry route), 2, 10, 43
Hutton, John Henry "J. H.," 83, 97–100, 150
Hydari, Akbar, 226

iced wings, 10
ICS. *See* Indian Civil Service
Imperial Japanese Army. *See* Japanese military
India. *See* Shillong, India
Indian Civil Service (ICS), 97–98
Indian workers in Burma, 21
Inner Line System, 105
intelligence concerns, 65–69. *See also* Office of Strategic Services
Intourist tours to Russia, 64

Japanese military
   attacks and invasion of Burma, 19–22, 29, 33
   fighting ability and commitment of, 27–29
   Japanese Zero fighter planes, 9, 10, 187–188, 218
   Pearl Harbor and Asian attacks, 19, 29
   Porter attacked ground positions, 218
   protection of Burma, 33
   rapes of nurses, 24
   "Regulations for Punishment of Enemy Air Crews," 32

ruthlessness and brutality of, 29–31
  as threat to crash survivors, 186, 188
Japan's Last Bid for Victory (Lyman),
  79, 192
jettisoned baggage retrieved, 183–184
John Company. *See* British East India
  Company
Johnstone, James, 87, 91
Jones, Craig, 206
Jorhat, Assam
  as air base, 4
  survivors arrive at, 213

Kachin tribe
  as British-led rebels, 33
  as Burmese hill country tribe, 16,
    21, 33
  Detachment 101, working with,
    67–68, 70
  as pro-British, 34
Kalyo Kengyu Naga tribe, 107–108,
  156, 164–166
Kaolikung Range, Burma, 9
Karen tribe, 21, 33, 34
Katzman, George, 162
Kempetai (Japanese military police), 32
kepruo (plane), 78
Kesiezie, Pfelie, 233
khel headmen of Pangsha, 108
khels (village divisions), 132–133
Khonoma village, 78, 86–87, 90, 91
Khruomo, Noumvüo, 78
Kittleson, Glen, 58, 178
Knight, Richard, 162
Kohima Educational Society (KES),
  232, 234
Kohima Educational Trust (KET),
  232–234
Kohima village, 87, 90–91, 99–100, 225
Konyak Naga tribe, 103, 191–192
The Konyak Nagas (Fürer-Haimendorf),
  103
Kramer, Joe, 217
Kukis, as Burmese hill country tribe, 33

kukri (fighting knife), 38, 195
Kunming, China, 5
Kuomintang, 44–45, 56–57, 67,
  226–227. *See also* Chiang Kai-shek
Kuthurr village, 119, 202
Kwoh Li, 74, 198, 203

LaBonte, Andrew "Buddy," 184, 191,
  229
lambu (sacrosanct ambassador), 141
Langnyu River Valley
  defenses built, 128, 130
  men missing from stockade, 133
  Noklak village on, 136
  planned pretend camp after
    Pangsha-Wenshoyl attack, 131
  protective party at, 181, 186
latitude/longitude of crash site, 163
Lee, Duncan C. "Koch"
  in charge of supply tent, 179
  on Eifler's SI reports, 70
  encounter with tiger, 212
  fitness level on march, 203
  as Flight 12420 passenger, 5–6, 15,
    58
  life after rescue, 227–229
  parachuted from Flight 12420, 74
  proposed meeting with Dai Li, 228
  as Soviet spy in OSS, 6, 62–65,
    228–229
  tasked by Donovan re Detachment
    101, 69–70
  tasked by Donovan re SACO,
    65–69, 67
Lee, Roland, 58, 212
Lee-Enfield rifle, 112, 116, 121, 134–135
Lemmon, Basil, 58, 175, 185
lend-lease material to China, 18, 45, 47,
  71–72, 230
Lewis guns, 130, 132
The Lhota Nagas (Mills), 102
LIFE magazine
  on C-46 problems, 11–12
  on ferry pilots, 4–5

Liresu village, 117
Loksan village, 151–152
Longmatrare, Nagaland, 222
Longmisa village, 153–154
Longon, P., 233
Ltu, Khrienuo, 92
Lunt, James, 29
Lushai, as Burmese hill country tribe,
    33
Lyman, Robert, 79

M1 carbines for survivors, 177–178
MACR. *See* missing air crew reports
Maddock, Thomas, 88
Manipur, India
    army to Khonoma siege, 91
    in Treaty of Yandabo, 85
march from Mokokchung to Jorhat
    airfield, 211–212
Mark I Eyeball, 162
Martin, Neil G., 22
Mason, Gerry, 5
Matche, 107–108, 140
May, Rob and Sylvia, 233–234
McKelway, St. Clair, 169, 171
McKenzie, William, 171–172, 178, 229
McKie, Ronald, 10, 54–55
Merrill, Frank, 73
Merritt, Joe, 191
Miles, Milton "Mary," 65–69, 227–228
military codes of conduct, ignored by
    Japanese, 29, 31
Miller, Ned, 3, 36–37, 159
Mills, Geraldine, 100
Mills, James, 231–232
Mills, Pamela, 114
Mills, Philip "J.P."
    Chang territory visit, 107
    on changes in Naga culture, 105
    as colonial administrator and
        anthropologist, 97–98, 100–102
    on death by Naga poison, 121
    on Edward VIII's abdication, 139
    first Pangsha encounter, 129–130

hope for nonviolent resolution in
    Pangsha, 112–113
journey to uncharted areas, 110
life after rescue, 225
overtures to neighboring villages to
    Pangsha, 122–123
perceptions of Nagas, 209–210
search for Wenshoyl, 133
on semi-independence for Naga
    Hills, 231–232
study of Noklat, 136
terms for peace with Pangsha,
    140–141
visits to uncontacted villages, 115
See also punitive expeditions
missing air crew reports (MACRs),
    162
mithan cows, 132, 149, 151, 184
The Modern Traveller (Belloc), 121
Mokokchung village
    anthropological studies in, 99–100
    as British administrative site,
        93–94
    march to, 208
    Mills at, 100
    Pangsha expedition launch from,
        111–113
    returning Pangsha expedition, 153
Mongoloid races, Nagas as, 82–83
Mongsen
    arrested in 1939, 158
    child treated by Flickinger, 188–189
    as emissary to Chingmei, 140
    first encounter in punitive
        expedition, 129–130
    gift to Flickinger, 195, 205
    imagined response to KET work,
        235
    injured foot treated by Vierya,
        141–142
    as *khel* headman of Pangsha, 108
    perceptions of white men, 189–190
    in Wenshoyl with crash survivors,
        174

Mongu, 108, 158
monsoons, 30, 96, 116, 175, 187
*morung*s (village dormitories), 136, 167
Mount Yakko, 143–144
Mozema village, 86, 90
Murrow, Edward, 59–61
Myanmar. *See* Burma
Myitkyina, Burma, 10, 16, 50–51

Naga expedition (1879–1880), 85–86
Naga Hills
  British surveying expeditions, 90
  danger of solo travel in, 107–108
  establishing peace, problems with,
    85–86
  as Savage Mountains (Chinese), 17
  sought independence from India,
    231
Naga Hills Military Police, 95
Naga Labour Corps, 115–116
Naga tribes
  in administered vs. unadministered
    zones, 105–106
  attempts to convert and civilize,
    88–89
  as Burmese hill country tribe, 21
  came to Pangsha to observe crash
    survivors, 199
  changes near civilization, 207
  continued quest for independent
    Nagaland, 232
  cultural dissonance problems,
    104–106
  dance celebration, 146–147
  different languages among, 111–112
  ethnological and anthropological
    studies of, 98–103
  exposure to foreigners, 9
  fighting methods, 119–121
  first contact with crash survivors,
    164–166
  gaonbura system and British rule,
    92
  history and culture, 82

internecine struggles for local
    power, 89–90
  Mills's description, 102–103
  offered tribute for British
    protection, 90
  playful natures of, 99
  as porters for Pangsha expedition,
    111–112
  power by fear, 84, 127, 129, 143, 146,
    209–210, 221
  retribution for Raj attacks, 87
  visitors restricted by British, 9
  war, enjoyment of, 84–85
  See also Raj; slavery among Nagas;
    individual tribes and villages
Nagaland, 232–235
The Naked Nagas (Fürer-Haimendorf),
    103
Nakhu, 140
Nanking Massacre, 32
Nazi Germany Means War (Stowe), 19
Neilao, 78
Neveu, Harry
  on bail-out, 39–42
  in charge of guard roster, 179
  collapse on trail, 212
  as Commando pilot, 1
  engine problems, 35–36
  fear of Japanese capture, 30–32
  leg sore on march, 204
  life after rescue, 229
  preflight checklists, 1–2, 8
  responsibility for crash, 160–161
  reunited with Sevareid group, 159
  route from Chabua, 14–15
  weight concern for Flight 12420, 11
Ngully, Phyobemo, 234
Nian village, 158
Nlamo, 111, 133
Nokhu village, 144, 156–157
Noklak village, 125, 127, 136–137, 142,
    197–200
Noklu village, 143, 144–145, 148
Nokluk village, 219

Not So Wild a Dream (Sevareid), 227
"Note on the Future of the Hills Tribes
　　of Assam and the Adjoining
　　Hills in as Self-Governing India"
　　(Mills), 231–232
Nye, A. R., 157

Office of Strategic Services (OSS), 6,
　　34, 62–65, 67–68
Olson, Lynne, 59, 227
Oropeza, Frank, 191
Oswalt, Walter
　　bamboo chair for return hike, 194,
　　　199
　　in Blackie's Gang, 216
　　as camp radio operator, 179
　　died with Porter, 229
　　emergency distress signals sent, 37
　　helped to village, 167
　　leg broken in crash, 161
　　preflight checklist, 2
　　reunited with Sevareid group, 159
　　worsening leg condition, 170
Ozukum, Bendang, 233

P-40 fighter planes, 5
P-43 fighter planes, 5
palisades against Naga attacks, 119, 121
Pangsau Pass, 24
Pangsha village
　　as allies of Ponyo, 79–80
　　attack on Law Nawkum, 219
　　attacking other villages, 108–109
　　attempts to get firearms, 178
　　at Chingmei, 140
　　counterattack at Wenshoyl, 133–134
　　feared by other villages, 97
　　mocking of military expedition, .
　　　119–120
　　Noklak *khel* elders to see crash
　　　survivors, 199
　　now in Myanmar, 231
　　peace terms agreed to, 141–142
　　personalities of residents, 188–189

reported casualties, 135–136
return to violent behavior, 157,
　　218–219
slaves relinquished, 123–124
treatment of survivors, 194–195
urge for Control Area to include,
　　220–221
See also punitive expeditions
Pangti expedition (1875), 94
panji traps, 96, 120, 127–128, 138, 149,
　　151
Panso village, 122–123, 143, 145–148, 157
parachutes, 1, 3, 37–39, 162, 163
Passey, Richard, 171–172, 178, 188,
　　201–203
Patkai Ranges. *See* Patkoi Hills
Patkoi Hills (now Patkai Ranges)
　　Flickinger parachuted into, 171
　　on Flight 12420 route, 15–16
　　geography of Burma, 16
　　head-hunting and raiding in, 220
　　Law Nawkum attacked, 219
　　Mills's eagerness to explore, 110, 118
　　Mt. Saramati in, 118
　　Raj rule in, 97, 129, 153
　　as remote to white men, 107
　　renamed Patkai Ranges, 232
　　route to China over, 9
　　search planes over, 168–170
　　USAAF watch stations in, 219
　　villages on Burmese side attacked,
　　　108
Pawsey, Charles
　　in Battle of Kohima, 225–226
　　as colonial administrator and
　　　anthropologist, 98
　　concern for Control Area, 219–222
　　on illegal behavior in remote
　　　villages, 156–157
　　against independence for Naga
　　　Hills, 231
　　perceptions of Nagas, 209–210
　　push to outlaw head-hunting in
　　　Control Area, 224

request for punitive expedition on
    Ukha denied, 223–224
unable to enforce authority in
    Patkoi Hills during war, 219
Pesu village, 157
Phire-ahire village, 114
Phony War, 60–61
Pitt Rivers Museum, Oxford, 125, 145,
    151
poisoned arrows, 115. *See also*
    crossbows with poisoned arrows
Ponyo village, 76–80, 137–138, 185, 219
Porter, John "Blackie," 215–216, 218
preflight checklists, 1–2, 8
Price, Mary, 64–65
Probert, Henry, 30
Pukovi, 116
punitive expedition (1936)
    ended at Mokokchung, 154–155
    first battle day, 131–132
    journey home from Tuensang,
        151–153
    launch from Mokokchung, 111–113
    march over difficult terrain, 113–114
    military strength of Pangsha vs.
        British, 119–120
    need for follow-up, 156
    planned procedure, 128–129, 131
    second battle day, 133
    withdrawal to Noklat, 135
punitive expedition (1937), 156
punitive expedition (1939), 157
punitive expedition (1943), 158

racism, 28, 29, 31
RAF (Royal Air Force) aircraft at
    Chabua, 1
Raj
    administered by ICS, 98, 100
    Chingmak's loyalty to, 138, 152
    conflict with India government over
        Nagas, 87
    cultural dissonance problems,
        104–106

enforcement problems with
    distance, 109, 120
expansion of control over Naga
    tribes, 93
involvement with Naga tribes, 83,
    86, 94
Panso's loyalty to, 199
range of authority to Patkoi Hills,
    129
security benefits from allegiance to,
    122–123
show of authority to non-
    Administered Area villages,
    122–123
See also East India Company
Randle, John, 28–29
Rangoon, Burma, attacks and invasion
    by Japan, 19–22
Ravenholt, Albert, 205–206
Reader's Digest article by Sevareid, 211,
    213
rebellion by Burmese tribes against
    Japanese, 33
red as social status color, 122
"Regulations for Punishment of
    Enemy Air Crews" (Japan), 32
Reid, Robert Neil, 82, 84, 93, 155–157
religion. *See* Christian missionaries
The Rengma Nagas (Mills), 102
rescue packs
    boots for return hike, 194,
        197–198
    caused cattle stampede in
        Helipong, 204–205
    instructions about natives, 163–164,
        168–169, 176, 180
    M1 carbines in, 177–178
    salt for Pangshas, 194
    survivors' trash of value to Nagas,
        182, 195–196
    unusual contents, 182–183
rescue party arrival, 190–191
return to civilization, 212–213
Roosevelt, Franklin D., 230

Royal Air Force (RAF) aircraft at
    Chabua, 1
rule of law, 210

sahib of Mokokchung. *See* Adams,
    Philip
salt as most eminent gift, 142, 184,
    193–194
Salween River, Burma, 9
Samagudting (now Chumukedima)
    village, 90
Sampure, Nagaland, 222
Sangbah, 107, 180–181, 186, 193, 201, 211
Sanglao village, 156–157
Sangpurr village, 121–123, 144, 148–149
Sangsomo village, 115
Sangtam Naga tribe, 221
Santing, 108, 140
Saul, Jamie, 99, 105
Schrandt, William, 58, 213
Schroth, Raymond, 57, 227
search-and-rescue mechanisms
    developed, 215–217
Sema (Sumi) Naga tribe, 99
Sevareid, Eric
    on Adams as sahib of Mokokchung,
        190–191
    on ambush possibility between
        Chingmei and Kuthurr, 199–200,
        202
    on bail-out, 39, 40–42
    on British Empire and Nagas, 208
    as camp diarist and chaplain, 179
    as celebrity in survivor group, 206
    on Chingmak, 181
    with cold, 212
    coverage of Blitz, 61–62
    on Davies, 6
    doubts about C-46, 12–13
    on Dumbastapur, 7
    early days as journalist, 58–60
    on feast from Nagas, 184–185
    on ferry pilots, 7–8
    first contact with Nagas, 164–166

    first report to outside world,
        205–206
    on fitness of crash survivors,
        202–203
    on Flickinger's parachute arrival,
        172–173
    as Flight 12420 passenger, 5, 15, 58
    on graft and corruption in Yunnan,
        226–227
    group reunited with Stanton group,
        167
    ill-fitting boots, 198–199
    life after rescue, 226–227
    on London's courage, 62
    loss of spear, 206–207
    messenger from Davies group, 166
    misperception of Adams, 209–210
    on Mongson's gift to Flickinger, 195
    on Nagas fighting over survivors'
        trash, 197
    Not So Wild a Dream, 227
    note to men at Ponyo, 81
    observations during flight, 35
    observations on Panso, 199–200
    as one of "Murrow's boys," 59–60
    on Pangsha personalities, 188–189
    Reader's Digest article, 211, 213
    on return flight from Jorhat, 213–214
    on return to civilization, 212–213
    on scenery between Noklak and
        Chingmei, 200
    sent by Roosevelt for objective
        viewpoint, 44, 56–57
    summary of experiences, 212
    sunstroke on fourth day's march,
        204
    survivor camp description, 187
    thoughts after plane crash, 159
    USAAF schedule, 13
    visit to Sangbah's home, 201
Shakespear, Leslie, 82–83, 87, 91, 239
Shans (Burmese hill country tribe),
    21, 33
shelters built for survivors, 177

Sherrill, Lloyd, 58
Shillong, India
  action needed re Control Area, 157,
    224
  extended Control Area, 155–156
  Fürer-Haimendorf permission to
    accompany expedition, 110
  inability to control intertribe
    warfare, 219
  letter re Pangsha raids, 108
  Pawsey promotion of punitive
    expedition, 156, 223–224
  Pawsey's concern for Control Area,
    220–221
  punitive expedition (1936), 109–111
  silent to requests from Pawsey and
    Adams, 224–225
  as site of Assam government, 109
Shingbwiyang village, 24
Shouba, 192
Sibsagar, 91
sieges, 91
Signer, Francis, 58, 159
Sikorsky R-4, 217
Sino-American Cooperative
    Organization (SACO) agreement,
    65–66, 68, 227–228
slavery among Nagas
  Christian missionaries against,
    104–105
  continued punishment for, 156–158
  final Pangsha slave returned, 149
  freed slaves, observations of, 149–151
  for human sacrifice, 108, 109, 142,
    149
  Pangsha and Yimpang rampage,
    108
  peace terms agreed to, 141–142
  punitive expedition (1937), 156–157
  slaves taken at Pangsha, 144
  See also punitive expedition (1936)
Slavery Convention (1926), 109–110
Slim, Bill, 26
Smith, Cyrus, 13

Smith, G. W. J., 111, 114–115, 133
Soong, T. V., 43, 44, 47
Stanton, Bill, 5, 40
Stanton, William "Bill," 15, 58, 167, 179,
    203
The Statesman
  as authentication from Mills to
    Nagas, 144
  on crash survivors, 188
  on Edward VIII's abdication, 153
Stilwell, Joe "Vinegar Joe"
  on Allied defeat in Burma, 26
  on C-46 problems, 11
  CBI theater created, 50
  on Chiang's ingratitude and
    demands, 56
  China experiences, 44–46, 48
  China position, vindication of, 230
  conflicts with Chiang, 46–49
  on Dai Li and Miles, 228
  Davies as adviser, 43
  as Flight 12420 passenger, 5
  lack of support for views, 43–44
  life after rescue, 229–230
  as Marshall's representative to
    Chiang, 45
  points made at Trident Conference,
    54
  policy disagreements with
    Chennault, 49, 52–55
  problems and goals for rebuilding
    Chinese army, 47–50
  in Washington to give viewpoint, 73
Stowe, Leland, 18–19
Straightway Mission School, 233
survivors' trash, conflict over, 195–196
Swinson, Arthur, 225–226
sword grass, 204

Tanaka, Shinichi, 27–28, 33
Tangbang
  as crossbow expert, 186, 193
  helped separate Nagas fighting over
    survivors' trash, 197

Tangbang (*continued*)
  home visit by crash survivors,
    201–202
  as protector of survivors, 180–181
  and returning expedition, 138, 143
telephones in Naga Hills, 169
Tenth Air Force, Kunming, 5
Thibaw Min, 17
Thirty-Fourth Native Infantry, 91
tigers and elephants, 207
Tobu village, 224
Treaty of Yandabo (1826), 85
Trident Conference, Tehran, 54, 55
Tsawlaw village, 140, 141, 219
Tuensang district, 107
Tuensang village, 150–151
Tyson, Geoffrey, 25

Ukha village, 157, 223–224
umbrellas on march, 206
unadministered area, 210
USAAF (US Army Air Forces), 13, 162,
    203, 210–211, 217, 219
US Joint Chiefs of Staff on China, 230
US Navy Department intelligence in
    Asia, 66–68
US support of China, 45

Vassiliev, Alexander, 229
Verona Project, 229
Vierya, Dr., 111
"vomit trail," 35

Wakching village, 103
Walmsley, Peyton, 1, 2
Wang Pae Chae, 15, 58, 167, 198
Wang-do, 202
war drills for Naga porters, 124
warning note with rescue pack, 169
Waterbury, Stanley, 15, 58, 194
Wavell, Archibald, 51–52
Wenshoyl (Pangsha *khel*), 131, 133–134,
    167–168, 176–177, 181–182
White, Theodore, 4–5, 7–8, 11–12, 217
Wild, Hugh, 162, 170, 229
Wild Bill Donovan (Brown), 70
Wilder, Evan, 58, 74, 80
Williams, W. R. B. "Bill," 112, 121, 133,
    139, 226
women, visibility of in villages, 167–168
Woodbridge, Stanley, 32
Wragg, Alfred, 21, 24

Yachummi expedition (1910), 94
Yimpang village, 108, 124–125
Yimsungr Naga tribe, 117, 118–119, 122
Yoke Force, 51, 53
Young, Hugh, 234–235
Yukso village, 144–145
Yungkao village, 157
Yungya village, 158
Yunnan offensive, 51
Yunnanese plateau, China, 10

zu, 113, 141–142, 153, 201–202, 209